DANNY MORRISON

MAD AS I WANNA BE

DANNY
MORRISON

MAD AS I WANNA BE

To be carl —

D Dlomei

Hodder Moa Beckett

Dedication

To the women in my family:
you helped create the dream

Acknowledgements

My thanks go to all the players whom I played with and against, at home and abroad, and to all the people, known and unknown, who have supported New Zealand cricket through my career (especially Dennis Kidd – the biggest New Zealand cricket fan of all time!).

Special thanks to my extended family for putting up with the madness; and to my wife, Kimberley, for her love and support in very full-on times and for always being there for me.

Many thanks, too, to all those talented people who assisted in the creation of this book and offered support, especially Margot Butcher, of Perfect Words Ltd: coaxed into listening to me by the daily promise of Kim's oven-fresh muffins, "Margs" penned my thoughts perfectly: thanks for your energy and creativity.

Thank you Malcolm Evans, graphic artist extraordinaire; Murray Deaker for your thoughts and enduring friendship; Francis Payne for your meticulous statistical analysis of our game; and thank you to the photographers for capturing the memories: Andrew Cornaga and Jo Caird, both of Photosport; Ross Setford, of Fotopacific; Margot Butcher; and an extra note of thanks to the Sunday Star-Times for access to its photo library.

Lyrics from "Start" are copyright Paul Weller/BMG Music Pty Ltd and are reprinted by permission of Music Sales Pty Ltd (Australia). Lyrics from "Comfortably Numb" are copyright G. Waters and D. Gilmour/EMI Songs Australia Pty Ltd and are reprinted by permission of EMI Songs Australia Pty Ltd.

All titles of chapters in this book refer to music that was the soundscape to special times and memories.

ISBN 1-86958-561-5

© 1997 Danny Morrison

Published in 1997 by Hodder Moa Beckett Publishers Limited
[a member of the Hodder Headline Group]
4 Whetu Place, Mairangi Bay, Auckland, New Zealand

Printed through Bookbuilders, Hong Kong China

CONTENTS

Management and staff at Crown are pleased to be associated
with Danny in the publication of this book as
we were involved in the sponsorship of his testimonial
season in 1996-97.

Danny and his lovely wife Kim have become very good
friends of Crown, giving us a wonderful insight into what
makes this dynamic duo tick.

There is a strong similarity in what our company tries to
achieve as our goals and what Danny has achieved in his
sporting life. To give 100 percent plus in effort and
commitment, coupled with always striving to be the best, is
the Danny way.

We trust you will enjoy this book and reflect on the person
who is Danny Morrison and his contribution to the game
we all love.

Brian Valentine
Managing Director
Crown Worldwide (N.Z. Ltd)

Foreword

Danny Morrison should never have been a fast bowler. Fast bowlers are normally tall and slim, all arms and legs. Danny is short, squat and heavy round the thighs.

Fast bowlers are meant to be mean and nasty, difficult to get on with, crazy in the eyes, completely focused and totally unreasonable. Danny is pleasant and personable, able to mix with all types and all ages, boringly sane, balanced and logical.

Fast bowlers have usually been brought up in an atmosphere somewhat akin to an elite Green Beret training camp. Sir Richard Hadlee was introduced to his art by his father Walter, a former New Zealand captain, in the family's backyard nets. Danny was raised in a liberal environment by his Mum where voices weren't raised in anger, let alone anything thrown at speed.

Danny Morrison became a fast bowler because he desperately wanted to be one. The first time I ever saw him was at the Devonport Domain cricket nets. I was unsuccessfully trying to run a First XI practice. Every time I made a comment, one of the team members would point to this sawn-off little runt of a fourth former imitating Hadlee and Dennis Lillee in the neighbouring nets and then the rest of them would burst into hysterics. I bellowed at the kid to "shoot through", but he just hung around the nets moping. Danny has one of cricket's most expressive faces and had taken on the demeanour of a spaniel who had just watched his favourite bone being devoured by the local president of the Rottweilers' chapter. I chucked him the ball and said, "Have a go, Shorty". The hang dog spaniel suddenly became the terrier, all bristle, fire and enthusiasm; trademarks that were to make him this country's second most successful bowler.

Like all kids Danny was a dreamer. The difference was that he not only dreamed of playing at the top level, but he was prepared to do anything to get there. Unquestionably there have been many others with more ability, more attributes to take them to the top, but none of them wanted it as much as Danny. In those early years he was like a sponge absorbing any ideas I may have had. When those were quickly exhausted he was able to move onto others far more knowledgeable.

Usually when I think of Danny a smile comes to my face. He is a real character and has certainly been the central player in some funny scenes. When Bay 13 of the Melbourne Cricket Ground first spied him, one wag immediately inquired, "Hey, Morrison! Where did your mother find you? At the bottom of the garden with the other gnomes?". Yet by the end of that 1987 Boxing Day test even the most hard-bitten Aussie fan had a new respect for the "gnome" as he supported Hadlee to take New Zealand to the brink of victory.

Danny's injuries are legendary. It is hard to remember any part of his body that hasn't been injured at some time. No matter how he was patched up, inevitably he broke down. In simple terms it was his body saying, "Enough!". Through it all the heart said, "Keep going". Heart is the biggest thing Danny has got going for him. No one could have tried harder – but in the end it wasn't enough.

It is a well-worn cliché that "sport develops character". Some top sportspeople become arrogant and puffed up with their own importance. They forget where they came from and who their friends are. That has never been a problem with Danny. His thirtieth birthday party was like a Takapuna Grammar school reunion. It was held at the North Shore Cricket Club and most of the guests were able to walk home which, incidentally, was a good thing. His mates are the same mates he was hanging around with at the nets all those years ago.

Les Coulson, who coached at those nets for decades and had trouble controlling Danny's enthusiasm in the early days, once told me that he coached cricket because "good cricketers made good citizens". Les would be pleased to see how Danny has turned out.

Danny Morrison is humble, modest, honest, straight and a thoroughly good human being. He genuinely cares for other people and generously tries to help kids when he has any spare time. In Les Coulson's words, Danny has become a "good citizen".

As a cricketer he epitomises the game in this country, probably more so than any other player. Not quite good enough to be a worldbeater, but certainly capable of turning on a matchwinning performance against all odds. Danny got to the top of his game in this country because of his grit and will to succeed. When New Zealand cricket has success it is not through technical superiority, but more because those qualities – guts and determination – come through.

Murray Deaker
July 1997

START

"It's not important for you to know my name, nor I to know yours,

If we communicate for two minutes only, it will be enough,

But knowing that someone in this world feels as desperate as me, and what you give is what you get . . ."

– THE JAM

My nerves were jangling inside me as I walked through the unfamiliar main gate, padded up the schoolish front steps of the grand pavilion and entered a wooden hallway. The hall, proudly lined with framed photographs of cricketers, was guarded by a crusty old Englishman in a white coat. He eyed me, asked me if I had permission to be there. I said I'd come to see someone.

The Whitecoat made me wait at the foot of a narrow spiral staircase that wound its way up to first the visitors' dressing rooms and then the Nottingham County Cricket Club home dressing rooms and balcony that stared down over Trent Bridge. The stairs he slowly climbed seemed to go so far up. You needed a special pass to get up there, to that male bastion, that haven. I didn't have one, so I'd had to write a note for the room attendant up there.

Eventually the Whitecoat came back down and said, "Mr Hadlee will see you now."

It was 1986, the first days of May in England where spring is chilly, still very dark and closed in. As I climbed further and further up the stairs I could make out the Notts team rustling about their dressing room, looking for extra socks and jackets to brace themselves for practising in the snappy weather. Then, as I walked through the doorway, the atmosphere hit me. Dressing rooms in England are small and old and intense, clothes everywhere, rows of coat hooks buried under layers and layers of cricket gear, players tripping over each other. It was different from dressing rooms at home, somehow authentic. I drank it in.

I looked around and saw the great man strapping on a large pair of shoes, wearing his whites with a tracksuit bottom and somehow making it look neat and tidy. He looked up at me. Unmistakably the wry, angular face I'd seen on television so many times. He seemed in an instant very serious, professional. Approaching him was almost like going to see the headmaster in the third form (which was a feeling I knew well – I was always getting caned in school).

"Hello, I'm Danny Morrison," I ventured.

And Richard Hadlee replied, "Good morning, young man."

That was my first meeting with the master. This was Hadlee's testimonial year at Nottingham and I was living down in North London, 20 years old and in my second year playing English club cricket. During the week I was working as a roadie for Canon photocopiers on a promotional roadshow. The crew had been heading up north-east, through Nottingham, when I'd asked to stop off at Trent Bridge to see Hadlee. I'd written him a letter asking if I could play in one of his testimonial matches. I was young, confident – and excited. Maybe he could tell. But he talked to me very matter-of-factly, politely asked me how I was, though he'd never met me before; where I was playing, how I was finding it. We were connected by the game. Guys were scurrying out to the nets. I felt I was almost in the way, an intruder on their rarefied terrain, so I had to be brief. I gave him my address and phone number and left, reluctantly, with a last backward glance at the ultimate pro in his natural environment. There was what I was trying to become, who I wanted to be.

I can still remember the intensity inside me then of wanting to achieve and wanting to be a professional cricketer. Meeting Richard Hadlee was the start, the first connection to the place I wanted to get to. I so much wanted to get into a side and play against someone like him, to show that I could. So I actively sought out that environment. I wanted to get into that fraternity and to be seen there, mixing it, playing the way I so strongly believed I could. I wanted to be amongst it, that excitement I'd seen on TV and watched from the rickety old West Stand of Eden Park.

Back in 1986, I still didn't know if I was good enough to get to that highest level. I'd only played a handful of first-class games in my first season back in New Zealand, 1985/86, when I was 19. If Hadlee had heard of me at all, it would only have been from a three-day game I'd played in October 1984 at Auckland's Cornwall Park, when I took 6-49 on debut for Auckland against the New Zealand side that was about to fly to Pakistan. Hadlee and Geoff Howarth weren't going on that tour; Jeremy Coney captained the side that included Lance Cairns, Ian Smith, Bruce Edgar, John Wright and Ewen Chatfield. Even as a young first-class player you were really quite distanced from stars like them back in those days, back when there was no academy as now, no real interaction with them – so for me just to play those famous men, let alone take their wickets, was a red flag to my ambitions. It was the only way you made your name.

Later that English summer of 1986, New Zealand practised at the lovely Maori Cricket Club in Surrey during their England tour. I watched them, this crew of professionals in their late 20s and 30s. Said hello to Willie Watson, the young bowler on tour who'd always been the bowling star when I'd played schoolboy cricket on the North Shore. I wanted to be in his shoes. Then I climbed into Richard Hadlee's car with Peter Webb, my Auckland team-mate, and we drove to Stevenidge, just north of Watford, where Hadlee had indeed arranged for me to play in one of his twilight testimonial games. We camped the night at his house in Nottingham with his wife, Karen, and their young boys.

Did Hadlee know me from Adam? I don't know. He no doubt thought I was this mad young kid, yet another one probably, who wanted to be a quick bowler. It was good of him to feed me that encouragement.

Now I look back and think of that time as a strange, exciting crossroads. Little did either of us know that just four years later, when Hadlee would be touring England for the last time, he would sit with me on the edge of Sussex's home ground on a cold day in Hove and formally hand over his mantle of strike bowler of the New Zealand team to me. No one thought then that this little gnome from Devonport would even be a real fast bowler, after all: I was short and built like an axe-chopping little batsman or wicketkeeper, rather than a six foot two, strapping, long-limbed quick. People never took me seriously enough. People thought I was pretending, I think. But I quite enjoyed that; it was quite a nice way of shocking people.

I was always breaking the mould.

START

INTERNATIONAL JET SET

It was for me the most powerful summer. The season before I'd seen Imran Khan, the great Pakistani allrounder, running in to bowl at Eden Park, but it wasn't until that summer of 1980 that I felt and breathed the excitement of cricket. That was the year the West Indies toured New Zealand.

The West Indies hadn't played in our country since 1969, when I was just a toddler – this was only their fourth tour here, and they were only popping through New Zealand on the way home from a successful campaign against Australia, their great rivals. So there was a lot of interest around the country and I remember the cover of *The Listener* carried a photograph of Clive Lloyd, the West Indies captain, punching a big, showy cover drive. It really captured me: the Caribbean flavour, cricket West Indies style. I would sneak off from school, wag to go and watch the West Indies cricket match on television, to watch Richard Hadlee dominate the series. The great opening pair, Desmond Haynes and Gordon Greenidge, were smashing it around. You saw the huge frame of Joel 'Big Bird' Garner and Michael Holding and Lloyd. They were big names, big people: cricket was larger than life. Then came all the controversy.

Colin Croft running into umpire Fred Goodall, Holding infamously kicking the stumps over in disgust as his side coursed to their first ever test series loss to New Zealand – a real sting in the face, coming as it was on the heels of success over Australia.

I wanted so badly to be out there in the middle of all that excitement, competing with people on that world stage. That summer, I really felt how insignificant and insular we were playing these big sides – and there was so much pride. How well New Zealand played at home in the 1980s is well recorded. It captured the imagination of a lot of New Zealanders, I think, and it certainly felt important to me. Cricket felt important.

In the following seasons, 1980/81 and 1982/83, the New Zealand side flew across the Tasman where the one-dayers between Australia and New Zealand were new, full on, addictive and splashed across our television screens with bright lights, coloured clothing, glitz and hype that you'd never seen before in cricket – and often we were winning.

I'd been playing cricket down at Stanley Bay Park in Devonport, Auckland one day, just charging around the park with my mates, when we came back to the house and flicked on the TV and realised, geez, there's a game on, Australia, the one-dayer! Lance Cairns was decked out in the awful beige pyjamas we used to wear then and was batting against Dennis Lillee at the MCG in front of 71,000 people. We'd tuned in to the exact over that riveted a nation's attention on New Zealand cricket like no other. I saw Cairns' last three sixes – we'd missed the first three – and the commentators were just going off. New Zealand had been right in the cart, six down for 44, but Cairns had come out and just slogged 50. Pick-up shots back over Dennis Lillee's head; flicking another of the great bowler's deliveries for six – one-handed! – heaving the ball high over Greg Chappell's head at fine leg. It was magic.

Our cricket had such a positive charge in the early 1980s. It wasn't long after the West Indies series win and those gripping scenes in Australia against their top guns that New Zealand won the one that had been for so long elusive: the first test win in England. That was 1983, and it was as if we had at last "arrived".

With all the excitement going on I was starting to wag school a lot. I wagged to watch a test match in 1982 when we beat Australia by five wickets and got suspended for three days. I was at Takapuna Grammar (just west of where I lived in Devonport), and the deputy principal there was none other than Murray Deaker. Deaker was also the coach of the First XI, and despite the fact that half the side had wagged to watch this match, Deaks was determined to make an example of us, though it meant he had to pick half the Second XI to play our match that weekend. "Another neat trick Danny did for me," as he recounts the story these days!

Eden Park became my focal point in summer. There was an old stand where the West Stand is now, dry, flaking wooden seats with the old, manual scoreboard behind it. We always used to sit down towards what's now the Taverner's end. Cars used to park on the number two ground in those days and we'd peer over the stand at all the people with their chilly bins and beers having boot parties. I loved the whole atmosphere of the park and the game. Cricket moved from being my sport to my passion.

By 1984 I'd left school and in the summer of 1984/85 I worked for the Birkenhead City Council with the parks and reserves department, with Paul Kelly, who was then the Auckland wicketkeeper and is now an ASB bank manager. It was the most frustrating summer of my life. I'd injured my back, bad enough that I couldn't play cricket for most of the summer and had missed out on making my Auckland debut after impressing all the right people in trial and club games around the city as a mad, young fast bowler.

Summer faded off to autumn and I got a job back at my old school, working on the grounds at Takapuna Grammar for 16 hours a week, and caretaking at Stanley Bay Primary as well, doing the lawns there and a bit of cleaning. Deaker had helped me gain a scholarship to play club cricket in England the winter before, but now I was recovering from my back injury, forced to stay back as the cold weather drew near, only able to think about the game I desperately wanted to play.

For those first few years out of school, my life was a case of just waiting for cricket, getting by until the summer. I was incredibly driven, very focused, and looking back, I put all my eggs in one basket. But I put that energy out there, that focus. I really wanted to get into the New Zealand side early. Make it, as soon as I could. Lillee had made it for Australia when he was 21, Hadlee when he was around 22; I reasoned quicker bowlers could make it earlier. Looking back, it was bizarre, like Tiger Woods saying he wanted to win the US Masters at 19. Only a young man would say that. But when you're 19, you're naive and confident. Only later do you look back and realise so many things could have gone wrong . . .

Early in 1986 I finally made my Shell Trophy and Shell Cup debut for Auckland. I was 19, coming up 20, and all I wanted was to be Richard Hadlee. In winter I worked again, laying concrete footings for a building trade gang, waiting once more for the next summer.

I'd become aware, around those mid-1980s, that the guys who were my boyhood heroes – the names like Hadlee, Wright, Smith, Snedden – were now towards the end of their careers in cricket. I wanted to be part of the atmosphere they'd helped create, the great 1980s side, but I was up against an amazing race against time to get there.

I really was driven, disciplined, committed and focused on making it before the gate closed on that era. I'd done a lot of my partying years from the ages of 16 to 20 with my mates, but I didn't drink a hell of a lot for a young male. Sure, there were times when you had a bit of a blow out, but I never partied to excess, whereas some kids at that age write themselves off regularly, at weekends and in clubs. Some people can hit the bottle harder than others and it just wasn't big for me. I'd got my driver's licence a bit later than most, too, and I'd already seen some of the hell messes some of my mates had got into with a bit of stupid drink-driving. We were only just getting to grips with the hard-hitting campaigns back then, and I couldn't cope with the thought of doing something like that. So I hung out at my club a lot, the North Shore Cricket Club, went to the movies, hung out around Devonport and the Shore. Caught the ferry to town sometimes where you could walk up to The Globe or De Bretts for a night out. And played cricket all I could.

Cricket is such a long game that inevitably my various girlfriends got fed up with me. The relationships never lasted and through my youth there were some turbulent scenarios, usually because my girlfriend had decided it came down to a decision between her or cricket. When you're 19, it's an easy decision! Cricket was my be-all and end-all and I wasn't ready to settle down. The girl I used to go out with at school and I broke up and got back together again a couple of times, with seasons in between. It wasn't that you didn't care about them, but just that cricket meant a lot of travelling, and, when you were home, a lot of practice. Having come from a very female-orientated home, brought up with my mother and sister, I was quite mindful that I didn't want to treat anyone unfairly.

Perhaps, in the back of my mind, I was also aware of my father having married young and having other commitments early in his life. I look back at it now and think of other guys my age that had got girls pregnant and were in de facto relationships or had married quite young. You saw how hard it was on other guys married with young kids. They couldn't be as selfish, and cricket can be a very selfish game, and a game that demands your youth. I was actually very driven for my age to do the career thing, which is how I saw cricket. I gave it my all.

My mother, Sandi, was a very balancing person in my youth and could communicate the idea of goals to me really well. But after I'd announced that ambitious goal of getting into the New Zealand side by the age of 21, Sandi worried a little in case I failed – because I wanted it so badly. Then, quite suddenly, it happened.

There was no phone call. My club side was fielding out at Merton Road, the University ground in Auckland, at the tail of the 1986/87 summer when the New Zealand squad to go to Sri Lanka in March came across on the radio news. Our scorer came walking over and shook hands with me: that was how I found out. Guys were patting me on the back, but it didn't sink in. It was all a little surreal, and Don Neely and the other New Zealand selectors remained distant beings you hadn't actually spoken to. I felt I was lucky that they'd actually taken me seriously – because I wasn't big and angular like Willie Watson, Brian Barrett or Derek Stirling and all the other guys they'd used a bit in the ranks behind the stars, Hadlee and Ewen Chatfield.

Cricket was a strange business back then, a professional sport run on an amateur blueprint. Believe it or not, I didn't know a tour to Sri Lanka was even coming up. There wasn't much communication at all between the national office in Christchurch and the players and so my selection was as much in that way as any other a bolt out of the blue. I'd just got on and played cricket and done well for Auckland that season, vaguely aware New Zealand would be in action again the following summer, somewhere or other. Even at the 1987 World Cup, which I played after Sri Lanka, I still hadn't realised there was a full tour to Australia at the end of that year. I remember the coach, Glenn Turner, in India saying to me matter-of-factly, "Look, you haven't played much here, but take some consolation in that at least you should be named for this Australian tour now." I was like, what Australian tour? You mean there's a full test match tour? Cripes!

Just as you'd find out you were picked by remote control, guys would find out they were dropped on the radio, too – often they would just be driving along in their car and hear the crushing public announcement from a stranger's voice.

To be honest, I was that focused in 1987 that really I was just living from day to day anyway, training, playing, training, and didn't think too much beyond my immediate season's goals. My mother says I became like a young monk, especially after being picked for Sri Lanka. I didn't go out a lot, because I'd be tired and chilling out after training hard. It was a real driving time for me, throwing myself at my goal – to make the World Cup that was coming up after Sri Lanka (a tour I had managed to find out about). I desperately wanted to be there, this event that only came along every four years and shone with all the world's great names . . .

But first I was to go to Sri Lanka and meet half the great names in my own team for the first time. Like my first, nervous meeting with Hadlee at Trent Bridge just a year before, that would be an exciting time of connecting myself to the environment I wanted to be in.

Martin Snedden came to pick me up for the airport that day late in March. Sneds lived down the road in Devonport, played for the same club side and had taken me under his wing a bit as I made my first tracks into the Auckland side after I'd met him in 1983/84. I was still living at home with my sister, mother and my uncle, who lived in the flat downstairs, and they stood on the doorstep waving and shouting "bon voyage". I don't know how far my family had thought I would actually go in cricket. It had been Dan's mad dream. I think they were quite amazed that I was actually on this tour going off with the New Zealand cricket team. My mother was happy just to see me go overseas and experience the planet – her brother, Uncle Rube, had been in the navy and learned about the world that way. They were both really proud that the dream had come to fruition, because I think there had been some concern about what my career would be, what I would do with my life, otherwise. Here I had been doing odd jobs and trotting back and forth to England to play sport, and while I was infused with the drive and desire, they were the ones left to worry on my behalf whether it really was all worth it.

I didn't have any "number ones" (grey trousers) so the new recruit made a slightly less than grand entrance at Auckland airport wearing a smart shirt, tie and blazer over tracksuit bottoms. The non-Aucklanders in the New Zealand side had been staying at the Airport Travelodge, so it wasn't until the airport that I met most of them, having glimpsed guys like Ewen Chatfield and Evan Gray only very briefly during my first Shell season that summer. Luckily a large chunk of the New Zealand side happened to be from Auckland at that time, anyway – John Bracewell, Phil Horne, Dipak Patel, Sneds, Martin and Jeff Crowe – so at least I knew some of the team-mates suddenly standing around me. I remember Bernie Bracewell, John's wife, got quite emotional saying goodbye to John there and that's always stuck in my mind.

The mandatory official photo of the touring side was taken before we flew out. It was Jeff Crowe's first assignment as captain (Jeremy Coney had just retired and John Wright was unavailable because he had a testimonial season with his county in England) and my first official photo. Looking back, it set the pattern for all the things that subsequently went haywire throughout my career.

Photos involve a time-honoured protocol. The senior pros, the stars of the side, always sit in the front row and the newcomers stand behind them. You know your place. When I started, Braces and Sneds used to jostle for that last spot on the front row. Martin Crowe, though a lot younger than them, had already secured a front row berth because he'd played a lot more test cricket than anyone else his age. From my first home test against England in 1987/88 to my last test, also against England in New Zealand, a decade later, I gradually worked my way from being a back row boy towards that team power centre in the front. But for my first tour, I broke the protocol.

Instead of going on seniority, the photographer had arranged us by height, with all the shortarses like me sitting in the front – and Jeff Crowe, the new captain, hadn't intervened. Here I was in the front row of a New Zealand team in my maiden New Zealand team photo, sitting right next to the captain, with Ian Smith on my left. Andrew Jones, another new selection, had properly landed in the back row, but Hadlee was in the middle row, a real faux pas, and I was seriously jumping rank. That photo was a bad omen for the entire tour.

We flew Air New Zealand to Singapore, then changed to Singapore Airlines for Colombo, arriving at 3am. I thought we were landing in an eerie fog, the sort of fog you'd imagine in Victorian London, but it was actually the density of the humidity in Colombo. It felt like we were commandos in a movie scene, sneaking in on a mission into enemy territory under cover of darkness. I'd flown away with a bunch of lads before, to Melbourne in 1984 with a New Zealand youth side, but I'd never been on any tour before this to prepare me for the culture shock of arriving there. It made Melbourne seem little more than a school trip, sweet and easy across the ditch. We arrived in the middle of the night and bright camera lights and flashes shone on you as you went through customs, faces stared incessantly at you, then you bounced along to the hotel in an old coach with seats hard as wood. The bus had curtains, and when I drew them to look out on the strange night roads, I saw people lying among all the junk and broken rickshaws. I'll never forget that shock – seeing people living, sleeping and cooking on the sides of the roads in poverty. It tempered the excitement I felt to be in that other new environment, the team itself.

I played one three-day tour match in Sri Lanka against a

President's XI at Galle, taking three wickets in what was my 15th first-class game. Then I watched the first test, a long draw. And then, disaster. A bomb shattered the entire tour. We were travelling by bus from the cricket stadium back to our hotel, The Meridian, when it happened. It killed 150 people and went off just 600 metres from our rooms in downtown Colombo.

After the bomb exploded, we were supposed to be confined to our hotel, but it felt really eerie and I wanted to get out and go for a walk along the Colombo promenade, which snaked along in front of the parliament buildings near The Meridian. A curfew had been imposed on people being out after 10pm and this was after midnight, but I went out for a walk anyway, by myself. I wasn't scared. People, guards and soldiers, just seemed to smile at me as if I was a nutter.

I thought to myself, "God, I finally get in the side and this happens. Blown away, the tour, my goals, all my ideas . . ."

The team had taken a ballot as to whether we should stay or go, as a unit, since there were two tests and four one-day internationals yet to be played. It was barely the beginning of the tour. Leading up to the ballot, my mind would oscillate back and forth – I'd want to stay, but then other guys would pressure me to change the thoughts in my head because they had families to go back to. I understood, because of Bernie Bracewell's emotion that time at the airport, but I didn't share that feeling and I wanted to stay. There was no reassurance that we would be safe – the police and army would come and tell us it was all no problem, but you weren't sure what to make of them. I looked around, confused. Hadlee was very uncomfortable. So was Martin Crowe – they had county contracts to get off to, Hadlee his last summer at Notts and Crowe, Somerset. Most of the senior guys wanted to go. It brought out the lawyer in Sneds, who thoroughly explained to us the consequences of staying or leaving from a legal perspective. Some of us did want to stay, to take charge of our futures, set them up. But it was not to be.

After this team decision it was a time of limbo, a quiet, flat time couped up in this hotel, washing away all the adrenalin and excitement I had felt before the blasted bomb and so I just had to get out. I walked through the clammy night air feeling quite down, depressed about having to go home from my first big tour with barely a chance to get involved in the side. The drawn test had been a long game to watch – Jeff Crowe had scored a test century on his debut as captain in 609 minutes, one of the slowest of all time – but I'd seen glimpses of what it meant to achieve at the highest level as a bowler. Chatfield had taken his 100th test wicket and Hadlee had equalled Lillee's haul of 355 wickets after exactly the same number of test matches, only two behind Ian Botham's 366; and Hadlee had also made his highest test score, 151 not out. To me, it was an amazing achievement. And now it was all disintegrating. I was sad.

We left as we had arrived, in the dead of night, 2am. We were catching planes to all different parts of the world, the team splitting up. Dipak, myself and Crowey went by Air Lanka to Gatwick in London.

It was an eerie trip out to the airport. The lights in the bus were left on. We wanted the lights turned out so people couldn't see us leaving in the middle of the night. It felt like we were tunnelling out, escaping. A few of the players' wives were on tour with us and they were freaking out. And maybe not only the wives.

"The curse of the Dan".

TAKE IT EASY

S ri Lanka had been a tantalising taste of the action. Afterwards I still saw the team-mates I had met as regular New Zealand cricketing heroes, but to have been around that starry nucleus even for just a couple of weeks . . . it only made me hope even harder that I could fit in with them.

My next chance was at the World Cup, which was being hosted by India and Pakistan at the beginning of the following season, October and November 1987. It seemed an aeon away, but through the winter I trained my guts out for it, after a short stint in England. I knew there were other guys the national selectors could easily pick ahead of me for such a big occasion, more experienced players like Derek Stirling. But, five weeks out, it was announced I was in the squad. What saved me was Hadlee didn't go, he was unavailable; and young Brian Barrett, who'd been taken to England in 1986, hadn't come on in leaps and bounds. It was consolation for my missed opportunity in Sri Lanka.

In those days sides got together only a couple of days before you were due to fly out. There were no organised squad practices at an indoor school – Auckland had only just got one of those – and it was pretty much left up to you to fire yourself up mentally and physically for a series. Even in the early 1990s, New Zealand team preparation really only amounted to going down to Twigger Street in Christchurch for a few nets at Canterbury Court, where the building was like an aircraft hanger: freezing, sunless, colder inside than out. Trying to bowl in those conditions, it was no wonder guys were breaking down with injuries so often.

But I'd been fired up all winter.

I arrived in Delhi wide-eyed. All the world players were converging for the opening ceremony and I couldn't help but stare as the stars – the big West Indians, the confident Australians – appeared across from me at the breakfast table, or in the lobby. I'd seen so few of them in person. My only disappointment was that Hadlee wasn't among them.

Discovering the team culture of the New Zealand side of that era and entering their dressing room environment meant learning from senior pros who had been on the circuit since the 1970s, when I was just a boy. Each had carved his own place in the dressing room: every time we were at a new ground I had to wait for them before I could sort out a possie, wait to see the gap, see where I could fit in – that whole time for me was as much about fitting in as getting a chance to perform on field. There was a pecking order, and that was part and parcel of the deal. I was the new kid, there to look and learn. I was raring to have a go myself, but at the same time grateful just to be there.

Chatfield, Wright, Snedden, Bracewell, the Crowe brothers, Smithy: that nucleus of the fraternity was quite a bit older than me. Only myself and Willie Watson, who was in and out of the side a lot from 1986 to 1990, were in our early 20s. Phil Horne and Dipak Patel had also only recently joined the team, but they were a good seven years older than me. I was not only in a different team, but in the middle of a different generation.

It would have been easy to feel a little alone and daunted by the status and experience of the players around me, if the senior guys hadn't gone out of their way to help my transition into the side. Chats, Sneds and Braces would make an effort to sit and talk with me, be it at an airport or on the team bus, and I started to absorb that the pros weren't these men who simply pulled on their V-neck sweaters and strode out to conquer as a unit. They were a collection of quite distinct individuals who'd worked out how to make their own personalities function within the team environment. Everyone was different, but they generally got along, and really stuck together on the road.

John Wright's nickname was either 'Rig' – for Rigor Mortis, because he was so stiff in the field; or 'Shake', because he used to shake his coffin out in the dressing room so that all his gear would tumble before him. He was the untidiest cricketer you could meet, gear everywhere around his nook in the dressing room, but that's how he felt most comfortable. He was the complete opposite of Richard Hadlee, who needed to be organised and neat as a pin.

I soon realised Wrighty was the real prankster in the team and liked having fun. He was the one who stuck the bucket of water above the doorway or the talcum powder on the top of the fins of the ceiling fan – he did that in the dressing rooms in India in 1988, the only time it's ever snowed in Hyderabad. At the World Cup in 1987, Evan Gray had brought a month's supply of chocolates with him to live on, little Mars bars and Moros and things. Wrighty got hold of his stash and left a trail of wrappers for Evan to follow with mounting dismay! There was another time in Australia when Wrighty took a bunch of bananas and gently sliced them inside the skin; Bert Vance came into the dressing room after he'd got out for very little and grabbed a banana to placate himself. Nice trick, he thought, as sliced banana splattered all over his lap. By the fourth banana he was thrashing the skins down on the ground and fuming. Then there were the more standard games – water pistols, coins glued to the floor, buckets of ice that would come shooting at you when you were in the shower. Welcome to the house of fun.

Wrighty was a good prankster because that wasn't all there was to him. He had real mana, a certain sense of what was appropriate in any given situation on or off field. He was widely respected. He'd been around a long time. I'd seen so much of him on TV and on the park. He'd been to Australia on three major tours in five years during the 1980s, and that cut mustard with a lot of New Zealanders. He made a huge impression on me. But I soon realised things were also quite an effort for him. Having played so much county cricket for Derbyshire as well as fronting for New Zealand, he had persistent back problems and his body took a while to get going.

Jeff Crowe was my first New Zealand captain and not nearly so much of an extrovert as Wrighty. Neither did he wear his heart on his sleeve the way Martin, his younger brother, did. To be fair, we had our fair few run-ins, Jeff and I, in my early years. There were times when I liked to get in and bounce guys, get up them but then have a wink and a smile, and he didn't like that at all. He thought that was being soft, unprofessional. I was bowling for Auckland one day against Wellington. Bruce Edgar was facing. I winked and smiled at Bootsie, tried to ankle-tap him as he ran through and got a little fine edge down to third man for a couple, then bounced him a bit, and smiled again. Jeff Crowe came over and said, "What the hell's going on?" I said, "What do you mean? Things are going all right, he's a bit lucky but I'm enjoying myself." Jeff goes, "*Fun?* You're having *fun?* Taking wickets is *bloody fun?*" He really was uptight about it. I think other guys in teams over the years have also felt I haven't been aggressive enough as a fast bowler because I haven't outwardly portrayed that, like a Merv Hughes or a Craig McDermott. But that was never my make-up. I liked smiling and enjoying being out there, because at the end of the day you played cricket because you loved the game, it was a passion. Sure, you got paid for it too, it was your bread and butter – but you genuinely enjoyed it. I don't think I ever lost that feeling.

I looked up a great deal to Martin Snedden and Ewen Chatfield. They were the medium pacers, and though I fancied myself as a domineering tearaway more in the mould of Hadlee and Dennis Lillee, I respected them for what they'd achieved as bowlers. Chats' dependability and durability as a pace bowler, right through to his retirement at 38, was inspiring. His experience was an incredible asset to New Zealand, when I look back at it.

Chats was hard to get to know because he was more of an introvert than myself and other guys in the side. Like Hadlee, he was an organised man, good with routines – and again a little bit like a schoolteacher in that he wouldn't stand for stupidity or too much tomfoolery if he thought it was going to be detrimental to our work at hand. He was straight up, you always knew where you stood with him. But he also had a nice, dry sense of humour himself, and was caring. He'd offer help to you in the nets when you were at the top of your mark, encourage you to concentrate on your follow through or offer a simple little tip in a very pleasant way.

Chats was a guy that had one speed, in life and in cricket. We called him the machine. He'd get up early each day on tour and go for these mad runs a good hour before breakfast, churn out his miles. Even today, in his forties, he's really lean, still going at the same speed. The team went for a 12-minute run around a racetrack in India in 1987; the rest of us just bunched in behind Chats' slipstream. He'd be 20 metres out in front, then towards the end we'd delight in dragging Chats off; he simply had no extra gear to flick into. He was the same in bowling, he could just run in all day. Javed Miandad said in 1989 that he wanted to take Chats back to Pakistan and use him as a bowling machine.

Martin Crowe and Hadlee were undoubtedly the two superstars in the New Zealand camp when I entered it, but the person who had the most influence on me within the team culture was actually Martin Snedden. He was very grounding, a friend and the home town hero at our local North Shore club. I grew up a bit with Martin, after I was formally introduced to him down at the club at the end of 1984 when he'd come back from a tour to Zimbabwe and Pakistan. I was still finishing school when he was making tracks with the New Zealand team, and had always looked up to him.

Sneds was about to start a family (he has a brood of four now) and was great for taking me under his wing in quite a fatherly way. I had different girlfriends around the country over various seasons at home and Sneds and John Bracewell, the family men who were at that settling-down stage of their lives, would often come out with lines like, "Geez, you two would look great together with kids . . ." – and they were serious!

I enjoyed just talking about bowling with Sneds, more so than even with Richard Hadlee. Paddles would talk to me about bowling in quite a professional manner, which was great, but I'd miss just chatting through things on the way to the airport like I did with Sneds. While Hadlee was the consummate pro, the essence of Sneds was a caring, family man who played cricket for the love of it. He was lucky his brother ran the law firm while he was away with Auckland or New Zealand.

While other people hummed U2 or Crowded House, Sneds used to love singing jingles from television advertisements. You'd be sitting there in the players' lounge when "Get your rice riso-otto!" would come floating at you from right of field. The big bottom lip would quiver again and you'd hear, "You oughtta be congratu-*laay*-ded . . ." He'd just pump out one after another.

A lot of the humour in that side seemed to be about keeping guys in line. Sneds was hard case and liked to take the mickey out of you – the lawyer would come out in him and he'd be almost flexing his intelligence on you sometimes. He liked to have a lot of fun, but, like quite a few of those older guys, he could be quite tough on people at the same time. It was flexing the authority – a bit like the prefects with the third formers at school.

He and Braces were thick as thieves. Braces lived in Mairangi Bay and played for Birkenhead so it was the Shore connection, and the two of them looked out for me as if, being from "Devo", I were family.

But Braces and Ian Smith in particular were also quite hard on us young ones at times. Braces was an old school guy. He was ever the competitor and gutsy, but he'd be the first to say he boiled over too much and got up people's noses, too hard sometimes, though his heart was in the right place. If Johnny had an opinion and wanted to express it, there was no holding back. He upset a lot of people, but he was there to win and to compete. His attitude, his strong personality that came from fighting his way through a large troupe of brothers, worked for some, not for others. But the bottom line was it worked for him. He was such a good player, such a tough competitor on and off the field. He gave so much. He used to brass people off with his appealing, but that was him to a tee.

He didn't get on with everyone, especially Martin Crowe. But you have that in all teams, a couple of players who'll tend to peg their gear on opposite sides of the dressing room. It's the norm.

The hard thing was it got a bit out of hand with some writings in papers in the early 1990s, which eventually led to New Zealand Cricket contractually forbidding players from writing columns at all. It had got too personal. Publicly Crowe and Braces had a go at each other when Crowe was captain and Braces had finished and was writing his column for the *Sunday News*. Then Martin would have a dig back, when we were playing England in 1992 and not doing very well, just before a dramatic turnaround in form and fortunes at the World Cup. Braces was young enough to keep playing beyond his 1990 retirement, but when Wrighty, who captained after Jeff Crowe, refused a tour to Pakistan and had therefore done his dash as captain, Martin was the next in line. That was it as far as Braces was concerned – he was forced to go, in a way. Around that time, when Braces was finishing up, the tensions could turn nasty, sometimes. After a great era, a lot of those senior guys finished quite flatly, and I thought that was a great shame.

Braces and Ian 'Stockley' Smith were always the first two to take the mickey out of someone if they cocked up – they were the ones who enforced the standards, in a way. Everyone pairs off within a team, and Smithy and Jeff Crowe got on very well, they were close within the team, and they happened to be the two I found hard work. It's fair to say I didn't really get on with Smithy, the way Braces didn't get on with Crowey. Smithy really did have his mood changes and swings – there was a running joke in the team that Smithy was "just having his period". He knew it as well as anyone.

With Stockley and I there was always a little bit of banter, but it would get quite snipey. He could be quite cutting, scathing. He could also be very funny. It just depended what mood he was in on the day. But it was always a case of he was one of the older guys and you were still doing your fellowship into the team. He made it his business to keep me in line, almost like the chief whip they have in English parliaments.

Smithy was big on etiquette. It seemed he was just waiting for you to step out of line so he could whip you back into shape. If you'd put on the wrong type of sponsor's shirt for a function, the wrong colour or style, he'd be right into you. I had these grey winklepicker shoes in 1987, but the team dress code for our number ones was black shoes. I'd been influenced by Joe Jackson wearing glorious white winklepickers on his "Look Sharp" album cover, but there were only grey ones left in the shop so those were what I bought to go away with. There was no room for fashion victims in the team culture back then and those shoes earned me plenty of backchat and a fair few fines in the team "court" sessions.

Another time I got on a plane late during a one-day series at home. It was packed, so I sat up the front in business class with sports photographer Ross Setford. There seemed to be no other seats, and although my economy seat was, in fact, vacant down the back, the air hostess had said I was fine up front. Willie Watson had been a mate and taken my shoulder bag down to the back where all the boys were sitting, so when we were getting off the plane I had to wait for it to come up, and also the ghettoblaster that I was in charge of, which was put into another cabin. As Smithy made his way towards me down the aisle he had a filthy look on his face and told me to pull my head in. *Who did I think I was sitting up here instead of with the team? What was I trying to pull, planting myself up in business class, unlike everyone else?*

Sometimes a moody episode could reflect into the day and around the dressing room. Smithy and I had a bit of a falling out during his swansong, the World Cup in 1992, over the wives being around. I used to babysit his kids a bit when he moved to Devonport so I was sad it ended with a bad taste. We'd have a bit of a set-to at the dining table in front of the whole team. It wasn't a good feeling at all, and yet the World Cup became a great feeling. To the credit of Wally Lees, our coach then, he'd get the air cleared in front of everyone, try to air our differences and just get on with it. I don't know why it was always so intense between Smithy and me, but it was.

Ken Rutherford used to wind Smithy up more than anyone, though. He'd take great delight in leaving a big bogey from his enormous nose hanging next to where Smithy would get changed. Smithy would just shriek at him. Ruds had a whole array of vulgar little tricks like that.

Despite the inevitable personality clashes, generally the culture of that side in the late 1980s was tight. That was the thing. Clashing with those older guys early on was actually a good learning experience and part of growing up within the team, and they all had their different methods of helping you into the traditional framework. These guys were older, they'd seen a lot more than you, they'd earned and they expected your respect. It's the starting order that you only get to go through once in your career, and I was very lucky to have those particular guys as the teachers.

Braces and those types of guys were good in the team because they'd also come out and have a beer with you, make a point of going out with you, sticking by you. A nucleus of four or five of us would go out a lot as a group – Braces, Wrighty, Sneds, Dipak and myself. I think the older guys had learned that from Lance Cairns, a great team man. I remember Braces stressing to me, in time, that it's important as a senior player to take young guys under your wing and help broaden their horizons, especially in a new culture. If they couldn't adapt to the inevitable culture shock touring other test nations, they weren't going to last long in international cricket. There were also certain etiquettes and protocols you had to adhere to, to gain acceptance, like wearing the right kit in the right place or making an effort to buy a round of drinks, and they made those things a bit easier for you.

I think I was actually much more extroverted than a lot of the young ones they'd inducted into the team in the past. And some that came after. But if I'd come in quietly and stayed in my shell, I wouldn't have got away with it. It seemed harder to survive in that environment if you were introverted, not seen to be giving to the team.

The special case was Andrew Jones. The aborted Sri Lankan trip had been Jonesy's first tour as well, but he was 28 and had played that much more than me, was known that much better on the circuit back home that he was more of a contemporary to the senior pros. Jonesy didn't say a lot or relate a lot; he did his own thing and was very unassuming and introverted. But the guys were quite accepting of that. He was never really the butt of jokes, or got too much of a hard time because he didn't open up. It was just the way he was.

I often roomed with Jonesy. He had great concentration, a unique player with a famously unorthodox batting technique. Though quiet, he could have quite a good sense of humour when he wanted to. But only when it suited him. It was always very hard getting into a conversation with him unless he'd had a few and loosened up. In fact, even living and breathing day to day with these men in the team environment on tour, I felt a lot of the time that I never really got to know the guys well enough and that they never really wanted to open up too much. Maybe it was the male culture, but also I think it was part of the professional ethic – you were essentially a workmate. They were intense, so involved in the game, that it took all those personal energies from them. At night you were tired. Guys didn't want to talk a lot about things, at times; they'd rather switch off.

I've found that even more the case in later years, and whether that's a trait of the television and computer generation, I don't know. But people don't seem to want to relax and talk more. It's made me more aware of how good it was of those 1980s legends to make such an effort to connect with me in 1987, because I must have seemed to have been from such a different generation myself. Willie Watson and I were a lot closer in those days, and I think it was because we were from that next generation, the 1960s babies. We hung out a lot with Mark Plummer, the team physiotherapist who started in 1988 and was our age. We'd known him as a useful batter for Papatoetoe in Auckland club cricket so he became the third amigo. Funnily enough Plums is now finding it very tough relating to a different culture – in his own country – an odd one out in a far younger New Zealand team.

In the late 1980s, the environment was so much different from what was to come in just a few, short (or were they long?) years. The players were such professionals, and mostly in their 30s. They didn't overindulge in late night activity – they might have a couple of quiet, social beers, but then they'd go up to their rooms to read or watch TV. They had a good sense of humour, sure, but their whole focus was cricket and wanting to be part of a fantastic side. They were giving totally of themselves, great role models and ambassadors in the twilight of their careers. I've never forgotten what it was like to be in that environment.

I soon noticed the more senior you were in the team, the closer to the front of the bus you sat. Maybe it was just more practical, away from us noisy ones up the back – it meant you got off quicker. Practicality comes naturally enough with maturity, but it seemed to me like a metaphor; the senior guys up front were driving the team. Paddles would always sit up the very front, Chats, Smithy, and the manager would be up there too. Braces and Sneds, the calm, cool guys, would be in the middle of the bus playing cards; they were the bridge. Over the years, sure enough, I gradually moved up to the front, too.

How they put up with some of my music I'll never know. Come to think of it, they usually didn't put up with it. I was a big British ska and Rolling Stones fan. Chats' generation would listen to The Eagles, mellow, easy-listening stuff, pure Radio i. Paddles listened to his family's own string quartet playing classical music, and Johnny Denver, Bob Dylan. Wrighty had a bit of taste and loved getting out his guitar on tour. He brought his Fender to Australia in 1989. He'd had a bit of a contra deal going with Dave McArtney of the Pink Flamingos; Wrighty brought Dave and his band along to get a bit of cricket coaching and in return Dave gave him some guitar lessons.

But they weren't ghettoblaster people and it was a lot more serious and businesslike in our dressing room back then. Hadlee didn't allow "music boxes", as he called them, in the dressing room at all. It interrupted focus. When Geoff Howarth came in as coach in 1993, he also leaned back to another decade and would march into the dressing room and tell us, "No bloody disco, thanks." You could always hear the music blaring from Aussie dressing rooms, where Allan Border let the younger guys cope with the environment in their own way, so it could be frustrating. I wanted to relax like that, too, have a good time at the end of the day. But Paddles and Chats and those guys really wouldn't have functioned well with that at all, and you understood and respected the status quo when you were the minority. But after 1990, when they'd retired, I was in charge of the music and it all changed!

New Zealand made two tours to India in my first years in the team, to the World Cup in 1987 and for a test tour in 1988. Because it was traditional on those long, hard tours of the subcontinent to focus on team-building and sticking together in an alien culture, a couple of special, extroverted characters on those tours really played an important role keeping our spirits up. They were the light relief in the midst of the seriousness.

Phil Horne, who was selected for the 1987 World Cup, was someone I'd played with a lot for Auckland. He was very genuine and integral, up front, but also just great fun to be around. We had a great bond because he was quite a livewire as well and enjoyed having a bit of a dance, but we really connected strongly during the World Cup because we were the two "spare parts" on that tour who didn't really play – the dirt-trackers, the specialist 12th and 13th men, the batter and the bowler who'd train a little extra together on our own and room together so we could lair up and blast our sounds without disturbing the pros! We used to sit at the back of the bus together singing Cliff Richard's "We're all going on a summer holiday".

It's quite deceptive how old 'Hornet' is – he's closer to Sneds' age than mine, but he has so much energy that he always seems younger. Unfortunately he was also quite injury-prone with it – his other nickname was 'Balsa'. Always banging into things and smashing himself up. He was very into everything, full on, a hundred miles an hour, always flexing his agility and charging around, but also had to be constantly very careful and aware of himself and wrapped in cotton wool because of his frame. It was very frustrating for him.

In Australia after the World Cup, the team played a game of forceback footie at the 'Gabba. It was just before a test and we'd had a few injuries. John Wright was getting particularly scratchy because it has been a long 12 months for his body, and there was a real chance of Hornet opening the batting. There was an old dog track at that time inside the fence at the 'Gabba, and we were cautioned to be careful, not to run into the fence. But Hornet went running back determined to take a catch off a big punt and, sure enough, almost impaled himself on this fence. He bounced off it like a barfly and ruptured his neck. On the verge of getting back into the test side, he refused to be touched by the physio, so much was he wanting to carry on. He just loved playing and was mad as a snake, really.

Hornet played badminton to international level at the same time as cricket, going to the Brisbane and Edinburgh Commonwealth Games before finishing up in 1990. He had so much energy, but he had one of those fast metabolisms that meant when the energy was suddenly spent, he'd just crash and burn. His special, hyper qualities made him an excellent fielder – he and Chris Harris were similar sorts as young guys, light as a feather and agile as a monkey.

When it was clear New Zealand couldn't make it to the semi-finals of the 1987 World Cup (a great disappointment since we'd managed it at the previous tournament four years earlier), Hornet and I got our first game on tour, at Nagpur against India, which was my one-day international debut. It was the last match and we'd really got our chance by default, a chance to bank a little experience when the team no longer had much at stake.

Hornet didn't have a great game. He got out for spit. Then, when we went out to field, the Indians wanted to bash it around, because to get themselves a home semifinal they needed to beat our 221-9 by about the 33rd over. So I got smashed round the park. Willie would have called it "like bowling in the highlights". Hornet hadn't played for ages and not only did the poor bugger not get any runs, but when a catch came at a beautiful height, sitting there for him to reverse-cup it into his chest, he reverse-cupped the hands but the ball bounced straight out. He shelled it. Those are the moments you just wish the ground would open up and swallow you whole. We lost by a country mile (and nine wickets).

The other different, extroverted head that rather stood out in that late 80s culture belonged to Tony 'Chill' Blain. Blainy had been on the 1986 tour to England before I made the New Zealand side, and joined it again for the 1988 campaign in India. The chief reason he stood out so much was because he'd peroxided his sunny head a Billy Idol blond.

He was an unusual one for a Nelson country boy. He was a real achiever, had a great, cheeky sense of humour, and at the same time would try to be quite suave, laid back and cool. He oozed confidence in social situations, and looked after himself, cared for his body. He's travelled around a lot and enjoyed taking almost a big-brotherly role with younger guys, teaching them how to enjoy themselves out on the road, expressing his legion of life experiences often in a very funny, entertaining way.

Chill was very open-minded and would throw himself wholeheartedly at new thoughts and ideas. The boys got quite a shock one time in Sharjah when they ran into him wandering around the hotel in a green face pack – he'd been told seaweed was good for the skin. He was the first cricketer, after myself, to take an interest in my wife's aromatherapy oils. He used to put Bergamot – for nervous anxiety – and calming Lavender on the tips of his collars before he went out into the field or to bat, so that he could just lean down and sniff at his shirt to calm his nerves in anxious moments!

Chill was a bundle of enthusiasm. He had a lifetime's supply of nervous energy. The most irritating thing about rooming with him was he wouldn't be asleep when everyone else was. He'd be up tapping his bat in the early morning when you'd be trying to crash out.

He was also the great romancer. I toured Zimbabwe with him as part of a Young New Zealand side. He picked up a girlfriend on that tour, the only one of the young guys there to do so, whom the rest of us very cheekily referred to as "Heather 10-speed". Heather was a big, Amazon blonde. They would go out and it would be the full Sylvester Stallone from Chill: he'd lay on this sultry voice, confident smile and Hollywood threads. He was rooming that whole tour with Martin Pringle, who could barely get in their hotel bathroom for all Chill's potions – for his hair, his skin, the whole bit. He'd have the longest showers in the team because he had to shampoo, then condition, then special rinse his hair, leaving everything to soak in.

When it came to fashion, Chill was a retailer's bunny, going through phase after phase, throwing his money wholeheartedly at his fleeting passions. On one particular tour of Australia he started a belt collection: he had belts with studs, colours, you name it, he had to have it. That led him into his buckle phase: there was one with a big chevvy on it, the bulldog, the confederate flag . . . He just

Mum's Nana Mouskouri impersonation . . . The Morrisons, circa 1970.

Grand matriarch Hazel Levin, my mother's mum.

'Mi-an-dad'. Out west on the farm, 1967.

The 1981 Takapuna Grammar First XI. Coach is none other than Murray 'Mad Dog' Deaker.

Test debut against Australia at The Gabba, 1987.

Wedding day, April 1993. One of my most cherished days.

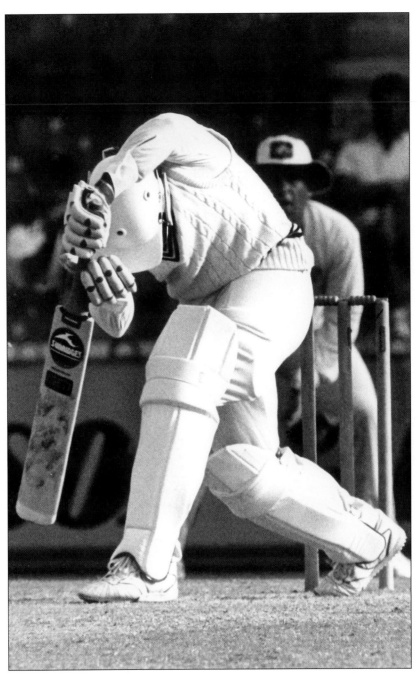

The Morrison forward defensive – head-butting a Carl Rackemann bouncer at the WACA, 1989.

Letting Dean Jones smell the leather, Perth test, 1989. Always enjoyed this sight . . .

. . . and this sight was even better!

I've got Dilip Vengsarkar caught behind during the Eden Park test against India, 1990.

wasn't a Country Road type of guy. You could certainly never miss him in a room.

Blainy and Chris Kuggeleijn, who also toured India in 1988, were thick as thieves. They had a similar sense of humour, both hard case country boys, a couple of mad blonds. They fancied themselves as entrepreneurs and in Sharjah in 1988 they got onto the fact that Lacoste shirts were really cheap there. They shelled out on about 50 shirts each and brought them back to flog off in New Zealand. Trouble was they missed the boat – they were just going out of style when we got back. They've probably still got rows of pristine Lacostes in the back of their wardrobes today.

TAKE IT EASY

STRAIGHT
OLD LINE

R ichard Hadlee was my role model. More than a role model. He and Dennis Lillee were the two men who'd inspired me to play cricket in the first place.

Hadlee didn't go to the World Cup in 1987; he was saving himself up for Australia. He'd almost single-handedly slaughtered the Aussies on his previous tour of their land – that was the series late in 1985 that he took 9-52, his test best, at the 'Gabba; New Zealand beat the Aussies 2-1 in the tests on their turf, then later that same summer won 1-0 from a three-test showdown on our own pitches. It was emphatic, a mesmerising, nation-grabbing season of cricket against our ultimate foe and there was hope and expectation that the next campaign across the ditch at the tail of 1987 would be *The Terminator, Part Two*. So, although I'd now already been on two international tours and was yet to play at home, Australia 1987 was the big one. It meant so much more to me, because although I'd briefly toured alongside Hadlee in Sri Lanka, I knew this time I would be seeing the pace master out hunting on territory that had a personal meaning to both of us. The touring squad was named just before we left New Delhi after the World Cup and I was ecstatic that both Willie Watson and I made it.

In New Zealand, Hadlee was a superfish in a small pond. He put New Zealand bowling on the map, head and shoulders above everyone else. He helped win our test matches more than any other individual. He was uncompromising. In 1979, in the English magazine *Wisden Cricket Monthly*, there was an article about the elusive 300 test wicket club: the writer would have scoffed if anyone had told him at the time that 11 years later a New Zealand man would be the first to 400 wickets. That was the power of this one man.

He'd simply achieved that much more in cricket than anyone else. That was what was daunting about him – those treasured statistics you knew so well, and that he flaunted with professional cunning. Cricket doesn't throw up great all-round players like Hadlee, Kapil Dev, Ian Botham, Imran Khan every generation. I was unquestionably lucky to be around when they were all competing for the crown of the great allrounder in the late 1980s, to witness the standard and intensity of their private competition within the game. To be in King Richard's court. To stand there at mid-off or mid-on, waiting for my turn to bowl, watching him stutter at the top of his mark as he always did, then glide in and take a batsman apart.

He was the unrivalled centre of my attention in Australia in 1987. In every dressing room I tried to sit opposite to Hadlee so I could have a clear view of the master and study him intensely. I was constantly wide-eyed about him, trying to see how he did it, how he was organised. And he was *absolutely* organised. When he laid out his coffin or his suitcase, everything had its place and it was tidy. The clothes would be ironed. Unpacking or packing, everything went into its place. I saw how he had his goals taped to the top of the lid of his coffin, reiterating key thoughts about being focused and like a well-oiled machine. Thinking about the positives, remembering that each day is a new day, remembering to do his homework on each player: all these points were part of his meticulous focus and visualisation routines.

I remember he'd hold a cricket ball in his hand, seam up, and just be flicking it into the air before he went out and bowled, getting his wrist action working and getting the ball to pop out seam-up. Then he'd do his stretching and exercises. All that left a great impression on me. I would just watch the ultimate pro, the freak, look for signs of how he'd survived so long, so well. He'd shortened his run up in 1982 and got a lot of flak for that from traditionalists in the game, but it allowed him to last in international cricket until his 39th birthday during his last test match in 1990. Right through to the end, I never really took my eyes off him. I was in awe of him throughout.

Hadlee had a different mana to anyone else in the team. He wasn't aloof, but there was always a pervading sense that he was a bit special, a different case. He was the professional going back and forth to England with the lucrative contracts and tunnel vision.

He also knew, by the time I surfaced in the team, that his time was finishing – and he was making the most of it. He was trying to eke out of the game as much as he could. As everyone knows, he was very stats and goal orientated. That kept him going. In 1987 he had test wicket world record holder Ian Botham in his sights and was closing in when I first got in the side. You knew in India, in 1988, that he probably wouldn't have come at all if he had managed to claim Botham's record on this Australia tour, a year earlier – he was coming up 38, and with age the subcontinent becomes an even tougher place to tour than usual. I still remember Paddles bent over, vomiting out on the pitch at Bangalore, looking like a ghost.

As a person, Paddles had a dry sense of humour – a lot of bad jokes and bad shirts! But that was him: the special case, always a bit different. You would see Sneds relate to him well. I remember times during games when Sneds would be raving away to him in the corner of a dressing room and they always looked very intense and serious. Cricket was discussed as business in the shed, it wasn't a muck around, slap your buddy type behaviour.

Richard was seven years older than Martin, and Martin was seven years older than me. Fourteen years is quite a sharp generation gap and it was very much like that between Richard and myself. Despite the age difference, a highlight of my first tour to Australia was rooming with him during the second test match in Adelaide. As one of the most senior pros, he sometimes would have his own room on tour, but it was a done thing, a tradition for experienced heads to room with one of the crazy young guys to pass on knowledge. He didn't mind, and so it was that the sorcerer and the apprentice, as the Australian cricket writer Patrick Smithers described us, roomed together high up on the 14th floor of Adelaide's Gateway Hotel.

If you were on one of the higher floors, your room looked back across the pretty, leafy grounds around the Adelaide Oval. Every practice day, or evening during the test that week, we'd come back to our room with the vista sweeping out below us and talk earnestly about the game.

We talked about the "KISS" theory – that's short for keep it simple, stupid. Quite often we did speak about very simple ideas, but when you heard them from his lips, they took on larger meaning.

Some of the words he said remain entrenched in my mind.

Always believe in yourself. Be totally focused when you're at the top of your bowling mark. No matter how things are going you must always keep running in because you never know when your next victim will come along. Never clutter your mind with too many things, always just focus on what you're going to do with the next ball. No matter what the obstacles are, you should always try to keep your drive and focus. Always have your goals in mind, make sure they're attainable and realistic goals, and always aspire to do your best and give 100 per cent.

I learned to trigger key words in my mind as I bowled. They were: focus, switch on, base of off stump (which gave you something to focus on whether it was a left or right-handed batter), rhythm, front arm, follow-through. Whether you'd set the guy up for a bouncer or a slower ball or got closer into the stumps, the bottom line was getting the basic elements of bowling right each time. Then you could have your guy on toast, as Hadlee was fond of saying.

It was a really cherished time, that learning curve, hearing those things from someone like him. Sitting around relaxing in the room with the great man after dinner, the TV going with the sound turned down so he could talk to me. The only thing that was disconcerting was that our room seemed almost too immaculately tidy. Having said that, in later years Chris Cairns always felt that Dan was just too organised, too. Maybe it shows the importance bowlers start to attach to their routines. It was fortunate for Paddles that I was quite tidy naturally, even as a teenager – I used to get a hard time about that from my mates at school. I just functioned that way. Some guys' rooms are atrocious on tour. It doesn't matter if that's what works for you. But Dan's shoes were always neatly laid out and everything was put away in the cupboard! Two hours on Saturday morning had always been put aside for chores and helping my mother around the home when I was growing up. Maybe all those hours of doing the compost and the bathroom had put me in good stead. When I saw how routine Hadlee could be, it was as if I knew that ability was already there in me, too.

That was big for me, that rooming experience, that whole time. Almost exactly a year later, Paddles and I were rostered to room together again, this time in an awful, cramped hotel in Rajkot, a sort of dry, industrial backwater in the western part of India. It was a refresher course, going over with him the elements I'd tried to absorb and control in my first real year of development as an international bowler. We were touring an even tougher place then, especially for fast bowlers, because it was so barren. It was a good time to speak of all those little things again, the goals, targets, what

I wanted to achieve, where I was at, going to the nets and practising quality rather than practising stale, or for the sake of practice itself.

It wasn't until the end of that first season, when I'd taken my first few test wickets, that I started to relax a bit more with him and feel accepted as one of the pros in the team. It always remained the schoolmaster-type role with Richard, we were too far apart in age to become firm and fast friends. It was hard, at times, more of a business relationship, one that never got as close as it was for, say, me and Martin Snedden. But certainly after that Indian tour, we could relate well.

I definitely connected with him as a person better once he'd actually finished playing. When he finished up in England in 1990, you could see quite clearly how intense it was for him playing in England, particularly with his father, Walter Hadlee, there watching. Cricket was a huge part of his life, a family tradition, his driving force and a business that kept him incredibly busy, not only on the park, but off it with innumerable commitments and contacts. Though he was a part of our team on that tour, we actually saw very little of him. I often roomed with Jonesy.

No one resented Richard's style, however, because his actions spoke louder than his words and it was hard not to be in awe of them. He was the superstar, and yet not the cocksure, Hollywood type. He was always too busy succeeding for that.

It was quite difficult for me to accept that the great man's career had to come to an end, and quite scary. The selectors had been looking for someone to take over from him, but no one really could and I doubt anyone really will. There'll be other opening bowlers and other fast bowlers who can get a bit of seam, but Hadlee is incomparable.

That I seemed earmarked to follow in his outsized footsteps (that's why he was called Paddles, after all) was a burden, a weight on my shoulders. It was going to be tough for anyone taking over from such a legend, but here, of all people, you had a garden gnome from Devonport. When I look at my schooling, my background, where I come from, it almost doesn't make sense. Why not someone like Cairnsie, who had the traditional cricket and family background, the classic physique, the natural dominance? Someone like that deserved his mantle, surely, not this shortarse from the North Shore from a non-cricketing background, breaking the mould, brought up by his mum and just plain lucky to have been channelled in the right direction by Murray Deaker at school . . .

The positive aspect to that was that at least there weren't the immediate comparisons. I was such a different stature to Hadlee that we were viewed as different entities on the bowling crease – had someone like England's Andy Caddick been following him, it would have been much tougher on the pretender from a public and emotional perspective. I'm more of a strength bowler, more explosive, whereas he had a lot more rhythm and timing in his action. It means I've found it more physically demanding to try to bowl fast, but it was a blessing not to have that immediate comparison.

But all too suddenly, just three years after I'd first played alongside him, it happened. It was a cold day in June and I was almost numb. We sat in a couple of cold bucket seats around the boundary at Hove, in Sussex, while our side was batting on that 1990 England tour.

Hadlee said that it was over to me, a formal handing over of power.

He said, "You're the strike bowler now. You know I'm finishing now, you're taking over from me. You've got to believe in yourself about taking the mantle, Danny. There's other perks that come with it. If you do well, there's other commercial and sponsorship opportunities that also reward you. It is worth it to want to do well and to make a career out of it if you want it badly enough. So do you think you want it badly enough?"

I did. I understood the point he was making, and I knew that for sure. But it was hard for me to accept, that conversation. My brain told me I'd just dominated against India and Australia at home the summer before, but the heart was shouting that Hadlee was the ultimate bowler and I didn't want it to end. I just wasn't within a bull's roar of him, to be dead honest. No one else would fill those shoes. He dominated so much. Look at the stats. He'd taken his 100th test wicket only in February 1979, but though he only played 11 years more, he chewed through 331 more test wickets at a time when New Zealand played a hell of a lot less test cricket than some other nations. He was the fastest man ever from 200 to 300 wickets – and obviously the fastest from 300 to 400, because the only other one to do that was the old Indian train, Kapil Dev.

To be told by Richard Hadlee on a cold day in Hove that this is where it happened for me, may the force be with me, was really quite a shock. All too suddenly it was over, that amazing period in my life where I got a chance to see a hero close-up, to room with him, to learn my trade from him. I watched him walk out the dressing room door as a player for the last time and a great era, far exceeding my own few years alongside him, was over.

THAT'S ENTERTAINMENT

I'll never forget the way it felt to be 20 years old and careering around the Australian continent with the full heat of international cricket shining in my face. My tours to the subcontinent, to the World Cup and Sri Lanka, may have been packed with culture shock and all the names on the international stage, but somehow I'd never felt part of the action – more a passenger in a land far away, quite distant and removed from any sort of real attention in the world of cricket. The *real* culture shock for me as a new player was going from those relatively quiet tours to a land down under in the full grip of summer cricket fever – and baying for eleven New Zealanders' blood.

Australia was a kind of cricketing Disneyland. The big difference across the Tasman was that no single winter code dominated the nation; it was split into geographic factions of rugby union, rugby league and Australian rules. So cricket, the summer code, was the binding force and you seldom met an Aussie who wasn't intent on seeing his patriotism expressed through the country's favourite team. The media thronged the big players; Allan Border was as famous as any man in the land.

As a youngster, crisscrossing that big, burnt continent was amazing, seeing the hype about the sport, the attention from the public and the media zero in on you in every city, the talk it generated as Australia's national sport. I was bursting out of my skin within days of landing in the country, pumped up by the energy and bright lights that suddenly surrounded us and the charge of being on tour again alongside Richard Hadlee. But the single moment that gave me goosebumps was when our plane first glided in to land at Perth.

Perth was Dennis Lillee country, which is tantamount to saying it was holy land. If R.J. Hadlee was my hero, D.K. Lillee was my idol – I treasured the fact that I had the same initials. He was the ultimate. I'd actually already met the great man a few times, having been to his fast bowling clinics in Auckland, in 1985, 1986 and 1987 (he ran these in a number of places around the world, on a mission to help young fast bowlers develop). Now it was me on his turf. The power of that feeling was unforgettable.

Martin Snedden said to me, "You're just going to love this – but don't get carried away with it, try to still be up there giving your ball the chance to swing."

Sure enough, the Western Australia Cricket Ground was heaven. I couldn't believe the practice facilities there. The nets had pace, bounce, consistency – it was so mind-blowingly superior to Eden Park. And in those nets, standing next to Hadlee and Chats throwing me tips like bits of meat to a hungry animal, all I really wanted to do was get carried away, run in and bowl hard and fast. I could see in an instant why Australia had produced an abundance of fast bowlers, especially since the war. The surfaces were great, they encouraged you. For both Willie Watson and I, I can't stress enough how wide-eyed we suddenly were. We were so lucky to be there, the apprentices to the sorcerers in these magic lands. I was having the time of my life. And I'd pinch myself catching a glimpse of myself on TV here amongst the players intent on giving the Australians more of their bitter medicine.

Willie and I thought we were pretty much the dirt-trackers on the tour, behind Hadlee, Chatfield and Sneds, with Martin Crowe able to back them up as a very useful part-time swing bowler.

We played the first two tour games against Western Australia at the WACA and a South Australia country XI up in Renmark, but then didn't play at Adelaide, a four-day game against South Australia and the last warm-up to the first test in Brisbane. I honestly didn't think I was going to play in the test match, and that was reasonable to assume, though I'd done quite well and picked up wickets at vital times in both innings of our Perth three-day game. But it was nothing to set the world alight. To be honest, it was such a dream time that I was happy just to be on the tour. Of course I was burning to play test cricket, but you were tempered by realism and just didn't expect it, particularly when you were among the league I was in. They could have easily used the same combination they'd used in 1985 – Sneds, Chats, Paddles. Sneds had bowled well enough so far on tour.

I'll never forget Jeff Crowe coming up to me on the eve of the first test. I was in the nets there at the Woolloongabba Cricket Ground in Brisbane and he said, quite simply, "You're going to play this test match. We want you to run in and bowl fast." It really threw me. Far out! As I realised I'd taken Sneds' spot, it quietly surprised me.

The adrenalin started pumping instantly. Here we were at the 'Gabba, the very ground where Hadlee had taken his 9-52, 15 wickets in the match only two years before. I'd watched that match live on TV, when I was getting over my back injury, wanting to be there so badly. Hadlee was just a sight to behold that day. It was one of the most perfect performances you could see in cricket, an artist's work. He'd bowled to a high mix of left and right handers in that match, got in close to the stumps, swung it at them, interrogated them, hardly using the bouncer – he was like a dentist with a fine probe, subtly picking the batsmen to pieces, being very controlled and patient. And now I would actually be there, that very place, playing test cricket against Border's Aussies at the 'Gabba. I could scarcely believe my luck.

We had a series sponsor's get-together at the Brisbane Sheraton the evening before the test. It was amazing to look around the room at the unmistakable faces of Merv Hughes, Craig McDermott, Bruce Reid and Allan Border, faces I'd seen so much on television, and occasionally from the terraces of Eden Park or from a distance in India. To think that tomorrow I would be playing test cricket against them. Mentally, the leap to test cricket was huge. For the Australians, Mike Velletta was also making his test debut; maybe he felt the same way I did when he caught sight of Richard Hadlee.

Cricket's a great sport for superstitious behaviour and the Aussies took it to extremes the following morning. They had decided that because they wanted to reverse the fortunes of two years ago, they would do the exact opposite in 1987 to everything they did in 1985. We were very surprised to arrive and find ourselves in Queensland's dressing room – the home dressing room, that was much bigger and more comfortable than the visitors', where the Australians had parked their gear.

Even though it was a typically humid, dripping Brisbane day, as far as I was concerned the air was snapping and sparking the morning of that first test match. The morning session of a first day is always like that, but when it's your maiden test match, every little thing becomes accentuated, blood rushing to all your senses. It was hard to stay calm. Border won the toss and sent us in on a wicket that was clearly going to assist the pace bowlers. We didn't make very many at all, only 186, Martin Crowe and Wrighty the only ones holding up the innings.

I took my first steps into a test match right at the end of that less than glorious first day. Down at ten (Chats wasn't about to surrender his number eleven spot), I'd been hoping not to have to bat, and I remember feeling foolishly inadequate going out there for the first time. I wasn't switched on or focused enough. There were only four overs to go to stumps, but it was the second new nut and the ball was fizzing. I was wearing John Bracewell's helmet and just wanted to survive. But, being young and cocky, I didn't wear a grill and that, from a raw tailender to a fast bowler, was like a red rag to a bull.

I suddenly felt quite daunted. Bruce Reid hurled a bouncer that went right over my head, as you'd expect with the slight difference in our heights. But Greg Dyer, their wicketkeeper, jogged past and barked, "You little shit, you'll get plenty more of that, too." The slips behind me became very noisy, yabbering to McDermott, "Come on Billy, let's get one up his snotbox . . ." I could hear Steve Waugh in there somewhere. He was their new whizzkid – and already a champion sledger.

I lasted seven balls and got caught behind for nought by Steve Waugh at slip. Yet again, a tragic sign of things to come! I was actually quite brassed off that I was good enough to nick it, instead of playing and missing. Chats, the wise old head, took my place and survived the last few overs.

I hit the pillow that night with a headful of thoughts about how different it was out there to any other cricket I'd played. It was such a contest, with a real gladiatorial atmosphere built around the one-on-one confrontations between batsman and bowler, the crowd questioning your parentage and throwing obscenities, the slips having a piece of you. It was so real! So much a contrast to the pathetic banter you got in a first class game at some small park in Rangiora or Levin . . . It was a step up and away from anything I'd seen in New Zealand.

The next day, I was far more nervous the first time I walked out to bowl than I was to bat. I have a low blood pressure and get into a very vague state sometimes, when it's as if everything around me is in a movie, I've stepped back from reality and am just watching it. I could feel my neck pumping and the clammy air around me and thought, hell, am I really here, striding out with Hadlee and Chats in a test against Australia? Wasn't I only just down in Stanley Bay running in on a concrete pitch with a painted tennis ball doing my impersonations of these guys?

I always thought Auckland was sticky in summer, but it was nothing compared to Brisbane and the sweat was trickling down my back before I even walked up to place my mark. Being very much the junior, I had to bowl up the 'Gabba hill – Hadlee came downward from the Vulture Street end. I was struggling to get up the slope and into their face in the sticky breeze and I went for something like 15 in my first three overs. It wasn't a very good start.

Then I went to clean my boot, which had become gummed up in my delivery stride with this black clay they have in Queensland. I accidentally flicked my nail back in the process, so that the corner of the nailbed stuck right out and blood was pouring down my thumb. That was a bit much for me and I started to feel faint. Thankfully the sightscreen attendant was near on the boundary and had some ice in a coke esky. I grabbed some, holding it round the thumb until it numbed. I'll never forget looking back up and staring along the ground from where I was fielding, towards the Clem Jones stand. It was humid, it was hot, I'd been caned and now I'd messed up my hand and was feeling nauseous. I thought, geez, I come all this way and this happens. If this is test cricket, you can stick it!

But that burst of pain from my nail was like a wake-up call to my brain. Hello, Danny? Switch on! We're here, smell the coffee, snap out of it! Then I was swapped to bowl from the other end – Hadlee's end, the end from which he'd got 9-52 – and all of a sudden the feelings within me lifted.

Hadlee had got an earlyish wicket, Geoff Marsh for 25, then number three, Dean Jones, for two. Border was in at four. I turned at the top of my mark, saw the nuggety little guy with the dark green cap, a moustache where a grill might have been on any other batsman, characteristically tap-tapping his bat as I ran in trying desperately not to feel completely overawed. I felt like David bowling to Goliath.

I was conscious of trying to swing the ball in the groove, but was aware also that I'd damaged my nail and the best I could realistically hope for was just to hang in there and improve my figures for a start. But quite quickly I got Border to blatantly tickle one down the legside and Ian Smith flashed across for the catch. I was delighted, my first test wicket, Border for bugger all – but then I turned and saw Mel Johnson, the umpire, his face as stiff as a board. He had decided to give it "not out". I look back on it now and think it was another little omen. It summed up everything that was going to come: things weren't going to be easy for me in cricket. Because of my physical non-attributes, I was always going to have to work extra hard, starting on day one.

Braces yelled across to me, "Come on Danny, dig deep."

I glanced at Hadlee and thought to myself, focus . . . rhythm . . . off-stump . . . here we go.

And then, not too long afterwards, I remember going up for the appeal, as if it was all in slow motion. I saw the umpire's finger go up: I had my first test wicket, A.R. Border, the Australian captain and number four, lbw for 9. I was floating on cloud nine, but as much with relief as anything else, because the let-off hadn't ended up costing us dearly. I didn't really leap around. As the first couple of guys ran in towards me, I just winked and nodded. Some guys wait an eternity to get their first wicket, but I'd got one. Got it. Got *him*. It was sweet justice more than sheer joy.

Unfortunately for us, David Boon went into limpet mode and ended up making 143. Ken Rutherford enjoyed the sight of me bowling to him. "Quite bizarre, isn't it," he quipped from point. "The two shortest men in the world playing international cricket. David Boon, the shortest batter in the world, and the shortarsed Danny Morrison charging in bowling at him."

The thing that really got me going was that none of the Australians wore helmets back then, except the openers and tailenders. Not even Greg Dyer, the keeper batting at seven, thought we were worth one. It was so arrogant. Steve Waugh would wear a lid just with earpieces, but he'd whip it off as soon as the new ball wore off its coat.

I'd nearly cleaned up Dean Jones as the ball fizzed past his face. It seemed such a contest that I couldn't help myself. These guys stared back at you saying, "Well come on champ, I'm still here buddy, I'm having a go at you." It was amazing to have that in your face when you were the guy holding the new ball and running in. Jones had obviously been stamping his authority on a new pup. But they all had plenty to say.

I had quite a duel with Steve Waugh. He was playing and missing a bit, but surviving. Then I hit him in the box. He was doubled over in pain. I saw it again on the Channel Nine highlights later that night. Richie Benaud was commentating and noted that Waugh and

I were both stretching our back/groin at the same time in the interruption. He purred, "Now isn't this interesting, there we have the opening bowler and the batsman doing identical stretches, but for entirely separate reasons . . ."

The contest was on and I was into it. Waugh played a couple of loose shots and ended up flicking out round the corner to Andrew Jones at square leg, right at the end of the second day's play. The next day Don Cameron wrote a lovely piece in the *New Zealand Herald* about "when Danny Morrison crossed the Border from make-believe land to reality . . ." It was very apt.

Sadly we weren't able, in the end, to repeat the glory of 1985, Australia winning with over a day to spare on the back of their 119-run first innings lead. Maybe changing the dressing rooms had worked after all. But although we lost the match, that test is still quite vivid in my mind, even though it happened coming up 10 years ago.

The four wickets I picked up in Brisbane in such elite company gave me confidence as we moved further into the tour, through the remaining tests at Adelaide and Melbourne. I started to really relish the atmosphere the Australian crowds generated at the magnificent venues in that country. The volatile, barracking Aussies really wanted a piece of Hadlee, because he'd been so successful there previously, taking wickets, winning the car, the whole bit. They began to chant, over and over, from ground to ground, "Hadlee's a wanker!" It was amazing to be in that different cauldron, and the energy of it, the excitement brought out the showman in me. I thrived on the banter. When I was in Melbourne, a guy yelled out, "Morrison, you garden gnome, where'd your mother find you? Down the bottom of the garden?" He followed that up with, "Listen mate, I've heard of sheep getting their tails docked – but who docked ya legs?"

The eleven Aussies inside the boundary rope would still be getting stuck in, too, but I never really got tied into the "verbal" after that first test and just smiled and winked at them. Jeff Crowe would get irritated and say, "Right, there's no smiling today, Danny. That's part of the rules for today. It's the full campaign, OK?" It didn't work.

It was a real shame we lost that test series, because we didn't deserve to. It would have been a fairer result if it had been one-all. It was actually Australia's first home series win for a long time, since Lillee, Rod Marsh and Chappell had retired in 1984. The great moment of high drama came in Melbourne, after we'd drawn the second test and were fighting for a win. Phil Horne and John Wright had given us the best starts of the series, Wrighty making 99 in the first dig before McDermott had him painfully caught behind, while Martin Crowe had scored 82 and 79. Hadlee, meanwhile, took bags of five in both innings. But whatever we seemed to manage, Australia return-served it straight back at us. The whole match boiled down to the final day, when Australia, batting for 247 to win, got off to a great start before Hadlee tore through them again in the last session, turning the game right back around in our favour. Finally there was just the tailenders, McDermott and Mike Whitney, left at the batting crease. Suddenly we were staring at a win instead of a loss.

Bowling to McDermott, my veins were on fire. McDermott wasn't the greatest of batsmen in the Australian brigade and when the ball rapped him loudly on his pad, I went up, certain that I'd got him out lbw. I think all of New Zealand and possibly half of Australia believed that too, but umpire Dick French got his hand stuck in his pocket. I couldn't believe it; the whole match and series came down to one, marginal decision.

But that tour has remained nonetheless nothing but a good memory for me. It was the realisation of a dream – one I discovered I really did want to be part of. Far beyond my initial expectations, I'd ended up playing all three tests of the series. As we left the MCG after the last day, I remember Willie Watson saying, "Mate, that's a good effort to be playing the whole three in the series." It was something he hadn't managed to do as the young pace bowler in England the year before. As we were heading out of the ground for the Hilton I also ran into Dennis Lillee, and he lifted me onto the moon with a smile and a few words of encouragement.

When I got back to New Zealand, I played a couple of Shell Trophy matches before the home test series against England was due to start. I felt like I'd got my whip and wanted to crack it against everyone I came up against. Bob Cunis was about to take over the coaching role for New Zealand. He caught up with me and explained what he wanted to see from me if I was to make my home debut against the Poms. He told me to show the selectors that I really wanted it by charging in on the more contrary New Zealand pitches. The competition was still quite fierce, with at least five guys vying for positions in the bowling contingent by my reckoning, so I had no problem giving it my all. In my enthusiasm I developed a side strain and ended up tearing my rib cartilage in Wellington. But it was going to take more than that to hold me back now.

THAT'S ENTERTAINMENT

SATISFACTION

I loved that time, when everything about international cricket was new and exciting. But they were also uncertain times, when I felt quite insecure as a young bowler trying to be accepted, trying to cement a place in that inspiring New Zealand side. The first battle was just to stay in it consistently.

Until Ewen Chatfield retired in 1989, Martin Snedden, Willie Watson and myself were competing for the third seamer's spot, behind Chats and Richard Hadlee. Sometimes they'd play four of us, but very rarely. In the tests, it would be Hadlee/Chatfield/Morrison quite often, while Willie would frequently take my place in the one-day internationals.

But at the beginning of the 1988/89 season, after a tour of India, I was on the outer a little bit and Willie and Sneds went to play the first test against Pakistan at Dunedin and I didn't. The fact that the whole match was washed out by rain and they never got a start wasn't much consolation to me.

You'd still find out whether you were in or out by reading it in the paper or hearing your name on the radio, or over the speakers at a ground. The time I didn't go down to Dunedin was the one time in that era that the convenor of selectors, Don Neely, did ring me and say, "Look Danny, we're picking some horses for courses here. Willie's been in really good form and Dunedin's a slow wicket."

I think that was the first time I was actually rung by any selector about a team selection. In those days they didn't really even have faxes – there would just be a press release and you'd find out through the media; then a day or two later there would be a letter in the mail from the New Zealand Cricket Council when you already knew!

For the second test at Wellington, Willie was left out and I was back in. It wasn't easy to stay in the team in those days, and even when we toured together as a group, the competitive nature of the situation never left you. Every time I was passed over, no matter what was actually said, I knew the message was I had to get out and perform yet again. Though it could be murder on the nerves, basically it was good for me.

Your natural insecurity was sharpened by the common knowledge that it was a time of imminent change in the New Zealand pace bowling department. Everyone knew that Hadlee and Chats, both in their late 30s, were coming to the end of their careers. There was a constant jockeying of position between the hopefuls intent on taking their place.

There was a lot of hype in the latter half of the 1980s about the greying of Hadlee's temples and the urgent need to find someone to "replace" him, particularly, upon his inevitable retirement. Through to that eventual day in England in 1990, the selectors experimented with a raft of pace bowlers: Sneds, Willie, Derek Stirling, Gary Robertson, Brian Barrett, Brendon Bracewell, Johnathan Millmow, Chris Pringle to an extent. Sean Tracy was on the verge of selection at times. But the bowlers always tended to be more in the mould of Chatfield than Paddles. They were really looking for someone who was quicker, who could swing the ball, to start taking over from Richard. That was my saving grace.

My biggest motivating factor in cricket had always been just run in and bowl fast. Dennis Lillee had reiterated the simplicity of it to me at his coaching clinics in the mid-80s. He'd said, "Don't ever actually forget that you want to run in and bowl fast. You're a new ball bowler, your strength is that you can bowl quicker than the rest. OK, you're not tall, but you do run in fast and skid at them and you're a natural swinger of the ball. Worry about the accuracy thing later. You'll only be trying to refine that basic talent, to get in the groove more, make the batter play, upset them with skidding bouncers and things."

My pace was my extra armoury. I was so lucky. Because Hadlee and Chats had both been so durable, a number of other, more experienced, but older, bowlers had really already missed the boat by the time a vacancy finally opened up. I came along at the right time in the right place.

Young bowlers were also coming and going at a rapid rate at the time, often losing a lot of confidence and form, or breaking down. Johnny Millmow and then, in 1989, Chris Cairns, were prime examples of young guys trying so hard that they ended up with stress fractures, forced off the park when they most wanted to be on it. But for me, apart from having an extra gear in my bowling, my other great saving grace was that I got injured young.

When you're a mad teen you think you're bulletproof. As a kid fresh out of school I'd got into the Auckland and New Zealand under-19 sides, making a short tour to Australia with the national youth side before I went over on my ankle, snapping my ligaments and ending up with my foot in a cast. Without really taking much time to rebuild my fitness, next I went away to play a summer in English club cricket.

Club cricket's a very relaxed environment at the best of times – games didn't start until two of an afternoon – and especially being in a new country with plenty of places to explore and other things to distract me, I never did enough training, warm-ups, warm-downs, stretching or conditioning routines. Got into bad habits. During the week I was humping quite heavy equipment for the Canon photocopiers roadshow I was working for, and just never looked after my back or my self well enough. Something had to give.

I came back to New Zealand for the 1984/85 summer and played my first real match of note at Cornwall Park, against the New Zealand side leaving for Pakistan. I was 18 and things were on the up. Then I played a few games for my club in Auckland, and was doing quite well, grabbing bags here and there in the one-dayers. But I'd felt like the tin man all season so far, quite knotty in my trunk. One morning I tried to get out of bed after a game on the weekend, and my back felt very uncomfortable. The best way I can describe it is to say it felt like the putty was going hard.

I kept on going, but it was hard enough jogging up to the wicket, let alone running in. My body had been changing a lot through adolescence and, in combination with the stress I was placing on it by trying to bowl like a demon, I was just asking too much of it. I knew something was really up and reluctantly sought a medical opinion.

The scan showed a tear in my back. There was swelling and scarring where the L5 disc of my spine had slipped out of alignment and was rubbing parts it shouldn't have been, messing up my whole sacral and hip area. I was lucky it wasn't skeletal; it was more muscular and ligament damage, mainly to the left lumbar area due to slamming my front left side down in my delivery stride. But in the mornings I couldn't get out of bed with the pain, and it gave me a hell of a fright, because I didn't play again until the very end of March 1985.

In the meantime I'd missed out on making my Shell Trophy debut for Auckland. Ray Hunter, our seasoned offspinner at North Shore, frustratedly told me that I should be trying to bowl anyway, because I was letting someone else take my job. And Willie Watson did. That's where Willie got the jump, pulled ahead of me and made that New Zealand tour to England in 1986, after having the inside running to play for Auckland that summer when its New Zealand bowlers were away on tour. I immediately thought of Dennis Lillee telling me, "Never give a sucker an even break . . ."

I was dispirited for some time. Auckland had a flood of good bowling talent at the time – Willie, Sneds, Gary Troup, Brian Barrett, Stu Gillespie – and I began to question if I'd really get another look-in soon enough. I seriously thought about moving to Northern Districts at this time and even went down to Hamilton and had a meeting with them, before deciding to hang in there and play for the Auckland Second XI.

In the end, the frustration of not being able to bowl gave me two gifts. It made me hungry, or hungrier, and it cautioned me to look after my body. I knew Lillee had been only 23 when he got stress fractures through his spine, so when I finally did get into the New Zealand team environment I was quite receptive to learning about maintaining your body as a bowler. Being professional wasn't just about being paid, but about looking after your body so you would be available to play as much as you could. Playing under Hadlee, Chats and Sneds really helped me appreciate those issues, and I recognised that though international cricket was a good lifestyle, one you could enjoy, it was also a tough lifestyle. My body was my living. I had to watch how much I ate and drank, get enough sleep, see the physio where necessary and get enough strengthening and stretching on a daily basis. I got into good habits early.

After tearing my back up, I'd also realised how much harder I had to train. It was almost a blessing. I'd realised what I was doing to my frame by trying to run in and bowl fast. Not being of the classical mould, not having a long, fluid and strong physique like Chris Cairns, I'd align myself to Malcolm Marshall, the shortish West Indian pace star, and concentrate on how successful he'd been. I look back now and wish I'd actually run through the crease a lot more, like he did; it may have been easier on the body. But, having spoken with him, whereas I've had groin and back problems over my career as a consequence of trying to run in and bowl fast, he's had back, shoulder, rotator cuff and ankle problems.

I had my first hernia operation in 1992 at the age of 26. That's when my body type really started to catch up with me. But in my formative years, after the early back injury, there were only niggling-type injuries, sore hammies and the like, that I tried to keep on top of with daily maintenance.

The selectors had used so many other bowlers in the ranks that it was nice that they persevered with me and gave me encouragement – because when you're young, you're going to be a bit erratic, wild and woolly at times, trying to bowl so fast; and form and niggles can also dictate a lot of your success, or lack of it.

Late in October 1989 the New Zealand squad was practising at Pukekura Park in New Plymouth, where we were gathered for a camp in readiness for a short, sharp tour of Australia in November. On the bus there afterwards Martin Snedden leaned over to me and said Hadlee wasn't going.

I said, "Piss off, of course he will!"

Hadlee never had injuries (he had niggles, but that was all), so you always just expected the great man to be there whenever there was action. But in 1989 Paddles' one weak spot, his Achilles tendon, was really starting to catch up with him and he pulled out of the tour.

Chats had retired earlier in the year so suddenly our horrible lack of depth was revealed. Five frontline bowlers were picked for the tour: Sneds, Willie, Gary Robertson, Brendon Bracewell and myself. As the quickest, overnight I had been elevated to the spearhead of the attack.

The only other genuinely quick bowler coming through in New Zealand at the time was Chris Cairns, a teenager who'd had a great tour with the 1989 youth side in England that winter. He wasn't in the initial squad, but when we had a few injury scares and Andrew Jones, who bowled a little offspin, split the webbing in his hand, Cairnsie and Dipak Patel were flown over as back-up, and Cairnsie ended up making his test debut before breaking down with a shattered back.

That return visit to Australia for me was a huge emotional leap from the test series two years earlier. It was a blast to be back in Dennis Lillee country, and I was really fired up about playing my first test in Perth. They'd just finished the Lillee-Marsh Stand at the WACA and I caught up with my idol again and had a bowl with him in those brilliant nets. I was glad that he was there, because somehow it gave me more confidence and impetus to take on the challenge in front of me. Although I hadn't played a lot of test cricket and was still very raw, for the first time in my life I was going to walk onto the field as my country's strike weapon.

Wrighty won the toss and, being an opening batsman, didn't want to bat first on the WACA wicket, which in hindsight would have been quite a good idea. In terms of confidence, Australia was like a new side. They'd just beaten England for the Ashes, won them back 4-nil after England had held onto them for the previous two series. Fortunes were turning around. David Boon got a double hundred and Australia made 521/9 declared. It was a long hard graft in the field, hot hard work with a 38 degree, energy-sapping wind coming from the Swan River. I remember feeling very light-headed, dizzy, constantly calling for drinks on the boundary.

The highlight for me was getting Dean Jones, but I was certainly made to work for it. Deano had been really mouthing off the whole way and I wanted his wicket bad. Near the end of the second day, when we were still trying to chip out the middle order, during a drinks break I looked up at the scoreboard and saw that Jones was on 99. I thought of Wrighty two years earlier at the MCG when the poor bastard had got out on 99. Then I thought, well wouldn't it be nice to zero in here and knock over Jonesy the same way? Here's a break in concentration . . . why not?

You look back and wish you'd had that power of positive thinking more often. He just fell over one and was dead lbw, out for 99. He'd played well, but his long vigil was over.

I ran through, playfully slapping him on the head as we crossed. The Crowes were staring at me as if to say, Jesus mate, if that was me, I'd whack you one with my bat! Jeff Crowe gave me a very dry, "Congratulations, mate." I thought, where's the high fives? They didn't like me doing that at all, and I couldn't work it out because they knew how much crap they got from these Aussie bowlers when they were sent back to the pavilion . . . We'd been in the field nearly two whole days and it wasn't nasty, just a spontaneous thing, a bit of light relief.

I got Border out again in that innings, too, when he was set on 50. Swung it through the gate. I'd had Taylor, the opener, out earlier, and had a few more dropped. If we'd taken our chances better we could have bowled them out for 350. But you've got to take them, and we ended up batting for our life, following on after making 231 in our first innings. But despite our predicament, or really because of it, it turned into an unforgettable occasion, with Mark Greatbatch and Sneds playing the innings of their life to draw and save the one-off test. The Australians had outplayed us through

MAGNIFICENT SEVEN

Up until 1993 I'd taken six five-wicket bags in test cricket, but never more. Willie Watson used to enjoy giving me a hard time about that. Chris Pringle had taken 7-52 in Faisalabad in 1990 and Willie himself, in the same series, had bagged 6-78 at Lahore. Then Chris Cairns took 6-52 against England at Eden Park in 1992. I was the supposed strike bowler, but everyone had a "big bag" except for me!

I finally joined the boys' club against Australia at the Basin Reserve. Seven's always been a lucky number for me and it turned out to be my seventh five-wicket bag in test match cricket on the seventh of March, which was a Sunday, the seventh day of the week. And I got seven for 89. Maybe I should have batted seven that match as well!

To break the drought against Australia, my favourite opponents, was the icing on the cake. It turned out to be the second best test wicket-taking performance by any New Zealander in a match on our pitches, after Hadlee's 7-23 at the same ground in 1975/76, but I was more delighted with the fact that Allan Border was one of my victims – again! I had him lbw for 30.

Having finally got the hang of the big bag trick I then backed that most of it, but we batted most of the last three days and literally blocked them out of the win.

When I stepped off the park, I felt the Australians' attitude towards me had shifted. They seemed to respect that I was dangerous enough now to bowl good outswingers – and that I gave it my all out there, a 100 per cent man. At various functions the Aussie guys started to mention they were impressed with the way this little runt from New Zealand would take them on. They loved you to bite back, to stand up to them. After that tour I never seemed to get so much of a slagging when I was batting against them, and if I did, it wasn't personally directed.

It was certainly that test match, bowling without either Hadlee performance up with 6-37 in the next test at Eden Park – in back-to-back innings, in fact. Willie and I bowled well in tandem and we helped win the match. I was at the peak of my powers, my nicks were being held, I was bowling people out and it felt fantastic. That six-for included my 100th test wicket. I was bowling to Ian Healy and Andrew Jones caught it in the gully. The milestone had been on my mind and I leapt up on Crowey's shoulder in sheer elation. To snare it in a test against Australia on my backyard strip (particularly since it had been a graveyard for quick bowlers so often) was right out of the script. I was lucky the pitch had a bit of juice in it because of wetter weather leading up to the match. It was still partly overcast that day and the humidity of advancing rain had helped the ball fizz and swing around – we cleaned the Aussies out for 139.

I ended up with 17 wickets that season and the series against Australia remains one of my favourites. Two good friends of mine, Warren and Holly Keene, got married the day, March 12, that I took my 100th wicket. I went to the wedding reception afterwards and felt it was just a great time to be alive. I was getting married myself soon; I knew I was good enough to play for my country; I knew I was in a good groove, felt the selectors had faith in me and Wally Lees, the coach, was trying to get the best out of me. It was a time of confidence, with no stress. You could see why a lot of us were performing. It was John Wright's last summer and a very special time for us all.

Later on in that Auckland test match Dick Motz, the first New Zealander to get 100 test wickets, sent me a telegram. It was very touching. It said, "Welcome to the 100 club".

or Chatfield alongside me for the first time, that I really started to get in a groove. Cairnsie's debut there had been the start of an era as well, and though injury prevented him from re-emerging for almost two years, he became another contender for the vacuum that would open when the senior pros finished up. They were still uncertain times, but from the beginning of 1990, I started to have a lot more confidence. I felt things were happening for me, that I was more of a wicket-taker, that I could do it, and therefore consolidate my place in the side. Those feelings buoyed me through a good home season against the Indians and Australia (the deal was that after India made a full tour here, Australia would come over for a tri-series and single test). I took three five-wicket bags in a row.

Then we toured England, but that wasn't a great time for me. It was a hard tour and although I was pleased just to be on it, I was struggling emotionally off the park. The only Lord's test I played, Richard Hadlee had just been knighted in the Queen's Birthday honours and the ground announcer would proudly introduce his spells, "From the pavilion end, Sir Richard Hadlee". It was most peculiar bowling alongside a knight, glancing up at the scoreboard and seeing his three-piece name right next to mine, which was quite humble in comparison! But we ended up sharing the wickets in that match, I got four and he got three. I would have loved another one there, of all places, but Paddles was pretty good by now at cleaning up.

So it took me a good three seasons, really, to feel more or less confident about my place in the New Zealand side. At the time it felt like an age. And by 1990, more of the country's young bowling brigade were knocking on the door to get in, which only added to your uncertainty.

Shane Thomson, who later switched to offspin, was still playing as a seamer back then. He'd made his test debut against India at the beginning of 1990 and, being quite fiery, presented himself as another quick bowler option. Chris Cairns, Willie and Chris Pringle were also well in the frame. Then Stu Roberts came away with us to Pakistan at the end of 1990. There was a sense that you might be expendable if you didn't perform. I never took it for granted. Although you didn't want to dwell on it, the bottom line was one person's opinion could change on the selection panel and that could be it for you. Even with confidence in your own ability, you were at the mercy of others. Security isn't a common feeling in cricket at the best of times.

I got on particularly well with Cairnsie and Tommo, the young pace bowlers coming into the side. Mark Greatbatch and I assumed the responsibility of helping them into the side as the senior pros from the 1980s started to retire around us; I started to be the one rooming with a younger bowler. It was a sudden time of enormous transition on and off the park.

Canterbury's Stu Roberts joined the team and was a great tourist in 1990 in Pakistan. In spite of getting very few opportunities to play, he had great spirits and was invaluable to the team in a tough place like that where you missed home and sometimes felt alienated. The loudspeakers bellowing the chanting that calls everyone to prayer go off at 5am each day all over Pakistan. It wakes you up and early on in the tour, when you're jetlagged, you get quite peeved with it, having woken up in the middle of the night and just started to go back to sleep before they blast you out of bed.

Stu would get a tea towel and knot it on his head and do a great impersonation of the early morning Urdu chanting. It soon became a ritual in the team room before every fines meeting. He was a bit like Stephen Boock had been just before my time: a hard case character on tour able to share a great sense of humour. It really lifted your spirits in times that could have been difficult.

Of all the new faces, Chris Pringle was a law unto himself at times, carefree, a great lover of life. Pringo would be out to 4.30 in the morning if he felt like it. Ken Rutherford was always a good one for having a pint with the boys too, something of a lovable larrikin. He got his triple century on the 1986 England tour after staying up through the night celebrating Willie's 21st. Willie was good in that he'd take a lot of the younger guys out, even though he'd be off in his own little world at times, so quiet and almost shy in the bar. He really was hard to get to know, though well liked for his dry humour. When he branched out, as he sometimes did, and got involved in a conversation, he was very hard case. But mostly he was quite reserved, sitting back and just absorbing it all. He had quite a different upbringing from myself and his family's old Scottish reserve was quite strong in him.

Willie and I had had a great time when we were young on tour trying to break into the side and there was still that old rivalry, the competitive spirit between us that dated back to our schooldays. But increasingly there were times I really felt for Willie, because as things started to go well for me, it was often at his expense, and I knew how hard he was trying, like me, to cement a place in the team.

We'd toured Zimbabwe for six weeks together with a Young New Zealand side at the end of 1988, immediately before the New Zealand test side was due to tour India. We knew there was one opening on that Indian tour for a fourth seamer after Hadlee, Chats and Sneds, but the selectors wanted to wait to see how we all went on this Zimbabwe trip before finalising which one of us would be picked (Tommo was also on that African tour as a seamer, and showed glimpses of promise until he broke his hand batting and Cairnsie was sent over in his place).

I struggled in Zimbabwe. Our coach there was Geoff Howarth, and I felt that as a bowler I didn't really have a mentor there, as such. It was a shame we didn't have a bowling coach to help, because it became obvious that I was doing things technically wrong, wasn't getting to the wicket well and things like that. I was left to my own devices pretty much as the senior pace bowler in the side, but I was suddenly in a bad trough. By contrast Willie was the seam bowler of the tour: he showed good form. But instead of picking Willie, the selectors took me to India.

Willie was really down about it, and I felt pretty angry, to be honest, that they hadn't picked him when he deserved it so much more than me. But the selectors had seen how I'd performed in the tests at home the summer before and wanted a bowler who could swing the ball with more pace.

I think that was the start of Willie feeling the frustrations of not breaking through. Sometimes he might have thought he should have been picked ahead of Sneds, sometimes ahead of me. The transition years were hard on him. And then he injured his thumb.

He'd been playing club cricket and had just got 100 for his side, Grafton, which normally would have been a cause for celebration for Willie, when he was standing at slips and tried to stop a catch. It was early in 1990 and both Willie and I were about to fly down to Christchurch as part of the squad from which the first test team against India would be picked. Willie, myself, Sneds and Tommo were the candidates, with Paddles still testing out his body in Canterbury club cricket after his Achilles problems. Willie was lined up to play because he'd been doing very well domestically, but his thumb was starting to feel very sore. He was taken away to hospital and when we next saw him it was at the hotel: he was wearing a cast. He was shellshocked. Hadlee ended up making an early return to the team and later Willie joked that you must be quite a decent player if Richard Hadlee's your replacement. But the levity didn't really disguise how disappointed he was.

Hadlee took his 400th test wicket in that test: the rest was history. Willie didn't play for the rest of the season and then didn't get picked to go to England. It must have been tough for him, having been on the one four years previously as the promising youngster. He missed out on such a lot of earnings, too, because back then a lot of us didn't have insurance. One freak injury cost him almost a year in cricket.

Willie's career always seemed to come to a halt just when he'd got it going again or was starting to really develop himself in the side. He showed a lot of commitment and desire to keep coming back. When the thumb had healed, he flew to England to play club cricket in Lancaster – mainly so he would be handy in case he got called up to the New Zealand squad. We had a lot of injuries and he did end up being drafted in with Chris Pringle to play some three-day matches at the end.

But whenever you're left out of a team for a while, no matter how close you've been to that unit, it starts to drift away from you. It's very hard to be around those other guys when you're on the outer, they're still playing and you're not. They are sharing experiences that you aren't and can't be part of. I feel that now around guys I'd played with for a long time, and I realise how Willie must have felt that badly back then.

It's funny how you can be very quickly forgotten, and it was quite sad that Chats retired so quietly, without too much comment by others on the hole he left in the side. It was a real contrast to the hype surrounding Hadlee's exit. Hadlee stuck out so much more because of his statistics, his dominance, the fact that he was an allrounder, but the role of Chats was vital to him. Chats was his hunting partner for so long. Sneds was another figure who didn't dominate, but who had also done a good job behind Hadlee for a long time. Sneds' worth to the team was often underestimated, but he lasted only one year longer than Chats, so there was really a double vacuum. Willie took over Chats' and Sneds' role and did the donkey work for guys like me on many occasions. But it never quite worked out for him. Satisfaction in cricket is always very fleeting, but I think he deserved more.

ODE TO MY FAMILY

It was the late 1950s when my mother's parents, Ted and Hazel Levin, decided to emigrate from South Africa to New Zealand. My grandfather had been in the Royal Navy and was taken prisoner during World War II. Like his father before him, my grandfather was a great sportsman and had many silver cups to prove it. For him, New Zealand represented freedom and a better life for his family. My mother, Sandi, had been born in Cape Town, but she and her brothers and sister found themselves growing up in small town New Zealand. In the 1960s the family moved to Auckland.

Thomas, my father, meanwhile, hailed from a large, noisy family of 10 further down in Hawke's Bay. One of the family – Uncle Syd – became our connection to Morrison Motor Mowers. The Morrisons were of mixed Scottish and Irish heritage. My grandfather, after whom my father was named, had married Rose Kyle, who died on my fourth birthday in 1970. Rose's mother was a schoolteacher who was on holiday from her home in County Armagh, Ireland, when she met and married James Kyle, a gardener and horse trader. They had five children, one of whom, Leo 'Lofty'

Kyle, was a very good rugby player in George Nepia's time. He was killed in the 1931 Napier earthquake, at the Masonic Hotel where he was apparently waiting to meet his good friend Winston McCarthy.

Like a lot of babies from the 1960s and early 1970s, I had young parents – my father was born in 1945. He and Sandi had two children. I was born in 1966, my beautiful mellow Aquarian sister, Zhara, two years later. Dad was very able with his hands, a builder by trade who would craft good furniture. But, possibly against the New Zealand grain, he wasn't hugely sport-orientated, though he'd actually been a good wrestler in his youth and played a bit of rugby at St Paul's. Unlike a little Hadlee, Bracewell or Cairns, I never really got to play cricket in the backyard or down at the beach with my family.

In the early 1970s in New Zealand a lot of marriages were splitting up. Our parents' was one of them. I remember the day Dad left for Australia. I was seven. My mother held Zhara and I stood next to her as he went out the door with his bags, all of us blubbering messes.

Sometimes Zhara and I wouldn't see Dad for a long time after that. There was good work in the building trade over in Australia and he started living there, off an on, in the 1970s, part of the economic drift across the Tasman at the time. We lived in Te Atatu North in Auckland. I remember in 1975 he sent me over a little Chopper bike – that fad was just hitting New Zealand then, little bikes with these huge metal back pieces on them. It was a huge blast.

In 1981 Zhara and I went on our first overseas trip to stay with the old man and his new lady in Melbourne in the summer holidays. The West Indies just happened to be touring Australia at the same time. Because the Australian cricket team were within inches of victory, it was free to get into the last day of the test at the MCG. I went along and for the first time in my life laid eyes on Dennis Lillee, charging in full of steam and power to mop up the West Indian tail. He dominated that whole series. I'd never seen anything as exciting in my life, sitting there in this huge, towering, historic, enclosed stadium watching Lillee charge in and win a test match for all the pumped up Australians around me. I had no inkling whatsoever that just six years later I'd be out there myself.

For years it seemed cricket was strangely incidental to my life; I didn't really play at all. Instead I got involved in rugby in 1974, which I loved. I spent two winters trotting along to footy practice at the Te Atatu North Football Club, playing games against other boys from clubs around the city. We used to call North Shore the "toothpaste team" because they wore green and white striped jerseys, and when we moved to Belmont on the North Shore towards the end of my primary school years, I felt for quite some time that I was joining the enemy. Uncle Rube, my mother's brother, had thought the Shore was a great place to bring up kids and it was he who encouraged my mother to move there. He always did have a lot of foresight.

Moving across the Harbour Bridge was like a whole, fresh start for me. Until I moved to the North Shore, my name had actually been Kyle Morrison (as in Daniel Kyle Morrison – the Daniel part had slipped off when I was two), but after a chat with my mother we decided I'd be a Daniel again and I felt like I had a whole new identity, Secret Agent Dan was on undercover assignment in enemy territory!

Over the next few years we moved along the peninsula from Belmont to Stanley Bay to Devonport, where Uncle Rube lived in the flat downstairs from us. We were a close unit, the four of us. Rube was like the father we never really had. He worked as cabin crew for Air New Zealand and would bring us back soccer balls, volleyballs and all the gear from Hong Kong or the States.

Living on the North Shore really did turn out to be a world away from Te Atatu and my life started to open up to the whole new environment. Mum had done a drama diploma in 1978 and had met another man, Stephen Dee, who was later general manager of the Victoria State Opera in Australia (before that he was with Auckland Opera, bringing productions like *La Bohème* to the Aotea Centre). Back in the 70s Stephen was a stage manager and so Zhara and I had a great time going to lots of shows with him, sitting up in the control room with all the dials and spotlight switches. Sport got pushed backstage for a while as I followed his lead and explored the arts. I learned the recorder and did drama classes at the Little Theatre. I'd go to all sorts of workshops on Saturday mornings so instead of playing footie I'd be making pottery whales.

In 1979, when I was in the third form at Takapuna Grammar, I got a part in a Crunchie ad through my drama. It wasn't the famous one with the Crunchie shootout on the train that played on TV, but the one on a plane, which played in picture theatres a lot. I'd go to the movies for a long time after that and suddenly there was me up on screen, dressed in a school uniform throwing Crunchie bars around with a big grin on my adolescent face.

I got caned within my first week at Takapuna Grammar. The local boys have this tradition of monkey apple wars with the intermediate school kids catching the bus across the road, and I got caught. Not for the last time. Rugby had faded away altogether by now as I'd started to hang out with a group of mates at school who were right into soccer. Mark Hadlow, the actor who was New Zealand's 1995 Entertainer of the Year, was a little older, just out of drama school at the time, but he used to join us down at Stanley Bay Park where we played a bit of informal soccer in the weekend with an old volleyball. He was, and still is, a bundle of energy and very hard case. He was our goalkeeper diving around like a mad frog in the slush.

In 1981 I made the first XI soccer team at school, a side that also included decathlete Simon Poelman. Sir Peter Blake, rugby's Brad Johnstone, and the swimmer Gary Hurring, who was there when I started and a full legend at school after the 1978 Commonwealths, went to Takapuna Grammar as well.

It was a very well-rounded school, a co-ed near the beach that had a bit of a reputation for sport and quite a reputation for a few other things. There was a bit of a drug problem, kids smoking marijuana when I started. The grounds were quite hard to patrol, sprawling with lots of nooks and hideaways. Kids used to slip off down to St Leonard's Beach, where the nudists hung out. You'd throw monkey apples at them as well. During PE we'd sometimes go down and play volleyball or touch on the beach, too, and that was great.

Murray Deaker took over as deputy principal at Takapuna Grammar in 1980 and immediately started cleaning the place up. Deaks had been teaching at Auckland Grammar with John Graham (the former All Black who's now the New Zealand cricket team's manager) and Orewa College before coming to us, and was big on two things: sport and discipline. He pretty soon got nicknamed "The Big D", as in the big detective. He used to walk round the school with a big piece of dowling and if you weren't in class by the second bell, you'd suddenly feel it on the back of your legs as he gave you a blast of his jet engine voice. He used to take it to cricket practice as well for when we got cheeky.

I was a full-on teenager at that time. As Mum says, there were times in my adolescence when she didn't like me very much. It was Deaks' influence in sport that probably kept me on the straight and narrow, because there was still a lot around in terms of typical adolescent craziness to distract me. Sport was a great saviour in that regard. I partied hard, but I had balance.

Influenced by Deaks and inspired by the controversial West Indies series, my big goal in 1980 was to get into the cricket first XI, and that's really where cricket became a serious sport for me. I'd actually started as a wicketkeeper – that's how I'd got into the North Harbour B under-12 side, keeping wicket to Willie Watson at the trials at Rosmini College. Willie was so much bigger as a kid than anyone else that he was the hero, so much quicker and bouncier than the other guys around. I was just a cheeky, pesky runt behind the stumps. It was only later that I wanted to be a quick bowler and run in and bowl fast like Dennis Lillee, changing from being a gloveman at intermediate to a paceman at high school. I'd wear sweat bands on each wrist like Richard Hadlee and do his trademark little side shuffle at the top of my run, wanting to be strong, fast, lethal and taller like them. I just never grew. Still, I went for the North Harbour

LOYAL

From the day when we were 12 and my mates Ben and Simon Chapple first took me down to the Devonport Domain, the North Shore Cricket Club has been my home in cricket. Whenever it was tough slog in Faisalabad or Hyderabad, that's what I thought about; the little seaside village cricket club in a cosy, tree-lined crater that used to seem so huge. I lived and breathed down at the Devonport Domain. With a double affiliation to it in junior cricket and soccer, summer and winter it was where I did so much of my growing up.

It used to be more of a soccer haven than a cricket club, with a rough little bar area in the clubhouse called "the shed" that had a concrete floor for sprigs until it was upgraded in the middle of the 1980s. The club always had a family, small village (which was what Devonport was then, before all the restaurants) feel to it, and people pitched in together, helped each other. Some were bankers, some plasterers, builders, many old boys of Takapuna Grammar and many friends. There'd be hard case characters. Champion sledgers in the field. Then sometimes you'd be halfway through your run-up when you'd see the slips crack up laughing – someone had told a joke – and you'd have to stop and go back to your mark all over again.

People were caring. One day in 1986 my cousin Anna-Marie died, she'd had cancer though she was only 14. That weekend down at the club I bowled six no-balls in a short spell – and I never bowled no-balls. But Ray Hunter, the Auckland offspinner who was our captain, had heard from family what had happened and no one gave me a hard time.

John Little, our opening batsman, was a club stalwart. When

Under-14 side – at the time it included Alex O'Dowd and Justin Vaughan, the glamour batsman, the pretty boy left-hander, and in 1981 I made it into the first XI at school.

Our big rivals were Westlake, King's and Auckland Grammar. Deaker, our coach, would fire us up in the dressing room to "get stuck into these single-sex school poofters". He never was one to mince words! Brent Bowden, the international umpire, was at Westlake; he was the big school sports superstar there playing cricket in summer and kicking the ball quite nimbly as their star first-five in the rugby first XV. Because I was still quite runty as a 15-year-old I swung the ball a lot then, more of a Martin Snedden than a Dennis Lillee. It's a shame I wasn't quick enough to bounce

former New Zealand opener Richard Reid batted for us after he came back from living in South Africa, those two smashed opening attacks, pretending they were Sri Lankans.

Then there were the men who are married to the club, faithful to it decade after decade. Peter Mitchell's opened up the bar religiously each weekend for longer than I can remember; Ross 'Rosco' Parlane, the ump who used to be the scorer, seemed to have been there even longer.

People talk about changing times, the old loyalty guys used to have to their sports clubs no longer being around. But even though players swap clubs more often nowadays, loyalty hasn't disappeared. When I had my Auckland testimonial season in 1997, it was people like Rosco who were invariably there supporting the golf days, the dinners, picking their way though the terraces at Eden Park flogging yet another book of raffle tickets . . .

I've always enjoyed going back to play for my club: it's never been a chore. It's such a spiritual place for me that it could never be. But there aren't so many older characters around in the club now, the way there used to be, and you miss them. You notice less people down the club, with Saturday trading, people having less time. Guys I used to go to school with and stand alongside in the field are tossing footballs to their young sons for 10 minutes in their backyard instead. The oldest player at North Shore now is only 33. All through the country, teams are getting younger. Even the national side. I wonder what they'll miss in years to come.

But I'll still be hanging out with the guys I played cricket and soccer with down at the Devonport Domain those many summers and winters. And when cricket's gone, I'll still have those mates.

'Billy' Bowden more often while I still had the chance!

Willie went to Westlake as well, I played against him in1983. He was a bit of a star on the Shore, playing senior club cricket before he'd even left school.

Seasons flowed into one another and I was happy as Larry playing cricket in summer and soccer in winter with my mates until, one July afternoon down at footie practice, I got flipped over hard onto my coccyx. I couldn't get back up, it was so sore. I remember grovelling around on the floor just trying to get moderately comfortable as I watched the soccer World Cup on telly. That was the last year I played winter sport. At the beginning of 1983 I made the decision to concentrate on cricket.

I have to admit I was a lot more interested in sport and chasing girls than in schoolwork by the time I'd reached the sixth form. I had to repeat my sixth form year. Whether I was in his first XI or not, Murray Deaker wasn't about to cut me any slack, and wanted me to get my UE So he dangled a carrot. "Danny boy," he bellowed, "you get off your chuff and get your UE and we'll send you to England."

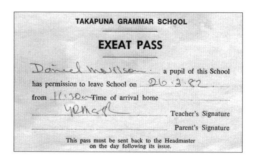

Deaker had had the vision to arrange a cricketing exchange programme, a "development scholarship" between Takapuna Grammar and a couple of cricket clubs in England for members of the school's first XI, which would turn out to be his legacy to the school. He was thinking longterm, not just of me, but it did the trick and I knuckled down, so much so that I got an aggregate of 205 for my sixth form subjects, a perfectly planned whisker over the 200 you needed to pass.

Bruce Warner was one of my team-mates in the first XI. He was seen as the next prodigal son from the Shore – a lot of people thought he would go on to play for Auckland, though he ended up more of an Auckland second XI player and premier rep for North Shore. Bruce and I were to be the maiden scholarship recipients.

Over the summer of 1983/84 Deaks set the fundraising in motion to pay for our airfares – back then it was still expensive to get to England, about $2600 for a return ticket between Auckland and London, so over $5000 had to be found, and once there we would be put up by club contacts and get jobs. Deaks got in touch with his mate Gary Ingles, who ran the Windsor Park Hotel, and Ian Hastings, a family friend and former police detective, and they and my mother organised a casino night at the pub.

It really was exciting, but we never dared believe the scholarship was actually going to get off the ground. You didn't think it would come to fruition. It was just one of Deaker's mad ideas. But I wanted to get to the UK with a passion. New Zealand had just beaten England in a test series here that summer, so my head was ringing with the names of the English stars – Gower, Lamb, Gatting, Botham, Willis . . . Cricket wasn't the only magnet. I'd followed British rugby league as well, and logged up years of watching big league soccer on TV on Saturday afternoons, flicking through soccer magazines with my mates in the first XI in winter, etching words like Chelsea, Manchester United and Liverpool on my mind. England was the headquarters of both the sports I loved.

But the biggest influence on me of all was the music scene in England. I ran into a guy named Derek Walker at a New Zealand soccer do recently. He has "The Jam" tattooed on his left shoulder: I can totally relate to that. British ska – The Jam, The Beat, The Specials, The Clash, Madness, Bad Manners – drove me all through school. I'd listened to their British voices sing about Eton, Richmond town, Kew Gardens, Slough . . . *slurp up your beer and collect ya fags, there's a row going on down near Slough* . . . places I felt so close to, but had never seen. I had a tremendous drive and desire to get to London. And within weeks I was there.

LONDON
CALLING

L eaving was traumatic, emotional, exciting and nervewracking all at once. Saying goodbye to my family, my girlfriend Wendy, my friends, flying Pan Am to the other side of the world, unsure what to expect, knowing I'd be met by strangers.

I had to change planes at Los Angeles and even though I never left the airport, I looked around amazed at all the different kinds of people around me – black faces, Hispanics – like the naive 18-year-old that I was. I got lost at customs, racing around in a mild state of panic trying to find my check-in point for the connecting flight to London. Finally I found the right place, took a few deep breaths and sat down in the passenger lounge. I opened letters from my family. My grandmother's and Uncle Rube's letters really choked me up. I could hardly read them. I had a traveller's journal, and wrote in it: "Realised how close I am to my family. I love them so dearly. Can't stop thinking of them. Photos of family didn't help either." Tears kept rolling down my face – and I'd only been away a day!

I continued, "Important notes. Be positive in your approach to life in England. Don't indulge in too much alcohol or anything I'd be ashamed of while living in the UK. Try not to get depressed, or over-thinking of loved ones, especially the family and uncles and my loved one, Wendy."

It was a hell flight. The other side of the world turned out to be a bloody long way away. You felt like you'd be flying above the clouds forever. But finally we glided in to land at Heathrow. It was April 15. England was just breaking into spring, and as I stepped onto England I looked up at clear, shining day, 15 degrees, bright and hopeful.

I made my way to the airport meeting point and waited. And waited. Waited some more. No one was there to pick me up. Shit! Starting to worry here. Know I'm at the right place. God, it's all going wrong already!

I had a little cash left on me so I found the Thomas Cook exchange booth, got some coins to use a phone and dug out my address book to call the club I was going to play for – I knew it had a flat above it where a couple of its people lived. The phone rang for an eternity. But just as visions of spending the night penniless and hungry at a foreign airport were starting to flash through my head, a tired English voice suddenly grunted on the other end of the line. It was Dave Pullan, the guy who was supposed to be picking me up. It was early on a Sunday morning and I'd got him out of bed – he was hung over. He mumbled about being unable to make it and gave me the number of the club captain, Stuart Young. So I rang another strange voice. Stuart was still in bed as well, and didn't really fancy hauling himself down from North London to Heathrow either (I suspect the boys had had a good Saturday night), but he was very apologetic and came down to collect me.

I settled down for the wait at the meeting point, reading the cricket magazine by which Stuart would recognise me. Then I stood up and stretched my legs, turned around and stared straight at a face I'd seen before. It was Cliff Richard. He was just going past me into the lifts. There were a couple of seconds of eye contact: he smiled at me, then the lift doors closed. I couldn't believe it. Ten minutes in London and I'd already seen my first rock star!

Soon enough I was in Stuart Young's car and we were pulling up outside the Harefield Cricket Club. I rubbed my eyes. It was a fully enclosed ground, with a mansion on one side and a farm down the other, pretty trees and a pond nearby. Around it were houses, New Zealand-type houses really, with weatherboards on a brick base. You didn't see that a lot in England. Separate houses were incredibly expensive by our standards, so usually houses were semi-detached, if not in Coronation Street rows. This was more like something straight out of Fendalton in Christchurch, really lovely.

The Middlesex County second XI used to like playing there a bit through the 1980s, though they don't anymore because it's too much demand on the sweet little ground. I've really fallen on my feet here, I thought. After a long trip and a nerve-wracking arrival, I suddenly felt a burst of energy.

The Harefield cricket side played soccer on Sundays. I'd arrived on the day of the final, so straight away they dragged me off to watch their game up in Watford, which was a suburb about seven miles away. I hadn't slept and was knackered, but I couldn't sleep anyway. My eyes were wide open as I sat in the unfamiliar grandstand in a new country. It was quite a hilarious game; the poor guys lost 7-2, but it didn't dampen anyone's enthusiasm for the party after the game. I started to meet people, and set about ignoring the advice I'd carefully written down in my journal by getting into the spirit straight away!

When I woke up jetlagged and hung over the next day it was already 1.30 in the afternoon. I'd been put up in the flat above the club itself, which technically was the secretary's flat, though he lived elsewhere so a few of the players used it instead. I got up and went for a quietish jog around the Harefield cricket ground. I'd come to London expecting a grey, rainy place, but my first 15 days there were uncharacteristically clear. The guys at the club thought I'd brought the weather in my suitcase and kept saying it was like the great summer of 1976. But when the Poms saw the mad Kiwi going for a light jog around the ground with just his shorts and running shoes on, or sunbathing on the boundary, they thought I'd had too much sun already.

Harefield was a bit like Devonport used to be pre-1985, when it was small and quaint before all the cafes and restaurants started happening. Harefield was on the end of the tube line, on the green belt where there was a bit more room than in London city itself. There were parks, there were ponds, a nice, green uncluttered village. Uxbridge was five miles down the road and that was a busier suburb: Harefield was a bit off the track. In a way I felt at home.

It was amazing how much the lifestyle there revolved around the club. The locals would invariably end up down there, and not just on weekends when the game was on. It wasn't uncommon to see people down there socialising on Monday, Tuesday, Wednesday, Thursday nights. Tuesday was selection night and Thursday was practice night, though I soon realised they weren't too big on practice at Harefield.

I started to discover the whole culture built around English cricket. Afternoon tea culture, club bar culture. It was very relaxed. Games didn't start until 2pm, a bit like in county cricket's Sunday league. They have long twilights in England so it wasn't unusual to kick on playing cricket past eight in the evening.

I wasn't being paid to play, so the pressure to perform as the "club pro" wasn't on my back. It was the last of the summer wine, really. But I was so serious about doing well in the game that sometimes I couldn't fathom how relaxed some of the Harefield guys were about their cricket – the guys would have a few pints and poles before the game. If you were fielding first, the main focus seemed to be the afternoon tea that would be laid on between innings. I especially couldn't get over the rule there that said you had to use the same ball for both innings: it would be old and roughed up before I even got a look in; I'd get smacked all over the park. But I'd bowl my guts out, looking for swing and cut on their dead tracks. I took 5-22 off 12 overs when we won easily over Amersham in one of my first games; I loved it. At net practice in the evenings I'd nearly take their heads off.

We played in the Schweppes 75 League in 1984. Later Harefield came second on the points table, the top two clubs being promoted to the Thames Valley league. Back then we were in the top four of 16 teams, a goodish side, but very inconsistent.

That's followed me around through my whole career. When I make sides, they stop performing consistently. Club, province, New Zealand, you name it. You actually start thinking, God, is it *me?* Auckland was really dominant with about eight recent or current New Zealand reps when I started, but after my first year there, it tapered off. I never played in the subsequent Trophy final-winning sides for Auckland, just the games here and there that petered out to draws. In the New Zealand side it was the same scenario, and even my club side, North Shore, started to have real ups and downs after I came along. Some days you really felt jinxed.

And Harefield was like that, too. That's where it all started. Guys were dropping catches left, right and centre. You'd just hope the fine nicks through to the keeper would stick. Great catches, low bullets where the guy just stuck a brave hand out at slip, would be taken, but then a couple of overs later it would ping off the same guy's chest because he'd forgotten to move, or he'd throw up his arms to protect himself from the ball as it bounced off his guts. I'd just have to laugh, look up to heaven and smile.

Catching behind the wicket turned out to be inconsistent throughout my career, which is a shame. For New Zealand I'd missed out on that great mid-80s slip cordon of Jerry Coney, Jeff

Crowe, Martin Crowe, John Bracewell. Those guys were such great slippers. It was the Harefield Curse.

Playing league cricket in North London was really all about meeting people, talking; not taking five wicket bags. I got on well with one guy who was playing the day of the soccer final; his name was Dave Singleton and he played mainly in the second XI. I was introduced to him at the bar. He had a great flat with another couple of the boys in nearby Denham, where a lot of stars hung out – Cilla Black had a place there, Roger Moore had one with a little airstrip, Elton John also. They said they could hear Elton's 40th birthday party.

'Sing' wore his hair longer at the back and shorter in the front like we all did back then – it was that whole V-neck and baggy trousers scene. He was a really friendly, chatty guy and he and Nick 'Tram' Lines would pick me up in Nick's TR7, taking me out on the town or down to Sainsbury's in Uxbridge to go shopping and get the groceries. We'd live on fish fingers and baked beans, a few vegies. Beers and bitter shandies at the club in the evening, French rolls. Up in the flat we'd blast my Rolling Stones tapes, David Bowie. Jordan Luck and the Dance Exponents had done the school circuit just before I'd left Takapuna Grammar and so I'd brought their "Prayers be Answered" album, which a few of the guys took a shine to. And we were all right into ska, it was the connection between us in a special place and time.

Once I'd got over the emotional, strung-out time of missing everyone at home I started to settle into English life. When eventually the weather broke and the dense, rolling European thunderstorms would come and pelt down rain, I spent a lot of time watching the world snooker champs in the afternoons, or England play Wales in soccer, live on TV.

Stu Young and a few of the other guys took me to Stanford Bridge, the Chelsea Football Ground, where they were playing Shrewsbury Town in a league match towards the end of the season. My first big soccer match! Then we went to watch Arsenal play Chelsea at Highbury – I was quite an Arsenal supporter at school, so that was huge. I actually liked both teams, so was terribly confused, but fortunately for me the result was 1-1. The atmosphere was superb: a typical London football match with rowdy fans, fast paced, full on football with hard tackling, Chelsea fresh up from Division two and out to make a point. It was unforgettable, I was in my paradise.

Being so close to London's heart, I started to take in all those things I'd only read about or seen on TV or in a video, the famous

London nightlife, the tradition and history by day. Simple things like catching the tube was a real experience. I thought of The Jam: "down in the tube station at midnight . . ." Went to the Lyceum Ballroom in The Strand to see Bruce Foxton live in concert. Caught up with my Uncle Rube at the Tara Hotel when he flew into town with Air New Zealand. Shopped in Kensington – I bought these grey slip-on shoes there that I thought were very cool for a tragically long time. Kensington was Princess Di territory, the wealthy area of London. She dashes past the papparazzi through that way, and years later I would stay with the New Zealand team in one of the grand hotels there, the Kensington Park Thistle, which was part-owned by Brierleys.

I played my first full round of golf in August at "Tricky Ricky's", parring the eight and the tenth and losing only two balls into neighbouring houses. It was just a magic, long, mellow summer, hanging out with a bunch of other young guys who had become my friends, sunbathing on the roof of our cricket club chilling out to the Style Council's "Cafe Bleu" album, passing summer evenings with pints down at the Rose & Crown, going out and hitting the town with lots of laughter and company.

There was certainly no way I was going to make money playing league cricket in England then; it was just exciting times. When I think about it, I was really fortunate to be put up in the flat above the club, which was really nice. And I didn't need a car, because I caught the tube or relied on mates to pick me up. But I still needed to earn money to get by, especially as the New Zealand dollar back then only bought you 30p. I'd taken over with me my savings from working on the milk run at home, three years of pounding those killer Devonport hills every day before school. I'd saved about $2000; when I converted it and only got 700 pounds, it was terrible.

I started working as a labourer, pebble-dashing. I'd mix pebbles up with concrete in a wheelbarrow to make a sort of plaster that the builder would smear onto the sides of houses. It was laborious work, but in a way I enjoyed it because it brought back memories of the tradesman in my father, days when I used to watch him doing up his sisters' houses.

The club chairman at Harefield was a man named Gerald Harmon. He was also the treasurer, and really got things happening, moving, the heart and soul of the club. He also happened to be the exhibitions manager for Canon UK Ltd, travelling around the country during the week, and got me a job as a roadie, travelling in the trucks, setting up the exhibitions and then doing the lighting backstage. It was vaguely glamorous, I loved it!

IRONIC

It was in Harefield that I first met my future mother-in-law. I even remember the date: April 13, 1988. I'd been down to Heathrow to pick up my friend Pat Hounsell and almost straight away we went down to The Plough, the pub next door to the club chairman's place. The pub closed at three in the afternoon and it was very quiet by the time we got there, but as we were sitting catching up over a drink we noticed this big black cab pull up. Out in North London you didn't see a lot of black cabs. The locals were all looking to see what was going on, while we just glanced through the lace curtains. Then this woman got out, dressed all in black with high heels, harem pants, leather jacket, big sunglasses; that whole eighties look! She came in and asked Big Mick at the bar if this was a bed and breakfast pub. Mick told her it wasn't. The woman replied, "Well, I don't know if you can help me, I'm actually looking for a New Zealand cricket player. His name's Danny Morrison and he plays at the local club."

We were sitting having our pub lunch just through an archway and round the corner. Mick called out, "Danny, the cops are after you, pal!"

I looked up rather startled and said, "Sorry?"

"The Mafia's after you! *Undercover D's* . . ."

Then in she walked. She said, "Danny Morrison. I'm Anne Talbot. I'm Kim Talbot's mother."

I was catching flies in my mouth; the jaw just thumped on the ground. I'd met Kim in Perth at the end of 1987 and her mother was from Mt Albert in Auckland. Yet here I was meeting her in this tiny pub in North London! Annie had been in Italy chasing up family connections and ended up staying and working behind the bar in Plough Lane for a couple of months. Of all the little pubs in Harefield she'd walked into mine – she hadn't even tried the club. But the most amazing things always happened at Harefield.

We'd be on roadshows during the week, getting back to Harefield in time to play cricket on the weekends. We got up through Manchester, Leeds, Bristol, Liverpool, Cardiff, Edinburgh, down into Somerset and Bagshot in Hampshire. I never really got over the sheer population of England, the amazing clutteredness of the motorways. Beyond would be lovely farm fields, full of the rape that looks like yellow snow across the landscape. Then you'd push into another town and houses would be jammed on top of each other, everyone in each other's pockets. In New Zealand we took a house and section for granted, though subdivision is trying to spoil that. Here a simple house was beyond the reach of most. I suddenly realised what New Zealand was all about, how lucky we are.

Work was spasmodic, perhaps two weeks on and then a few weeks off. But you had enough cashflow to get by. I was earning 30 pounds a day. It wasn't bad. I probably spent 30 pounds a week on food, and I didn't have to worry about much else. It was a good life. It was also a great way to see the country, and it gave me the drive to taste more of it, to be a travelling showman on the county cricket circuit. Life on the road. Staying in great hotels. To see the world for a living, playing cricket for a living. I wanted to cross over into that whole dream.

I was only 18 that first year in Harefield, but it's funny, I never wished I was older, able to do other things. I can get terribly melancholy about those days now, when I was away from home for the first time, hanging out with these great guys living in a great flat. That feeling of freedom. It was a carefree time. I had a ball. And I had a focus – cricket.

Because I was breaking the mould, not coming from a traditional family cricket background like the Crowes and the Hadlees, the Sneddens and the Bracewells who had the cricket fraternity in their genes and in their upbringing while I was playing soccer seriously until I was 16, experiencing genuine English cricket life was an important touchstone for me. It was my crash course in the whole cricket culture, a big time for me.

I was drawn back to Harefield time and again over the next 10 years, in a way the little club became part of my roots. Even though I wasn't earning much and it wasn't a great standard of cricket, I'd enjoyed it so much that it fired the desire to keep going back to England, to seek the professional cricket lifestyle.

After the summer of 1984, I went back and played there again in 1986 (after I'd torn my back up in 1985), and in 1987 popped back over for a couple of months after the bomb went off in Sri Lanka. And again in 1988. I'd stay at the chairman's place, a kilometre from the club. I loved catching up with the old guys, doing the old pilgrimages, haunting the old locals – and searching out more touchstones, like the historic old pub at St Catherine's Dock that was on the cover of The Jam's "Snap" album, and Henley Bridge, where famous photos of three of the band had been taken. I never really lost the thrill. It was only in 1989, when international cricket itineraries were rapidly increasing, that I reluctantly started to spend the winter in New Zealand to give my body a chance to rest. But in 1990 I was back in England again anyway, because New Zealand were touring.

A lot of the guys at Harefield used to laugh at me when I got them by the collar and growled, in my best Clint Eastwood voice, "Just you wait buddy, you'll be paying to come see me play next time!" They'd just piss themselves in the dressing room at stumpy Dan's mad plans to open the bowling for New Zealand; I don't think they really knew what to make of it. But six years later, there I was playing their finest.

Shortly after the New Zealand side had arrived from Sharjah, eight of the Harefield boys drove into London and caught up with me at a pub called the Burlington Bertie, which was behind Conduit Street – we were staying in West London, near Piccadilly Circus. Sneds, Crowey, Wrighty, Braces, Smithy and most of the cricket team were there having a jar when these guys arrived, and we had a great time together with the Harefield guys. Afterwards Wrighty took me aside and said, "Mate, you've obviously made a hell of an impression there, you're a great ambassador if those guys turn up for you like that tonight." I think that's what cricket was about for a lot of Wrighty's generation. People and respect.

I'd been at Harefield during a real boom time, before the '87 stockmarket crash. Guys were surveyors, couriers, sales reps, schoolteachers. A couple of guys worked for Rank Xerox or cigarette companies, generally guys in the commercial bracket with steady jobs who just enjoyed life. They lived for their club. There were a lot of us of the same age group, early to mid 20s, some late, a lot of the guys not yet married, or just married (the wives played in the ladies' cricket team on Sunday mornings). Harefield had 500 club members who paid about five pounds a year membership; older people would come in and play dominoes, cards and crib in the back lounge over a pint. It was a big social club because the beer was a lot cheaper than in the village pubs. And kids would play on the grass.

Harefield was such a big part of my life, a time of so much personal growth, that I always thought I might end up getting back there as an old fart finishing up his cricket, just for the fun of it. Going back to see places and friends. But when I went back recently, on the way back from the West Indies in 1996, it was quite sad.

The club had waned. A lot of my age group were starting to drift away because they were having families and had a lot more commitments. Maybe they come back for the odd Sunday lunch and quiet beer, but they don't play anymore, even though they're only in their 30s. The club hasn't got that huge 500 membership now, either; at least half have gone. It's lost a lot of the character and warmth I felt when I first arrived.

Gerald's gone too. There'd been an asbestos factory in the area once, and a lot of people around Harefield had developed asbestosis later in life. Gerald was just over 50; he'd worked in the factory as a very young man. He had three daughters, and had seen the eldest get married shortly before he died early in 1993. You watched a large, muscular man just shrivel up. He'd been the life and soul of the club, its driving force, and it seems part of the club went with him.

JE SUIS UN CRICKETER

– WITH APOLOGIES TO BILL WYMAN

I'll never forget how down and emotional I felt standing in the arrivals hall of Auckland International Airport the first time I came back from London. After all the uncertainty I'd felt flying out, five months later I'd created another life for myself in Harefield – and was quite sad leaving. I suddenly had two lives, and wherever I went from that moment on there were people and things I was going to miss.

Driving home across the Harbour Bridge with Sandi, it was like I'd been in a time warp. Things had really changed. The tolls on the bridge had gone. Houses had been painted, appeared or disappeared. Friends had left school, moved on, got jobs, moved away. It was a bit of a shock. I realised how much I'd missed the sea, running round the waterfront, living in Devo. In London all you had was the Thames, and that was brown, like a river of deep, bitter ale. I'd been to the coast in Exeter when I was working for Gerald, but their beach was just hard pebbles. So I got a lungful of the salt air of home, relished the open spaces and food and faces and everything that I'd missed. But at the same time I knew for sure that I wanted to go back to England.

It was the beginning of a nomadic 10-year period in my life, from when I was 18 to when I was 28, when I would be regularly shuffling back and forth between hemispheres. I'd enjoyed the lifestyle so much that I wanted as much as I could have of it, because I knew cricket doesn't last forever, or even very long. I was living in the now, trying to figure out a way to make the dream happen.

For half of every year England was your world stage, the place where you'd make a name and doors would open for you – if you were good. After touring there in 1990 with New Zealand, I went back in 1991 for half a season to do some paid pro-ing in the Yorkshire leagues and play in a series of World XI games. I lived up in Preston with John Farrar, a friend of Richard Hadlee's who ran his own PR business and used to get Richard and Dennis Lillee to do a lot of speaking for him. Farrar would be the World XI's manager, helping set up the festival-type matches.

One of the events I played in was Allan Lamb's charity six-a-side tournament for cystic fibrosis. It was at Althorp House, which was Lady Di's father's family home in Northampton. Her brother, the Viscount, was there with their father, who was pretty crook at that stage – he was on his way out and seemed vacant. He hadn't shaved for a few days. But the Earl still welcomed us into an enormous dining hall which was cluttered with those ostentatious gilt-framed portraits of forebears and all the formal paraphernalia of peerage. The cricket oval was set up at the back of their grand estate, fringed with marquees that buzzed with spectators, society and papparazzi. It was a fullscale cricket village, for just one day.

Geoff Howarth and I were the only two New Zealanders playing, and I was introduced as "Danny Morrison, who opens the bowling for New Zealand and went on last year's tour with *Sir Richard Hadlee*". Lamb was there, with Graham Gooch, David Capel and a few of the Northamptonshire players, but the big attraction was the celebrities – Kenneth Branagh, Peter O'Toole and Bill Wyman.

I couldn't believe my eyes; I was playing cricket against a Rolling Stone? Pinch me now! The Stones had been a huge influence all through my youth. My parents had taken me and my sister to see them live at Western Springs in the early seventies when I was seven and I'd sat up in the concrete terraces by the speedway with the binoculars glued to my face as I watched Mick Jagger strut and pout around. Now here was Bill Wyman keeping wicket behind me. You felt like saying, "I saw you at Western Springs!" except you knew that would be so dorky you'd just die afterwards, so I just looked back and smiled and said, "Mate, you're looking as accomplished as Alan Knott there." He just sort of smiled and coolly purred, "Thanks maaan." When I was bowling to him, I pretended to charge in, then halted and bowled a gentle offspinner, or a Jeremy Coney-paced outswinger. It didn't seem right to bounce a Rolling Stone.

Peter O'Toole was frightening. He'd been in New York, and I think he'd been ill. He looked like he'd been dug up for the game. He was so thin that his legs looked like matchsticks and his face was opaque. He wore these white stovepipe jeans that were worse than Sam Hunt's – I couldn't have got those skinny little pants past my calves! But it was amazing to see him in person.

There was a formal dinner laid on afterwards and I talked to Kenneth Branagh there; he liked New Zealand and had played at His Majesty's Theatre in Auckland. There were all these high society people around, Princess Di's brother's set. I couldn't believe it. New Zealand cricketers sometimes rub shoulders with our celebs at home, but this was on another scale. The county stars in England, guys like Lamb, Ian Botham, Robin Smith, hung out with Elton John, George Harrison and Rod Stewart. Cricketers, thesps, rock stars and royalty – it could only happen in England.

When I saw the county lifestyle up close, I wanted more than ever to have a crack at it. The glamour was magnetic, but more than that you really wanted to prove you could handle it, cope with a relentless workload of cricket against a barrage of the game's wily, seasoned pros.

My chance came quickly. I was asked to fill in for Wasim Akram at Lancashire County Cricket Club in 1992. I'd played with some of the guys from Lancs on the World XI circuit, and when England toured New Zealand just before the World Cup the following Southern Hemisphere summer, the chairman of the Lancashire County Cricket Club, Bob Bennett, happened to be the England manager. Lancashire had had the South Africa quick man Stephen Jack lined up to play as their overseas pro, but his ankle had gone on him and he needed an op. So Bennett asked me instead, during the World Cup. I'd been approached by Leicester not long before, but it had fallen through after they decided to keep on Winston Benjamin. I'd been really disappointed, I thought I'd missed my shot at county cricket. Now it seemed as if it was meant to be, and I didn't hesitate to say yes.

The reality of being a professional cricketer in England turned out to be a world away from my dreamy summer days at Harefield. To really make a living I had to go to the north of England now, in Manchester, which was more of a concrete jungle with row after row of terrace housing. And you sweated hard for your money.

Lancashire is the biggest club in England. It has the largest

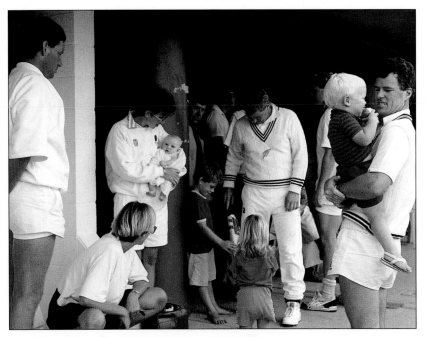

The summer of 1990, and it's all about togetherness. Above: Senior pros with their kids. Below: Another one bites the dust.

Superstars. Above: The incomparable Sir Richard Hadlee. Below: New Zealand's greatest ever batsman, Martin Crowe.

The great Allan Border offers me some batting tips.

Coaches come and go (and there were plenty in my time). Above: R.S. Cunis, who was a great help to Willie and me and, right, Wally Lees, who was also a pleasure to work with.

Tony Blain, aka Billy Idol, meets Zimbabwean head of state Robert Mugabe in Harare, 1988.

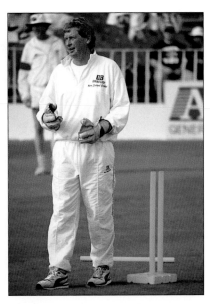

Ian 'Mr Grumpy' Smith . . . the best gloveman I ever played with.

Wasim 'the freak' Akram . . . incredibly fast arm action to match an equally fast mouth.

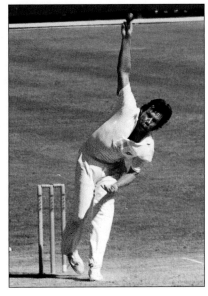

One of my mentors . . . the wonderfully caring legal eagle, Martin Snedden.

The Victorian Salute – demonstrated at Eden Park by Big Bad Merv and recently reintroduced by Shane Warne in England.

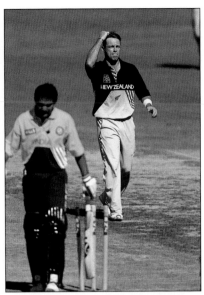

Shane Warne . . . who says spinners can't be strike bowlers?

Getting one over the great Indian batsman, Mohammed 'Mr Wristy' Azharuddin, Basin Reserve, 1994.

Sachin Tendulkar, the little Indian genius . . . and a master of timing.

The long and the short of it . . . You can see why 'King Curtly' gets a wee bit more bounce than me!

membership and a lot of history, the red rose county. The members demand a lot; they bitch when you're not bowling well, but the deck at Old Trafford was flat, far better to bat on than bowl. In county cricket you also waited 100 overs before getting the second new ball.

The Lancs side had Graeme Fowler and Paul Allott, the two legends who were thick as thieves. Mike Watkinson was a bit like Willie Watson with quite a dry, hard case sense of humour. He was only 31 in 1992, but he'd been around a long time. Philip de Freitas was in and out of the England side that season. Mike Atherton was trying to play his way back in; Neil Fairbrother was Lancashire's captain. Athers took over as captain when Fairbrother tore his hamstring a couple of times. The England physio, Laurie Brown, was also from Manchester and I knew quite a few of the faces around from having played England and in the World XIs.

County cricket was the harsh reality of playing the game professionally, making the game your life. You did play at classic grounds and stay in good hotels, but for most of the county guys cricket was work, almost a nine to five grind. They weren't like the big football stars; they had to train hard, play all week, and there was a lot of tiring travel up and down those monotonous English motorways. There were a lot of back to back games, which meant you'd be travelling almost as soon as you'd left a long day in the field, say from Middlesex up to Manchester. Then your team would lose the toss and there you were back on another cricket field, after having driven all evening and crashing at midnight . . .

It was day in, day out and non-stop, the counties contesting the County Championship, the NatWest, the Benson & Hedges Cup and the Sunday League – a lot of cricket. In 1992 the championship was the last year of only three-day games – they introduced four-dayers the following year, which meant the 18 counties played each other only once.

Kim and I lived in Nick Speak's flat in Didsbury, which was a nice suburb about 5km away from Old Trafford. Mike Atherton was just round the corner and we hung out a bit at our local, the Didsbury Crown. We had a car, learned to navigate the motorways and caught up with a lot of old friends – Lancs played quite a few times down in London so seeing Singy and the Harefield boys once more was great. The arrangement at Lancs was that if you had a partner who wanted to travel with you, that was fine as long as you stayed in a different hotel to the rest of the team – their compromise to the constant division inside teams over whether there should be wives on tour – so we'd stay in a bed & breakfast across from the team hotel.

I took 36 wickets in 13 first-class games for Lancs. It wasn't great, but often I'd only be bowling in one innings, because we weren't batting well and so were following on a lot. Against Hampshire we were 130 without loss at tea and got bowled out for 180. It was embarrassing. That was us, though, that year. The curse of the Dan had struck again!

I only lasted until the middle of July. We were playing at Northampton when I had my first serious breakdown. I left it, hoping the pain through my trunk would come right for the last few weeks, but it wasn't going to happen. I saw a specialist. He diagnosed a hernia: my summer in county cricket was over. Under the Lancs insurance scheme I went into a private hospital in early August for the operation and then laid up in Speaky's flat watching the Barcelona Olympics. My last month at Lancs was a paid holiday, but it felt like the most miserable time of my life.

I really enjoyed my time at Lancashire, the camaraderie with the boys and the taste of their lifestyle. It came at a good time for me. I was 26, I'd been in the New Zealand side a good five years – midway, as it turned out, in my career. I was ready for it, not overawed, because I'd absorbed what being in England was all about in earlier years.

I was grateful for the experience. I would have loved to have been able to play more on the county circuit, but it wasn't to be. And in a way, it wasn't really for me. It was simply too physically demanding bowling to that intensity year round. From 1990 through to July 1992, I'd bowled a hell of a lot of overs and stood on a hell of a lot of outfields; international itineraries were becoming very full on. Playing in the off-season started to take toll on your professional career for your country. There comes a time when you have to weigh up and choose between fitness or longevity – and I knew that more than anything else I wanted to keep playing for New Zealand.

I had to take my cap off to guys like Hadlee and Wrighty, who played so long on that circuit. But there wasn't nearly as much international demand in their era. By the time guys like myself and Chris Cairns tried to follow in their footsteps, that had all changed. Cairnsie's done well to play four solid seasons for Nottingham, but when you look at it, he's missed so much other cricket in the same period, since 1992. The lifestyle comes at a high price.

If I'd had a different type of physique and been fit enough, and perhaps been more of an allround player like Cairnsie is, able to bat at six or seven, county cricket might have been an ideal lifestyle for me, too, something I could have done for a much longer time. But I'd look around at other specialist bowlers, like 'King Curt'

Ambrose and Courtney Walsh, and see they weren't enjoying the county life. It was a job, it was how they got paid.

Walsh played in England from 1983, and I admired the way the big man lasted there so long. It really was a relentless grind of slamming yourself down on thankless pitches, day after day. You could see why Wasim Akram developed the reverse swing there, so batsmen couldn't hit it as well or time it as well. There were bonuses to playing so much cricket there. For me, I really enjoyed crafting subtle variations that season at Lancs, using a change of pace more often, more slower balls. I worked a lot on that slower ball. I wasn't very good at coming round the wicket either, and worked on that. I used to have success swinging the ball back into the lefthanders and getting lbws, so it was good to bowl lots of overs and work hard, trying new things when your selection for your country wasn't being assessed. You got so many overs under your belt. Martin Snedden had said to me before I left for Lancs, "Mate, you're not going for the money, you're going for the experience and knowledge." He was dead right.

I did end up going back to England for one last season after that, to play league cricket in Rochdale in Lancashire. I'd got married at the end of the 1992/93 New Zealand summer, so it was a bit of a working holiday and honeymoon for Kim and I. Chris Harris and his lady Linda were living close by, Harry playing for a neighbouring club, and it was a good, relaxed summer. The Sunday league didn't start until 2pm so people had time to eat their Sunday roast before cricket. I'd had a good run of going back and forward to the UK and I knew it would be my last English summer.

Playing as a pro in England wasn't the riches you might imagine. I did save some money through the early 90s, but nothing major – about 21,000 pounds from Lancs and the World XI games. Kim and I brought it back and used it to do our first house up. Of course, by then the pound had dropped against the New Zealand dollar to two-and-a-half to one. Just my luck. And though I enjoyed realising my ambition of making a living from the game as a professional cricketer, it never equalled the romance of Harefield in my youth.

When I was still at Takapuna Grammar, Frano Botica was at Westlake Boys' High. I never really met him, but I used to see him going into the North Shore Rugby Club and everyone on the Shore knew his reputation as a good player. Years later, in 1992 when I was with Lancashire, I went along to an event at Central Park, Wigan's home ground, where a huge marquee was laid out with dinner for 1000 people. It was a male fraternity-type black tie do, and I went with Mike Atherton and Nick Speak from Lancashire – you moved in those circles as a county pro. Frano was there. He'd started to make a big name for himself in rugby league then, and I caught up with him. I saw him again at the 1994 final between Wigan and Leeds – it was when New Zealand was touring and we all got tickets to go to Wembley through the New Zealand High Commission – and in 1995, when he came out to play for the Warriors.

Glimpsing the world of professional rugby league through Frano's eyes made me realise the precarious nature of your living in sport. Naturally league was a different world from cricket. Frano lived in a perpetual winter, and he and his wife, Tracy, really missed their New Zealand summers. Some years, they wouldn't be able to come back to New Zealand so would just go down to Italy for a holiday to see some sun and sand, but it wasn't the same. And the winters in that part of the world are long and dark. But it was the reality of making money from his game and you just had to go with it. Their kids came out to New Zealand in 1995 with Northern English accents – it was quite bizarre to see a lovely little brown Maori kid with this foreign accent pouring out of his face.

Wigan was a glamour club, and I couldn't believe how much more professional rugby league seemed than cricket, how laid on the facilities and resources were, how much more money there was in it. It was a million dollar lifestyle. Frano would work with the Wigan fitness professionals who knew his personal biomechanics and body type inside out, which I thought would be a great advantage over using commercial gyms and pools here and there the way I was doing in my training. At club level, league was far more professional in that sense than cricket at *international* level.

But that envy was really tempered when Frano came back to live in Takapuna. It was really neat to see him do well for the Warriors, but then came the moment in the middle of 1995 when a tackle from Mark Geyer broke his leg.

I went and visited Frano in Middlemore Hospital. He'd been just about to sign on for a longer term, but now there was this crippling injury – and then the money stakes suddenly dropped, because the club was talking to Matthew Ridge, trying to get him to come back from Manly. With screws and plates holding his leg together, overnight Frano had gone from highflier to noncontender.

Frano ended up going and playing in Castleford, and now he's gone back to rugby union in Wales. But I'll never forget how it could all change so quickly. I saw how his life had been turned upside down by a single, split-second injury, just like that. I realised playing sport for a living was like being on a knife edge. You just hoped you wouldn't get cut.

ALL AROUND
THE WORLD

A lot of being in a cricket team is about tolerance and understanding other people – and never do you feel that more than when you're away on tour in a foreign country.

Your position as an international cricketer gives you a real insight into different cultures as they surround you, and I was very fortunate to be able to return to some amazing places overseas quite a few times in my career. As I grew older, from my late teens to my thirties, I think I saw other cultures with more maturity, and was very fortunate to have that opportunity to grow and learn. I'd see young guys come in wide-eyed and sometimes go through that experience themselves, though some don't, and sadly just dread going back to some of the places. But everywhere's different – and that's what made life on the road so absorbing.

Even a country like England turned out to have a totally different cricket culture to New Zealand and Australia. I could never get over the large number of spectators who would come along with scorebooks and sit the whole day filling them in, using all the different coloured pens, clipboard, the transistor in one ear – the works. You get the odd eccentric doing that in New Zealand, but in

England they were coming out of the woodwork at every ground. The counties would all sell scorecards for 25p, which people were encouraged to fill in and keep.

You'd see English spectators sitting there in collared shirts, even woollen sleeved cardigans and duckshooters' peaked caps, boiling away in the June sun. Comfort didn't seem to matter so much as seemliness. They won't change. A lot of the walk-shorts generation still don't wear sunglasses and just squint into the glare all day.

That formality ran right through English cricket. You always had official room attendants there, staff whose job it was to make your tea and serve you biscuits. If you needed a stud prised out of your boot, there'd be a man at your shoulder to whisk it away to his workshop. At Lancs we were looked after by a great old guy called "the Major" – he used to go on about the war. He'd do anything for us and get his absolute money's worth out of it by teasing us for being prima donnas wanting to be looked after all the time.

I used to stay at Chris Cairns' house in Notts when Lancashire played there or I happened to be up that way. It was good catching up with him to break the grind of travel in England. They used to call him 'The Sheep' at Notts. At first they put him up in a biggish old semi-detached place in quite a rough part of town, an area known for car conversion, but he was generally well looked after and got better digs when he proved himself.

Cairnsie was big on taking his own supplies over. We'd have barbies and get into our tins of tomato sauce from home. I even used to take my own tomato sauce with me to a do, because the ones in England tasted different. Mother would send over the Wattie's rescue pack. And Vegemite! We used to put that on our "white death bread", which was about all you could get in England. That was the thing I missed the most – you couldn't get multigrain breads like Vogel's or Burgen, and the only brown breads were tasteless and overmilled. I'd take my own Complan and Beroccas with me to England, because the ones there tasted hideous. They had Marmite too, but it was horrible, like Bovril. You'd take your own Vegemite to lunch and the other cricketers would stare at you like you were mad, eating this ghastly brown stuff.

The game took me to the outer reaches of the UK, too. I went up to Inverary, near Aberdeen in Scotland, for the opening of a new club on one occasion. With the World XI in 1991 I also played in Edinburgh, picturesque cricket against all these hard-case Scots in a neat old city full of crusty old buildings. Then we played at Swansea in Wales, a miserable night game by the howling, stormy sea. It was a white ball and got soaked on an artificial wicket, splatting like a wet tennis ball. But the place that really impacted on me was Northern Ireland.

The Irish cricket team play in the Natwest and Benson & Hedges in England, but the English game hadn't really caught the wind in Ireland. They had a league, and a lot of New Zealand and South African guys (including Hansie Cronje) have pro-ed there, but soccer, rugby and even hurling are bigger than cricket. It's not traditional, and is very wet, which isn't great for cricket.

I first got to Northern Ireland in May 1990 with the New Zealand cricket side – we were warming up on tour playing an Irish XI at Downpatrick. I really enjoyed Downpatrick because I'm a big Van Morrison fan, and lapped up all the scenery around Coney Island, Strangford Lough, Killyleagh and the little fishing village of Ardglass, places "Uncle Van" had talked about on his "Avalon Sunset" album. It gave me goose bumps. Downpatrick was a beautiful village green, but then we played at Ormeau in Belfast, which was surrounded by concrete walls, with armoured vehicles rolling down the road past the club.

Belfast was nothing compared to Harare in Zimbabwe, where the president, Robert Mugabe, had his official residence directly opposite the main cricket club. There were armed soldiers with machine guns on permanent duty at the top of the road, and only Mugabe's men and cricketers were allowed to pass. That was 1988. I was there with a rather old "Young New Zealand" side – most of us were around our mid-20s, if not pushing 30 or slightly older. During the first 'youth' test, Mugabe came to watch and we all had to line up to shake hands, like meeting the queen. Then we played, with his security soldiers and their dogs strategically dotted around the boundary. A couple stood in front of the sightscreen, but since they had machine guns you tended to let them stay there.

Arriving for the first time in Africa in the dead of night was unforgettable. It was unnervingly quiet, the air smelt strange and out of the dark black faces would glide past you, militia watching you carefully as you got off the plane. We played most of our games at Harare, which has a beautiful Cape Dutch-style pavilion and purple jacarandas in flower during the cricket season. We also played at a country club in Harare South, in Mutare, down by the Mozambique border where shells had come flying over the hills and landed around the cricket ground during the civil war, and in Bulawayo as well, which was the only place we saw young black cricketers.

I loved travelling through the sparse, open savannah in the team bus; you could see for miles. Zimbabwe was one of the few times I got a taste of what cricket tours used to be like, the great hauls on the boat when there was far more time to relax and take in a country. Our team went to a snake farm, watched the black mamba eat a live mouse, jumped out of our skins when the mad old snake handler whipped the odd poisonous reptile out of its cage for us to get a closer look. We went to an Amnesty International rock concert that had Tracey Chapman, Peter Gabriel, Sting and Bruce Springsteen performing in a soccer stadium packed with a swarm of 75,000 people and pickpockets (the crowd was mainly South Africans who'd come across the border – it was a free Mandela campaign). It was huge. We went on safari, watching beautiful zebras and giraffes gallop away from us – we struck the coldest day of the year for that, sitting in these safari jeeps shivering in borrowed blankets and jerseys; it didn't seem like Africa at all. But when we went on a day trip to Victoria Falls, on the border between Zimbabwe and Zambia, it was 42 degrees. You'd rush for patches of waterfall mist, where the temperature was 10 degrees cooler, then step back into baking, oven-dry heat, guzzling coke after coke out of the old-fashioned glass bottles they had in Africa.

Africa was like being in a time warp. The Mashona and Matabele people on the street wore wide ties, polyester dresses and flares – as if the whole place had got stuck in the seventies. The buildings were like that too. Most of the time we stayed in the same hotel, The Hotel Jamieson, where the doorman wore a suit that was two sizes too small for him. You started to realise that a lot of the people around you, the black people at least, were poor. A lot of the ones who worked in the hotel were from country areas: they got two days off every two months to see their families. Some of them had 10 children, yet they were so thankful just to have a good job.

But cricket unfurled for us mainly the other side of Zimbabwe – the wealthy white enclave. Cricket was their game. I remember we were treated to a huge braii (barbecue) at a beautiful estate, a magnificent house and a vegetable plot the size of a small market garden – tended by blacks. There was an open bar set up in the garden, anything we could have wished for, tennis courts, a pool house, the works. Ken Rutherford, who was in charge of the New Zealand flag that tour, had a great time. He ended the evening by running around the estate wearing nothing but the flag like a cape round his shoulders crying, "Batrudder returns!"

Our Zimbabwean liaison manager throughout that tour was Russell Tiffen, a hell of a nice guy who's now an international umpire – he umpired a match New Zealand played in Lahore in 1996. The Zimbabwean cricket set were very hospitable, but you could sense there was a certain resentment against Graeme Hick, who'd turned his back on their efforts to gain test status (the ICC had yet to recognise it when we were there) and had just made 1000 runs before the end of May in the English county summer, playing for Worcestershire. He'd made a huge hundred against the West Indies and the video of it always seemed to be playing at the clubhouse in Harare whenever we had a function.

The freakiest thing about Zimbabwe was that it was my first taste of playing at altitude – Harare was 5000 feet above sea level. When you kicked a rugby ball at practice, it would go for miles. It was hard to breathe, my lungs were burning. Other guys' noses would bleed with the change in air pressure.

South Africa was another enjoyable tour, though again there was a certain edge that you sensed when you saw the hostile, high walls around houses with shards of jagged glass embedded in the top. All the grounds had uniformed security guards with rottweilers. When the ball went their way you didn't field it; the guards had to throw it to you. It was total overkill. When we'd go out for a night at the Sports Cafe, a chain of nightclub-type bars across the republic, they'd frisk you for weapons before you went in. You'd go into some exclusive bars that were full only of fat little white kids, no blacks around. That really impacted on me. You could sense the wealth.

We toured South Africa well after the official rejection of apartheid, but you could feel the tension around. Blacks were conspicuously in service or manual jobs, or running stalls for tourists. They would call you "Boss". They'd always be the ones cooking the braii. Being Kiwi, we wanted to muck in and help, but that would alarm them. They'd timidly insist, "No, no, Boss, I'll do that, Boss." You weren't allowed to be seen to be helping, because then they weren't seen to be doing their job and they'd get into trouble, or get the sack.

The whole concept of keeping that race down was sad. What freaked me out was you'd see blacks jumping up and down on the beach. Before 1990, they hadn't been allowed on the beaches. Most of them didn't know how to swim in the sea, so they'd just jump up and down knee deep in the water.

I never went into a township, but I saw the famous shanty town that slaps you in the eye when you first drive out of the airport in Cape Town. It reminded me of parts of India, the third world side of South Africa. Virtually across the road were large vineyards with Cape Dutch-style mansions . . . it summed up the inequality in an instant.

There was a stubbornness about the South African cricketers. They were hard and gritty on the field, and some of them, like Daryl Cullinan, had a swaggering arrogance. Perhaps it came from the two years' compulsory military service they all had to complete. Their warm-ups were like a military drill, very organised and regimented. You saw it in their umpires, too. Cyril Mitchley's signals were like a salute; he was very officious. The bonus for us was that we were taken up for a scenic flight over Cape Town's Table Mountain in army camouflage helicopters, hovering over the famous rugby and cricket grounds at Newlands in these great, noisy Iroquois.

But nowhere was the culture shock so great as around the Indian subcontinent. From my first taste of Sri Lanka on my first international tour, I never really got used to it. From the minute you arrived you'd be seen as movie stars, surrounded by officials and customs men who wanted to be seen having an important job. And as soon as you got out of the airport, there was the smell, the stench of the third world.

I'll never forget sitting in a rickety old Bedford bus bouncing over the potholes on the way out from Colombo airport that first time. I'd experienced homeless people in London, but nothing like the view out the bus window. Sri Lankans would be sitting on the side of the road cooking food in rusty tin billies hung between two poles, or just huddled round 40-gallon drums of open fire. That was their lot. Then you'd pull up at a five star hotel with 24-hour room service.

Phil Horne and I were getting over the flight when we went for a walk the next day. Hornet's quite a sensitive soul at the best of times and felt quite nauseous, overpowered by the smell of the streets where people lived, slept and pissed. We were heading for the markets when we heard this sound like a little lamb, a bleating: it was a leper coming begging. He had a leg missing and was on a crutch. One of his arms was mangled, and he had a very strong odour. He came up behind us and tapped Hornet on the shoulder. I'll never forget him turning round, then jumping back with fright. That was our first real encounter with the subcontinent.

You could see the English influence in the old colonial style of the clubhouses, but it was cricket in another world. I remember thinking, Jesus, we're going to play in this heat? It was energy-sapping. You could go through seven shirts in a 90-minute practice quite easily, and watch the perspiration come out of your pores.

The nets were just rolled mud. Dragonflies would ping off your forehead as you ran in to bowl. One of the most hilarious memories I have of Colombo is the time we went for a stretch after our first warm-up run, lining up against this brick wall to stretch our calves.

Then someone said, "Was that a tremor? Bit of an earthquake?" The brick wall had started to shift. We all freaked and leaped back from it as the whole thing collapsed. Then we all burst into hysterics that this New Zealand cricket team was so physically strong it had flattened a brick wall that was 20 metres long and two metres high! But the wall had no foundations. That was the subcontinent to a tee: the basics always went wrong.

I went to India straight after the Zimbabwe tour in 1988 – half a dozen of us flew from the African continent to meet the rest of the side, which had flown up from New Zealand. While we'd been in Zimbabwe, two of India's airbuses – on routes that we would be travelling – had crashed and killed hundreds of people.

Planes on the subcontinent were always dubious. I was sitting with Sneds, Smithy and Trevor Franklin as an Indian Airlines flight was getting ready to take off. They couldn't close the back door – it was just behind us and you could see the bolts had rusted. These men outside the plane just boofed it shut. I remember all of us looking at each other, cracking up in very nervous laughter. Were we going to be sucked out at 10,000 feet?

Then in 1995 one time we were squashed onto a different flight because ours had been cancelled. Because the plane was now vastly overbooked, they started throwing luggage down the aisles – they don't bother with the "please ensure your cabin baggage is stowed safely under the seat in front of you" line in India! An old woman in a sari sat down across from us with a dog in her lap. We looked around half expecting to see cages of chickens falling out of the overhead lockers. So many times you got on a plane there and started feeling nervous. Everything was out of control.

You often stayed in hotels that were like palaces in India. A lot of them had actually been maharajahs' residences at one time. The marble foyers, air-conditioned restaurants and breath-taking views over the orange/pink horizon of the sea beyond the Queen Victoria's Gateway of India in Bombay were your escape from the madness all around.

It was terrible the way you almost became accustomed to the maimed kids in the streets, their hands or tongues cut off by their parents so they could earn more money as beggars. You saw women walking on their twisted hands because their legs were deformed – there were no wheelchairs. Begging kids would pull at your shirt. A lot of them didn't want money, they wanted milk powder. They said it was for their families. But the scam was that they'd get the milk powder, take some and then sell it back to the black market where it originally came from. Some kids asked for clothes instead – you sensed that if you gave them money, it would just be taken away from them.

The taxi drivers would turn the engine off at the lights, and the beggars would absolutely hound you then. Hands stretched out through the windows. They'd keep pointing to their stumps. You became so immune that you started saying terrible things, like "Well, you should have thought about that before you cut it off." You had to build a wall, because there was so much of it, you couldn't afford to get emotionally tied in. You just couldn't help them all; and it was a real dilemma whether to give, whether to encourage more tragedy.

In Delhi, if you blew your nose after hitting the smog of the streets in an open, three-wheeled autorickshaw, your tissue would be black. We used to have autorickshaw races which was, in Indian traffic, really taking your life into your hands. Traffic would go through roundabouts en masse with no lanes or sense of organised direction. Then a sacred cow would stroll through the middle and everyone would suddenly swerve out at wild angles. We crashed into the sides of each other a couple of times, got the speed wobbles round the roundabout.

I'll never forget seeing life go by from those taxis. You'd see the men sitting round smoking while the wiry, dark women with baskets of concrete on top of their head worked as human conveyor belts all day. Life was hard. And it used to freak younger guys out when they first saw the men in India walking round holding hands or linking arms. That's just a cultural trait, nothing to do with being gay, but guys would think, geez, look at those fag cops – rifles over their shoulders, sucking a cigarette and holding hands! But the biggest thing that gets you in India is simply the incredible amount of people everywhere, the intensity of being there. Because you stuck out like dog's balls, and the Indian people were so passionate and knowledgeable about cricket that they all knew when a match was on, what you looked like and who you were, it was hard to feel comfortable wandering around alone. At times people would flock around you, or follow you.

Players, especially the Indians, were treated like rock stars. Their faces were in advertisements everywhere you looked. In 1996 we couldn't go past a billboard or lamp post without seeing Sachin Tendulkar holding up a Pepsi. He had just bought a holiday home in Goa when we were there and it was like a palace. Guys like Sachin, Kapil Dev and Mohammed Azharuddin were our equivalent of multi-millionaires. They had lush lifestyles and hung out with the "Bollywood" stars of Indian cinema – I think Azza married one.

They were India's royal family and treated like gods, given lifetime memberships of the best hotels. Given apartments. Cars. The Pakistanis were given parcels of land for winning the 1992 World Cup. It's no wonder subcontinent countries win those tournaments: it's such a big deal for them.

But the Indians and Pakistanis are put on such pedestals that if things aren't going well, the public comes down on them heavily. I think the Indian cricketers really feel that pressure, certainly when things aren't going well for them on the park. We saw a classic example during the 1996 World Cup, when Sri Lanka started to get on top of them in Calcutta. The crowd started rioting, throwing stuff at the cricketers and letting off fireworks. Clive Lloyd, the match referee, had to call off the game.

The crowds for a close test match are huge, excitable fans jammed in like sardines. When their players are under pressure, it can get quite scary out there. I've had fruit biffed at me, and in Bombay once I got stung by a battery on my shoulderblade – I was just lucky it was an AAA instead of a D.

The crowd would flash mirrors behind the bowler's arm when we were batting too, and sometimes even when one of their own was in. Playboy/film star/cricketer Ravi Shastri was out there in 1988 when he hadn't been performing well and there was real pressure on him to hold his place. Some of the crowd thought he shouldn't be there, and that was how they protested: by flashing mirrors into his eyes. Braces was bowling at the time and couldn't believe it when Shastri stopped him in his tracks and marched past the umpire to the big wire fence at long on and started angrily shaking his bat at the crowd. He stopped the game for a full five minutes, told the crowd off, came back and carried on. The stars really were a law unto themselves.

At the other extreme, the Indians could get off on the crowd going mad. They fed Kris Srikkanth into a frenzy against us: he hit Braces for a six first ball, then belted another right out of the park. Dilip Vengsarkar at the other end was telling him to settle down, but you could see from his eyes that Srikkanth was just pumping with adrenalin, and he hit out again.

We'd often get from one match to the next by train – it was like travelling back in time, living in the 1930s. We went in what the Indians called the first-class compartments – they had bunks so you could sleep, but we wouldn't call them first-class. It was all a bit of a novelty, but when you saw the locals crammed into the cheap class like bony cattle, you were grateful.

Being a cricketer in India is like being in the Beatles. We'd travel at night when there was likely to be less disruption to the schedule, but every time you stopped somewhere there would be all this banging on the side of the train: if you pulled back the curtain, there were 15 Indian faces pressed up against the window staring at you. You'd arrive at 4am in Baroda or Vishakapatnam, and it would be pitch black – but there'd be thousands of people gathered at the station desperate to catch a glimpse of a cricketer. Then the militia men would come through with their big bamboo canes, bashing people with these sticks like they were cattle. A whole sea of people would open up to make way for you, because they'd see these flying sticks charging in the background. Then when the Indian guys got off the train you'd hear all this shrieking. People would be screaming *Sachin! Sachin!* and *Azza! Azza!* as the militia men bashed them back. Tendulkar wasn't a cricketer; he was a god. People just wanted to touch him, because they felt if they touched him, they'd be blessed with his fortune.

There were times you didn't feel entirely secure. On our way to fly to Calcutta late in 1995, the team was delayed at Cuttack for three hours because a car crash had started a riot, and the riot was blocking the main route to the airport. Buses had been overturned and set alight so we had to abandon our team coach and squeeze into a convoy of taxis to follow a detour out through a dusty old snakepath. It was like the gumball rally, big sweaty sportsmen squashed three in the back and one in the front with the driver racing over potholes that were as big as craters. A mad adventure within a mad adventure.

We were flying to Calcutta to connect with a train, and I was getting quite worried about the delay because my wife, Kim, and Adam Parore's girlfriend at the time, Greer Robson, had flown up from New Zealand and were supposed to meet us at the station. A crowd of thousands had started to gather there because they knew cricketers were coming through any minute. Kim and Greer had never been to India before and huddled with their gear at the station freaking out: they were surrounded by 200 Indian faces staring at Kim and Greer's light hair and eyes. Greer's bumbag was snipped and whipped away by a pickpocket.

I got off the bus from the airport at Calcutta and anxiously started looking for the girls. Javagal Srinath gave me a hand and asked one of the local men to "find the two white women". When we spotted them, Kim just lunged on me and held on for all money.

Greer was on her way up to Europe and had stopped off to see Adam on the way. They'd had a bit of a wild romance that was splashed across the cover of *Woman's Day*, but Adam had started to go cold on the whole idea and had really taken her for a bit of a wild goose chase, a ride. It was a shame, because she's a very sweet person. Kim and I have caught up with her since.

Anyway, it wasn't really happening between Adam and Greer by the time we got to Goa. Our one-day international was rained out there, so the guys were taking some time out at a player's function laid out at a beach resort there. Greer doesn't drink alcohol at all, but some of the guys wickedly encouraged her to partake of the vodka and orange. There was also a marvellous chocolate cake. Poor Greer didn't handle the drink too well at all and flaked out. Adam was nowhere to be seen, so I had to carry her from the cafe on the beach back to our hotel, and as I lifted her up she threw up molten chocolate cake all down my arm. I couldn't believe how much a little person like Robbo could throw up – more and more just kept pouring out! Luckily it was a team issue shirt.

It sounds terrible, but laughs like that were great for keeping you going in India. You felt so claustrophobic and alienated at times in the culture that it was too easy to get grumpy. It was the little things, like losing your gear in the laundry, not being able to go out of your hotel, the wrong room service coming up, having to argue with someone about it – nothing seemed to be easy in India. You were hounded in the street and ripped off shopping. You started snapping at people after a while, the mad energy got to you. Then you'd start thinking like one of the locals, doing a deal with the laundry guy in your hotel, giving him one of your team t-shirts as "baksheesh" for getting your washing back, because you knew if you didn't all your DB laundry would go missing anyway, souvenired by the cricket-crazy staff.

I'll never forget Ian Smith going slightly round the twist in Jammu at the end of the particularly long and traumatic tour of 1988. It was raining in Jammu, quite a cold snap, and our game was called off. Everyone was getting a bit toey after six weeks on the road, but now, because Jammu was a security area up near the Pakistan border, we weren't allowed to leave our hotel and everyone was getting a bit of log cabin fever cooped up in this very basic and freezing hotel – the rooms were like cells. There was talk of us being rained in at the airport, which would mean we'd be unable to get back home to our families for Christmas. Smithy got his bat out and just started hitting the wall, over and over again. That was just how you felt sometimes.

But Pakistan was the worst. Sometimes Pakistan felt like a sentence, not a tour. The Pakistanis seemed harder people, fiercer and less amenable to you, after years of fighting for their scrap of land. Playing around Amritsar, only 20km from the border, you really noticed the military presence. Cairnsie once got some fireworks off some militia guys as part of a social committee event. We put these bombs in a tennis canister and when they exploded, all the guards came running with their guns. Their faces were like stone. They didn't seem to have a sense of humour, or really know English as well as the Indians. There was a greater barrier. You got an unfriendly energy that, for all its madness, you didn't get in India.

In a country that size you know there is corruption. You're told by liaison officers there, "For God's sake, don't trust the police, because they lie to Calcutta." It never really surprised me when the accusations of bribery, gambling and corruption in cricket, the Salim Malik affair and all the rest of it, surfaced in Pakistan.

It was the place you felt the cultural differences most acutely, mostly because of the religion. During the 1996 World Cup it was Ramadan, a time of year when Muslims don't eat or drink from dawn to dusk, so we had to go into the dressing room for drinks in case we frustrated the locals. It was ridiculous because the dressing rooms had these big glass windows and everyone could see us anyway.

Obviously there were no bars or licensed restaurants in Pakistan so you really depended on your team-mates to lift your spirits and break the monotony of the daily grind when you were there. You'd make your own fun, because if you didn't you'd very quickly stop enjoying cricket.

One of our few escapes was to the British Consulate, where they laid on a great function for us. There happened to be a couple of air hostesses there, and air hostesses are fairly renowned for being great party girls. There was no cricket on for a couple of days, only practice the next day, so it was a good night to go a bit mad. Radio New Zealand's irascible comments man Bryan Waddle got thrown in the pool later on in the evening, and Waddle being Waddle got a bit stroppy on us, wanting to find the culprit and toss him in – but, oh dear, next thing you know, the girls had ended up going in instead, clothes and all!

We got back to our hotel around midnight, nothing too late. The hotel had tall Pakistani guards wearing sikh-like turbans and lovely traditional gowns on the door – they were the same height as Willie Watson, who's about 6ft 3in, but these men seemed so much bigger.

Willie and I had gone back to Ruds' room, where we were having a cold drink, a nightcap, running around in just a singlet and shorts because it was still quite warm. Practice was the next morning at nine o'clock so we were all about to hit the sack, but then we got a message from downstairs that there were a couple of wet females in the hotel foyer. The concierge had come up and said, "Look, this is a Muslim country, this sort of thing freaks us out, it's not good for the guards"; so we went downstairs and here were these air hostesses who had been thrown into the pool.

The girls were actually staying at a hotel across the street from us, but Grant Bradburn had invited them back for a nightcap. We seized the moment and took our ghettoblaster down there to the hotel lobby for a dance. We were actually waltzing. Willie, he was dapper – it was like seeing James Bond in action. But because the girls were soaked, it soon degenerated into a bit of a clothes-ripping competition. It was a bit of an uneven contest because while we'd put on some rough old sponsored polo shirts, the girls were wearing these rather light, lacy outfits that ripped easily. We'd be waltzing away elegantly and then all of a sudden, *riiiiip*: there goes the back seam! Then they'd try to rip our shirts, but ours were too strong. One of the hostesses actually started using her teeth trying to rip Willie's shirt. Before long they were down to their undies, and these two big guards on the door couldn't believe their eyes. Was this some strange Western cultural dance?

The girls wanted to come upstairs for a nightcap so we thought we'd do the decent thing and let them change into some more substantial gear in our rooms. Ruds and Dipak Patel turned up to see what all the noise was about and couldn't believe their eyes, either. Willie joked that we'd told these girls it was a toga party so we had to rip their clothes. They went into the bathroom to put some towels around them, at which point Ruds decided to do his John Cleese impersonation. This involved walking around like a mad waiter with a tray carrying a couple of rum and cokes and a wine bottle. It was very elegant, except that he had no underpants or trousers on at the time. The girls came out of the bathroom and turned to see Ruds standing in front of them saying, "Ladies, how are you, may I offer you an hors d'oeuvre, or a small aperitif?" They freaked and ran straight back into the bathroom.

It was all innocent fun, light relief in a part of the world where it was normally very hard to let your hair down. Wally Lees, our coach, understood. He happened to pass by and just said, "Practice in the morning, gentlemen . . ."

Without doubt one of the best tours to get on is the West Indies. It's the complete opposite of Pakistan, like going to play cricket in Fiji. Everything around you is straight out of a holiday brochure and it's hard not to be distracted. At times in 1996 some of the guys found it hard to switch on, since none of us in the team had actually been there before. Having started my career two years after the 1985 tour to the Caribbean, which was only New Zealand's second trip there, I'd waited all my career to get there. In that period the side had been totally cleaned out. I cherished every moment I was there, because it was such a rare opportunity.

We landed in Kingston, Jamaica, which was the home of Bob Marley and reggae music, which I was really into. Barbados and Antigua, the Grenadines, St Vincent were more like backwaters. Every island was different and you never tired of the spectacular coasts and different vegetation, the mangrove-type trees hanging from cliff faces. You'd stand on a white sand, palm-fringed beach facing tranquil clear water, piano grins on the faces of the locals throwing fresh fish onto spits over a fire for you. Guys on the beach would sell you beads, and if you didn't buy their beads they'd offer you "the best ganja on the island" – cannabis. We saw the resort where they'd filmed the James Bond flick *Dr No*, and some of our hotels were just astounding. In Antigua Kim and I were put up in a huge condominium on the beachfront – I think it was supposed to be the manager's room! All in all it's one of the last tours in cricket where you can really mix work and pleasure, where touring loses its inevitable monotony.

It wasn't all sunshine and sand. It was dangerous to be out in certain parts at night – you sensed it was still a bit anti-white, a hangover from the oppression of the Brits. You would also drive past shacks with broken cars, hungry dogs, chickens and rubbish outside in the streets of Antigua. It depressed me that so many of the locals' houses were like baches, almost shanties. The government there takes a one per cent tax on the value of your house each year, so a lot of these big Caribbean people lived in small, half-finished houses that seem quite run down.

We were invited round to Courtney Walsh's mother's place in Jamaica for a party after the one-dayer, and even her house was relatively humble. His sisters were in there with Mamma Walsh and after that there was hardly any room. I remember trying to squeeze into this narrow entranceway, the oven squashed into this tiny little kitchen. Everything was laid on outside – the DJ, big speakers in the garage, good music pumping and this goat's head soup with all this grommetty stuff in the bottom, perhaps chopped up cockles or squid – I didn't really want to ask. Though it was virtually a street party, it wasn't gatecrashed because people seemed to know you didn't intrude on Walshy. That was the way.

A lot of the West Indian players seemed to live quite humbly, but a lot also had property back in England, and you didn't know whether they had money stashed in the Cayman Islands.

The common bond between all the islands of the West Indies was their religion, and that was cricket. It was just like 10CC sang in "Dreadlock Holiday": "I don't like cricket – I love it." At the matches it was an amazing carnival atmosphere. It was such a different culture. They love yahooing, having a good time. You could smell the dope down on the boundary, this sweet smell wafting across the ground. Music blared from hundreds of ghettoblasters, calypso bands singing hits like "Rally Round The West Indies!" There would also be official, eight-foot high speakers at the grounds pumping music between deliveries. If I got hit for four, the volume would blare up and it would be a 20-second party all round the ground. DJs controlled it and they were game-wise – it was loud, but it wasn't used in a way that would put anyone off. It was actually quite enjoyable. Yet in New Zealand, if we have a few Zimbabwean drummers in the stand, they get their snares confiscated!

We won the toss on a particularly flat deck in one match, but it was decided that we would bowl first, which pissed me off because sure enough they got 500. But even though it was a long, hard day in the field, the reggae really kept you going. Paddles wouldn't have liked it so much, and Glenn Turner, our coach, thought it was "too loud and you couldn't hear yourself think".

But despite the relaxed atmosphere, you never forgot that the West Indians played hard cricket. The West Indies' bowlers have charged in and dominated from the late 70s, a real force, with fantastic batsmen at the other end of the line up. They'd been raised in a tough cauldron, and when you played there you were expected to show what you were made of.

I generally suffered on the decks in the Caribbean, they were quite slowish that year, which was unusual. But Phil Simmons and Brian Lara came up to me at the end and said, "Man, you earned your stripes of respect from us for running in on those flat decks over and over again."

I'll never forget the end of the last test match, which the West Indies were about to win – they only needed about 30 in the second dig. This middle-aged guy, no spring chicken, was dancing away in the middle of the crowd. I was at the top of my mark and one of the boys called over to me, "Danny, take a look." Peter Willey, the English umpire, turned around too, and we just could not believe what we saw. Here was this 50-year-old guy with his fly down, his penis hanging out, just shaking his whole tush to the squealing crowd. This was apparently the done thing, and much more interesting than a Mexican Wave. Before long there was a line of guys at the top of the grandstands with their pants off, swinging from the rafters. It was definitely a cut above your regular streaker at the Basin Reserve.

It was quite surprising that despite the absolute passion for the game that you saw in the locals, a lot of the grounds in the West

BEAST OF BURDEN

I actually batted at five for Takapuna Grammar and once got 150 not out for North Shore in an under-18s quarter-final versus Parnell – the highest score in the club! It was at Walker Park in Point Chevalier, where the boundaries are tiny and I could half-chip it over the bowler's head with my big, heavy bat, but at the time it felt like the MCG.

Later on in my career, for a tailender, I had a good run of batting form, including 27 not out at Perth in 1989 and 25 at Faisalabad in 1990. I'd been promoted to nightwatchman and I was just starting to come off some good time at the crease when I went through a really bad slump, getting four noughts in a row in a series over in Australia. I was given Mark Waugh's nickname of "Audi". If I'd got one more I would have been called "Olympic". But I got 20 not out instead; contrary to popular belief I could still bat.

It was when I had about 20 test noughts that I first realised I was on course for a dubious world record – which was then 23. In India in 1995 I shot to 22 in Cuttack with a nice lbw and then equalled Chandrasekhar's world test duck record in my very next innings, at Lancaster Park against Pakistan in 1995/96.

By the time we landed in the Caribbean at the end of that summer, people thought that, being in prime duck-hunting country, it was a safe bet that the record would soon be all mine. The West Indians would give me a hard time, chuckling away in the slips that I was "looking for dat world record, boy . . ."

I had a really good chance of getting it in Barbados. We were bowled out for about 195, but I frustrated all the punters by getting

Indies were like their houses, quite humble and carefree. Some had terrible, stony outfields. It turned out that the local associations had to pay their stars so much – often in US dollars – that there wasn't much money left to spend on facilities. There's a third worldness about it, a sense of getting what you can while you can, because there's not much about. In a lot of the countries we toured cricket was much more than a game. It was a ticket to ride.

four not out in the first innings and 26 not out in the second. But in Antigua it was practically written into the script. I bowled my heart out all day but couldn't take a wicket with catches dropping like flies. The West Indies were none for a hundred and kept going. Then when it was our turn to bat, sure enough there I was as nightwatchman facing Curtly Ambrose, a world class fast bowler who'd been around 10 years feeling fired up by his noisy home crowd. I dug the first one out quite well, but then I got a jaffa that nipped back and was adjudged to be leg before. That was it, the world record; I'd averaged one every second test match!

Before we went away to Sharjah in 1996, the Queen Street Cricket Club presented me with their annual Duck of the Year award. Sneds had previously won it for the slowest test duck, spread over three days, as had John Bracewell for ducking one that went around his legs! But though my brief hold on the world record (Courtney Walsh, the great West Indian bunny, overtook me in the northern hemisphere summer of 1997) earned me a lot of light-hearted ribbing and was the source of a lot of fun, I was actually quite down the day after I got it.

It showed you how often the New Zealand tail had been forced to bat in tests over my career, how little I'd bowled in the second innings of a test match because we hadn't bowled that well or the opposition had batted particularly well, or we hadn't batted well and were facing the music twice.

I think I was also a better tailender than the record actually indicated. I could hold a bat. Generally in test matches I wasn't overly trying to play shots: I was guarding my end, batting time, getting into line and being a defender rather than an attacker. If it meant not getting off the mark, so be it.

MAD DOGS AND ENGLISHMEN

One of the things I enjoy the most about cricket is the mad personalities you get to meet along the way. Cricket's always been a great game for characters, and some are really quite eccentric. England seemed to produce more than its fair share of the larger than life oddballs and, as the old Noel Coward song goes, they used to come out in the midday sun. Geoffrey Boycott is one that stands out. There was a whole mana and arrogance about him. He'd made it to the very top of the game in England, where it really was as much about social status as sport, and seemed to live on a different tangent to everyone else. It was always up to you to make the effort in conversation, and all conversations seemed to lead directly back to him raving on about himself again anyway. I was talking to him about the pitch at Trent Bridge once when suddenly there I was listening to the day when he was facing all these West Indian bowlers on a wet pitch just like this in 1968 and he . . .

Boycott's almost a law unto himself. I notice a few women have come out in England's tabloids about how he'd walk past them at a match or a function and just hand them his room key. He's simply very confident about himself.

I first met him when England toured New Zealand in 1988. I remember winking at him down in Christchurch as he stood out on the pitch yarning to Neal Radford. I'd just taken my first five-wicket bag in test cricket and he probably thought I was being a bit cocky. He laughed at me and looked at me quite arrogantly, as if I was an upstart daring to wink at the living legend, so I kept out of his way. At the next test, at Eden Park, I was sitting in the dressing room when Trevor Franklin came in and piped, "Boycott wants to speak to you, Dan." I thought Franko was having me on as usual so I just ignored it and carried on getting a bit of treatment from Plums, our physio, just sitting there in my undies. Suddenly Boycott stuck his Panama hatted head through our dressing room door and said, "Oi, you! Danny! What are you doing? I want to talk to you!"

He came in and started raving in that slow Yorkshire drawl of his about me coming to play league cricket for Barnsley, his old club in Yorkshire, that season. It was totally out of the blue and I said to be honest I was just looking at having a bit of a break after New Zealand went to Sharjah in April. He got quite irritated with me, almost as if I was offending him by not jumping at the opportunity. He almost stormed off, as I think was his habit. He never did like being dismissed.

Fred Trueman was another Yorkshire legend who made a big impression on me. You really only said hello to Fred, he was such a great man in your mind. I said hello at the 1990 Headingley one-day international when we'd been chasing a big score, 295/6, and most of the Poms were delighted, thinking we'd lost before we'd even come out to bat. But then Mark Greatbatch got 102 and we got up and won it by four wickets. Trueman was the man of the match adjudicator and Headingley was his home ground. But he came into our dressing room afterwards and said he thought it was a great laugh that we'd got up to win and was happily basking in our glory, having a couple of quiet ales with us.

The following year, 1991, Trueman was the manager of the World XI side that went to Northern Ireland, which included myself and Mark Priest, Imran Khan as captain, Winston Davis, Roger Harper, John Morris, Sanjay Manjrekar, Atul Wasson and Maninder Singh. The match was part of the Belfast Festival and during the official dinner there Trueman said he wanted to have a talk to Priesty and me. Any full-blooded Yorkshireman goes on about how it was in his day for hours if you let him, so we didn't think too much of it when he later cornered us at the bar of our hotel and started talking off the cuff. Priesty and I had not long before been on tour in Pakistan with the New Zealand side, the infamous occasion on which the

Pakistanis had got the ball swinging all over the place and ripped us apart in the tests. The balls they used would have a curious absence of leather on only one side. We'd figured the Pakis out and fought fire with fire, scratching up half of our own ball with a bottle top. The umpires actually took the ball off us, inspected it, and then handed it back saying it was now fair for both teams! Trueman was very interested in the ball-tampering business so we gave him the whole story about how the Pakistanis had swapped the ball during the match for one with these neat and tidy gouges in it, how Priesty had run off and taken a photo of it. He was intrigued, listening intently. The next thing we knew it was splashed across a newspaper. Trueman had a contract with one of the English dailies for a column and we'd played straight into his hands. *I was on tour with these lads and they were talking to me and I found out . . .*

I thought, Jesus, the man's a law unto himself. But Trueman was a good laugh. I asked Freddy about the wedding between his daughter and Raquel Welch's son. He said, "Ah, what a woman, what a *robust* woman, very *full* woman as you know, Danny . . . but she wouldn't let me too near her."

The Boycotts and Truemans were the eccentrics of the game, but players also get very good advice out of them – a lot of our batters in the past have listened to Boycott, and Fred's been happy to pass on tips about swing bowling. They're guardians of their craft in some ways, and there's so much downtime in cricket that there's always time to talk about cricket and life. Fred was forever sucking on his pipe, reeking out the room and holding centre stage for anyone with ears. For people like him, cricket was their whole life. They lived and breathed their careers, wrote and talked about it for a living. He's done it for over 30 years since he stopped playing. It's incredible.

Henry Blofeld was another guy who always dominated conversations. He really was quite eccentric, quite different, which you only begin to get a taste of when you see him commentating. The story went that he got hit by a bus while at Cambridge, ruining his promising cricket career so he'd never actually played that much himself. He was over the top with his cultivated upper class accent. A lot of his commentary was pure waffle about seagulls, cravats and bizarre things; his writing was like that too. But he strutted around happily, quite inflated with himself.

'Blowers' seemed to move from one television network to the next. His only overseas international job now is in Sharjah – people elsewhere have got quite sick of the over-the-top carry on. But he's had a good life cruising around writing and watching the game. You'd run into him quite a bit, all around England, always holding centre stage and simply raving his tits off.

I thoroughly enjoyed taking the mickey out of him in Sharjah last year after we'd tied a game with Sri Lanka. He went, "*Danny*, my *darling*, haven't seen you for *so long*", and I replied in his pompous accent, "*Henry*, my dear old thing, haven't seen you for an *aeon*, what's going *on*?" He got quite irritated about it but we thought it was a great laugh.

Dickie Bird was the most lovable of the great English eccentrics. Many other people have commented on what a good umpire he was – he certainly had the respect of the players. He played county cricket for a long time before becoming an umpire and standing in many tests. He was great. There was always this energy about him that there was just going to be no nonsense going on while he was on the park. If a situation was getting a bit ugly, he'd be in there diffusing it quickly. When he was in New Zealand in the summer of 1994, stood in the match at the Basin as we played Pakistan in the second test, it was quite different from the first game of that series, where it had got quite nasty and heated out there between the teams, the Pakistanis barking and biting at us. He'd observed the situation and strode out intent on controlling it. He didn't umpire the third match in Christchurch – and it was noticeable that the Pakistanis were trying their antics on again there. After Dickie had umpired the second test, he'd stayed on to holiday in New Zealand – which to him meant following the rest of the cricket, keeping his finger on its pulse. I caught up with him when the verbal was flying out on the park and he just said firmly, "It wouldn't be happening if I was out there, pal." Bryan Young and Shane Thomson both made 120; we won the game and that shut them up.

Dickie's idiosyncrasies, eccentricities and the manner he had on the park helped the whole energy of the game. He had madcap ways. He'd be on his own in the corner of the hotel restaurant, always dining alone. He was quite a private person away from the field. It was taking the professional ethic of not fraternising with the players to extremes. When we saw him in India in 1987, he refused to eat anything else but canned drink, steak, eggs and chips. That was his breakfast, lunch and dinner, the whole World Cup! He used to drawl dramatically, "If I eat anything else I could die."

On the park, Dickie was so flamboyant with his very individual signalling and the calls in his big Yorkshire accent. His hands would often twitch in his front pockets as if he had a touch of Parkinson's. I used to like to get in close, looking down that channel of middle and off stump, and as I'd come into bowl I'd sometimes suddenly just catch the white coat pockets flicking out – sometimes it put me off. But he was a very professional umpire.

Dickie retired after the Indian series last year and was very choked up about it. Cricket had been his whole life. They say he's married to the game he loves so much.

Every cricket nation has its own cluster of celebrities, people who are just a little bit larger than the game, and it was interesting playing alongside some of them in the World XI tour in 1991. Towards the end of that summer we made a short tour of Northern Ireland. At best, Ireland were quite good club players, really no match for Imran Khan, the great Pakistani allrounder and our captain.

Imran was charging in, wanging it in to these two lefthanders, getting it to go through and stand up on a length on a wet, sticky dog. Then he decided to come round the wicket, angle it across them with his big inswingers. I was at mid-on and he called across to me in his lordish Pakistani voice, "Danny, I won't be long, I'll just be bowling about five overs from this end and you can come on after me." Then, at the top of his mark, he called across to the four guys fanning out from the keeper and said: "Slips! Get ready!"

At first slip was John Morris, the Derbyshire pro who's a bit of a dag. He'd just been in Australia with the England Ashes side, his wife was just about to give birth and here he was on a cricket jaunt!

The poor batsmen weren't getting any bat at all on Imran as the ball fizzed past and so instead of bowling just five overs, Imran kept himself on. Finally John Morris called over in Imran's distinctive accent, "Immy! We're still waiting!" Imran looked at him in disgust and strutted back to his mark. It brought the house down.

John Farrar was in charge of the event for us. Later Imran took him aside and said, "John, I've got to go to this *Moriaaaarty.*"

"Sorry?" said John.

"I've got to go to a Moriaaarty. You know, a paaaarty."

We had back to back one-dayers and Imran wanted to fly from Belfast back to London for a party and then fly back to play the next day's match, skipping the official function that night. He boarded a 7pm flight, went to his Moriarty in London, did the full socialite scene and then got on another plane 12 hours later to get back to Ireland. We arrived at the ground about 9.30 the next morning, opened the dressing room door and there was Imran flat on his back with some jerseys folded up for a pillow. He hadn't changed out of last night's gear (the black Lacoste shirt, black pants, gold chain hanging out like the full legend) and he hadn't showered. I couldn't believe how much he honked, and I haven't got a great sense of smell. He had a quiet smirk on his face. "Great Moriaaaarty, lads . . ."

Imran didn't talk to many people, didn't fraternise, and had a perpetual arrogance about him. I'll never forget him declaring on Hadlee in 1989. Paddles had just got his fourth wicket, and one more would have been his hundredth five-for, a big event for Hadlee, who was driven by statistics at that stage of his career. There was a certain amount of professional jealousy between those two.

Looking around at the great names in cricket during my time, Graeme Gooch stood out for me, as a batsman and player. He took over as captain in 1990, inheriting a beleaguered England side that was getting a hiding wherever it went. He turned that around, and led by example. He had a classic upright stance, was menacing on the drive and loved to pull or cut anything too short. He had a high backlift to curve against quick bowling. It was his trademark, a stand and deliver-type technique. Standing there at the crease in his helmet with his big droopy moustache, black stubble scattered across his face, he almost looked like an English knight, St George fighting the dragon. All he needed was the coat of mail. He was very much like that. He commanded respect at the top of the order, such a good player of quality bowling, standing head and shoulders over his team-mates. He was always a big threat, and very mentally strong, as his 333 against India proved beyond doubt. I enjoyed my duels with him.

The English always had a certain arrogant streak, while a lot of the Asian cricket stars, and even the West Indians, were noticeably quieter and more unassuming than many of the Westerners when you met them – although some were quietly arrogant, treated as they were like movie stars at home.

The subcontinent seems to churn out small, strong batsmen with very flexible, slight wrists, so that they are able to play very wristy, squash-type shots and nudge the ball where they want to, often very late. You noticed with the Sri Lankans, in particular, that the batsmen's stances were very different, so open, with their feet and grips in unorthodox positions. They don't always worry about taking the copybook, side-on stance because of their amazing wristiness: you could bowl a good delivery through the off-stump and they'd pick you up and whip you through the legside. You'd bowl to a righthander, swinging the ball out from middle to off, and they'd stand back, square up and whip you through straight midwicket: you'd wonder how the hell the ball had got over there.

Aravinda de Silva was the stand out. He was very difficult to bowl to, at times. His whole game plan was looking to cut and pull everything and he would happily play you off the back foot if you were too far up. Then you'd think you'd bowled a good length, but he'd punch back a backfoot drive to that as well. He was a good judge, knew what to hook and leave alone – it was a waste of time bouncing him. He'd make his runs in quick time, off good deliveries. Your best form of attack was to keep the ball up there and swinging away, trying to nick him out because, like a lot of the Sri Lankans, Indians and Pakistanis, he liked to go for his shots. They weren't afraid to take you on because they'd been brought up on flattish, good surfaces where the ball didn't deviate much. You could see why they often came undone in England or New Zealand, on tracks that varied more. They started anticipating the ball and that would be their undoing.

Imran's great contemporary in the Pakistan side, Javed Miandad, was a hard customer to deal with because he used to square up a lot at the crease, a vicious cutter of the ball and a beautiful executioner of nudging dabs, a bit of French cricket. Like Aravinda and Sachin Tendulkar, he would occasionally unleash a swivelling pull shot where he rocked back and the ball just exploded off his bat. He'd smash it through midwicket with nonchalant ease. In Pakistan Miandad used to get away with murder; the umpires there never gave him out lbw even when it was plumb. In 1990, during the first test in Karachi, I went for the old three-card trick, two bouncers and then one right in his blockhole. It hit him square on the ankle – but when the umpire actually gave it out, I couldn't believe it. I was dancing on air. I said to the guys, "I don't care if I don't get another bloody wicket on tour; I've got Javed Miandad out lbw in his home town!"

Javed always had plenty to say, a notorious streetfighter. He could be nasty, and when he was Pakistan's captain he encouraged a kind of orchestrated nastiness from his side to try to get on top of the opposition. I remember Merv Hughes saying he once gave Javed the full earful and Javed just looked straight back at him and piped, "Mervyn, you should be driving buses!"

In the bowling department, Waqar Younis and Wasim Akram working in tandem are matchwinners for Pakistan and gave some of our top order quite a few sleepless nights. More than anyone else in recent years those two players have been a nemesis of New Zealand cricket. In 1990 they were the difference between the two sides, blowing us away with both barrels. In 1993, in a one-off test at Hamilton, we had the match in the bag, only chasing 127 to win, but they took five wickets apiece to blow us out of the park for just 93. The next season, yet again, they were the two heroes, with Aaqib Javed backing them up.

The unusual thing about Waqar and Wasim was that often it looked like they just meandering along, but all they needed was a sniff of victory, it seemed, and they were in. They'd close in like killer sharks for these devastating spells. They do exceptionally well with the old ball and can both reverse swing it, one with a very fast left-arm action and the other charging in like a bull at a gate with great inswinging yorkers. Pakistan is blessed to have two bowlers of their calibre in their side at once. I'm sure there's a rivalry between them that they both feed off, subtly competing against each other like a Lennon and McCartney. It was so frustrating that we couldn't have seen them off just a little bit longer, most times. They loved touring New Zealand, and it wasn't just the scenery.

Thankfully Pakistan's arch rival, however, was India, not New Zealand. India had the ultimate wrist king in the form of Mohammed Azharuddin; he was the classic Indian player who could whip everything on off-stump through the on-side with ease, more so than even Aravinda or Miandad. But the Indian batter who stands out is Sachin Tendulkar, this boy prodigy who's very adaptable to anywhere in the top order. Like da Silva, although a little guy he plays with a very heavy, three pound bat. They're like railway sleepers with a banana bow in the middle. He isn't scared to loft the ball; no matter what stage of the innings, he backs himself to go over the top, often with devastating effectiveness. He has a good stance, a little more copybook and upright, and superb timing. He's powerful all round the wicket, and can play late. It was always a captain's nightmare playing him; how could you set fields to that?

Tendulkar can look like an angel with his schoolboy face, but he can have a bit to say out there and can mix it with the best of them. He and Cairnsie always have a bit to say to each other. But he's got a way to catch up with Javed.

When Tendulkar was young, he tried to smash everything, quite a petulant player. He slashed out at me when he was on 88 in Napier in 1990, Wrighty took the catch and that's how he missed out on becoming the youngest man in cricket to make a test century. He was near tears by the time he got off the field. But he learned to control his shot selection later to tremendous effect, often against us. It was always payback time.

Interestingly the only guy who's come close to teasing oppositions the way the Asian players have often teased us this decade is Andrew Jones. Jonesy's technique was very unorthodox and wristy, hitting the ball late. He really played more like an Indian than a New Zealander, possibly because he'd learned the game in a country area away from traditional coaching methods. I hope our new Brierley academy won't stunt the innovators like him.

Of all the international acts I came up against, the West Indians held the most fascination for me. When they toured New Zealand in 1986/87, I met them in Hamilton in a President's XI, then again in Napier in a Shell XI; I was still a new kid on the tracks and quite in awe of the dynamic names I was up against – kings like Viv Richards, Gordon Greenidge, Desmond Haynes, Richie Richardson, Larry Gomes. They were a great side.

The track bounced a bit at McLean Park and it was an exciting challenge, these guys having a crack at you – they certainly weren't scared. I bounced Richardson a bit when he was quite new to the crease: he went for a couple of hooks, then played and missed before going for the hook again. This time it skidded on a bit quicker than he thought and as he pulled out of the shot and turned his face away to the offside, the ball hit him an inch above his left ear. I'll never forget the hard whacking sound it made against his skull. The ball flew off so fast that John Wilson, Jeff Wilson's uncle, ended up jogging in from fine leg to collect it. Richardson was visibly shaken. As the physio held up fingers for him to count and checked him out for concussion, Jeff Dujon came out to the wicket and picked up the ball. He said to the ump, "Listen man, this ball's gone a bit flat on one side, it needs a bit more air in it!" We all cracked up laughing at the reference to Richardson's thick head and Richardson shot back a bit of verbal at him. He carried on and smashed a hundred. I couldn't get over how hard his skull was. They say it's the reason African-American boxers are so good.

Later generations of that team, Brian Lara and the like, showed the same swashbuckling style. In Antigua, bowling in the second innings, I remember bouncing Lara and he top-edged me over fine leg for six. Then he thrashed me between fourth slip and gully. He's a very unassuming and gifted player, but likes to have a go at you, dominate, score runs at a free rate, even when you're bowling well. Lara, like Allan Border, was a lefthander and it was a good duel trying to go across them. Funnily enough, just like Border, almost every time I played Lara I'd get him out, which was some satisfaction – three times in four tests, during times when we usually only got to bowl at them in one innings.

Watching the West Indian fast bowlers, meanwhile, I was just envious. They had big hands to hold the ball – it must feel like a stripped-down tennis ball to some of them. And they had great leverage with their long arms, giving them extra pace; and the height for extra bounce. They had it all. The West Indians have never been big on trying to reverse the ball; maybe they feel they have enough artillery as it is. In the late 1980s, when Shane Thomson was still bowling fast, Tommo and I used to feel like West Indians trapped in white men's skins. We wanted to be Malcolm Marshall and Michael Holding. You envied their physiques, their fast-twitch muscle fibres, small pelvises, tight glutes . . . It was the romance of these fast bowlers who'd been dominating world cricket for more than 10 years.

I was enthralled watching Courtney Walsh and Curtly Ambrose at close range. Walsh got 13 test wickets in a match at the Basin Reserve on an absolute featherbed. Everyone else was struggling, made to look very mediocre, but he had the ability to get that little bit extra out of it, using his frame to full advantage. You don't often get to play the West Indies and it was always special playing them. It was also tough test cricket, but as Wally Lees used to say, "It's not called 'easy cricket', is it?"

I never played much against the South Africans, either, but I enjoyed the opportunity. Hansie Cronje always reminded me of Pete Sampras more than an Afrikaaner. He was a strong captain – he has mana, and shows his emotions quite a bit for a cricketer, but he plays hard and always wants to win. It was always a hard duel against that country, though with Cronje personally, he seemed to get out too much fending off the short ball. Fanie de Villiers was hard case, a good example of a South African who'd compete fiercely hard on field and then be a charming man off it. He had so many broken toes he had problems getting boots to fit. Then there was Brian McMillan, a mountain of a man, but a quiet achiever. I'll never forget how big his head seemed – it was like a horse's head.

I've admired South Africa's quicker bowlers, too, more so than their batters. Allan Donald's very graceful, with a smooth run-up to the wicket despite his large, 6ft 3in frame. Fanie was the foil at the other end, bowling outswingers, wide of the crease, at that difficult angle with bounce extracted from his height. They complemented each other nicely. Then there was Craig Matthews, who was like a bowling machine – their Chats. He bowled very straight and kept it tight. They tended to play four seamers, with Stephen Jack or McMillan, a genuine allrounder, and they were all big men. I envied the support they had from each other, able to hunt in a fast, steady pack. I played with guys like Simon Doull and Cairnsie, Dion Nash, Murphy Su'a, Chris Pringle, Willie, but we were never all fit at the same time. It was so frustrating.

It's the Australians who are our unrivalled rivals, this big bully brother of ours across the Tasman, and Australia always seems to have an abundance of real batting talent coming through to take us on. Perhaps it's because across their continent, from slow Hobart to humid Brisbane to hot, dry Perth, their domestic players play hardball on such a variety of surfaces and in quite different climatic conditions. But whatever the reason, Aussie ultraconfidence oozed through their stars.

I first met Shane Warne at the Lancashire County Cricket Club in 1992 when he was playing at Accrington. He was very garish, with beach-blond hair and a loud singlet on, the new kid on the block, and was about to head off on tour with his national side to Sri Lanka. The next year I played against him when New Zealand toured Australia and I was amazed to see how quickly he had become so confident. He was cocky. I'll never forget at Perth, he yelled out over the dressing room to Allan Border, "Hey, AB, *AB!*" – like he was taking over the show. He'd had a great Ashes series that year. I happened to go to the test match in Manchester where he bowled Gatting first ball; a star was born.

There's an Americanism in Australian culture where they pump up their big stars and that happened amazingly quickly to Warne. He's sometimes the full Dennis Rodman type. A lot of the Aussie guys smoked, but only Warne would have the audacity to sit smoking in a press conference, the cameras rolling. He was always just having a good time riding his own wave.

Dean Jones was always cocksure and never shut up. He was a hive of activity. You never knew whether it was nervous energy with Dean, or just plain confidence in himself. Steve Waugh is the one the Australians say they'd get to bat for their life, but his brother, Mark, was a more elegant batsman, consistent and very gutsy. With their superb reflexes, the Waugh brothers both played indoor for Australia as well. David Boon was the little guy who loved pulling and cutting and wasn't scared to have a go at you on the up. Like Boony, Ian Healy was belligerent against us too; the anchor man at seven and difficult to get out.

But of all the Aussies the big one for me, and for a lot of people I'm sure, was Allan Border. He had a huge mana about him. The crowds would chant "Bor-der, Bor-der"; it was ringing in your ears as he came out to bat. You'd look down the wicket and he'd be glaring at you. The challenge was there. Or sometimes he'd deliberately totally ignore you, and you couldn't even get into some banter with him or put him off with a wink and a smile. There was all that steel, that gritty energy about him.

I'd rise to the occasion. He wrote in his biography that he believed I had the wood on him; every time I played him I got him out, more or less, except for the last time, which was quite a nice way for him to go out. For him, I'd look through the off-stump to the keeper and hug it in to get him lbw or, because he tended not to get off the crease a lot, sometimes I'd try a surprise bouncer. But generally I wanted to be up there doing something. He often stayed back, backing himself to hit it, playing a bit of French cricket.

New Zealand was having a nightmare in the test series against his team in Australia in 1993, and the match in Hobart was particularly frustrating. Border's was the only wicket I got, and he was grumpy when it happened because I'd bowled a slower ball to him and he'd just patted it back to me for a simple caught and bowled when he was set on 60. I gave it the full little dance through to Blainy, the keeper, and Border just growled, "Look at the scoreboard" – as if to say, *you cheeky little loser.* So I gave him the verbal send-off then, told him he should have retired years ago, but afterwards I felt annoyed with myself. I should have jogged up to him, put my arm round him and said something back without losing my cool. That would have been so much more satisfying. I normally would have smiled and winked, but that test was very frustrating. I'd taken the bait.

The most unusual dismissal I got against 'AB' was at Eden Park in 1993. He was given out caught behind for a duck. Steve Waugh was at the non-striker's end and I asked him if he thought Border was out. He said he thought he'd just feathered it on the way through. But the television replay showed the sound that the umpire had heard probably wasn't Border's bat, but the top of the stump as the ball went past him and just whiskered it. The bail had flicked up, but then dropped back down onto its cradle, so Border wasn't really out at all. He'd turned round and couldn't believe the bail was still there. Then he shook his head and walked off; he just got no luck against old Dan.

I had huge respect for Border. He'd been around for so long. You also respected the Aussies for the way they treated you off the field – usually we'd all pile into one or the other's dressing room after any match between us for a beer and yarn together. Border was great like that. When the Australians came over to New Zealand for a tri-series in 1990, he tapped me on the back when he saw me and said "How are you going, I hear you've been going quite well lately Dan?" I'd just got three five-fors on the trot against India. So I started to have a rapport with him, and I was honoured when he and Dean Jones flew over to play in my testimonial match.

I thoroughly enjoyed our rivalry. I loved taking him on, and vice versa. To have got Allan Border out so much in test cricket (eight times in all; more than I got any other international player), to have had those duels with him, is something I treasure. He was so durable that when he retired it was weird seeing Mark Taylor as the Aussie captain. Australian teams didn't seem the same after that. It was like the king had died.

PUMP IT UP

I had a love affair with Australian cricket. The ultimate place to tour was always just across the ditch. I liked the psychology that went with having this big, loud cousin over the sea, the rivalry. You went there to play against the best in the world, as the Aussies were for much of my time in cricket. I liked the way they did things, liked the way they treated cricket as their national game, the way their cricket facilities were fantastic and their crowd support strong and vocal. I had a love-hate relationship with the crowd, blowing them kisses and getting abuse, but it was great fun winding them up. I thrived on it. I think that's why I've often performed my best at the international level – playing to the gallery brought out the showman in me.

Everything about the Australian game seemed so much more grander and professional than our own. You especially envied their facilities. In New Zealand grounds are very much rugby-orientated, apart from the Basin Reserve (though cricket may lose even that to the multipurpose Wellington Stadium after 2000). Ours are *rugby* grounds that also have cricket. But the great stadia in Australia prioritise cricket, and as a result Australian nets, changing room facilities and playing surfaces are the best in the world.

In most States the climate was good cricket weather, and consistent. Whenever it was a beautiful summer's day at the WACA or SCG, it really made you feel like you wanted to get out there and charge in. Brisbane was a harder place to play because of the sapping humidity, while Tasmania could be plain wet. Perth, if you haven't got the Fremantle Doctor, could be pretty demanding too. But generally you relished the atmosphere, whether it was Adelaide, which was sedate and so picturesque, surrounded by churches and trees and looking in parts like Wimbledon, or the awesome energy of the MCG with a full house. I loved playing them all.

I had a special connection with Melbourne, having first been to the MCG on a trip to see my father as a kid, when I'd seen Lillee charging in against the West Indies' tail. It seemed such a famous ground – I'd watched the underarm delivery on TV as a kid, heard the commentator ad-libbing that it wasn't a great day for Australian sport, seen the aftermath with people jumping over the fence to give Greg Chappell a hard time. Then, seven years later, in my first test series, I was the one out there in the middle of controversy as Dick French turned down the lbw that would have given us the match. Twenty-five thousand people were watching on that last day, the largest crowd I'd ever played to. The feeling of being there, of bowling in tandem with Richard Hadlee trying to get that last Australian wicket at the MCG was amazing.

Playing under the searing lights of the SCG was another great experience, an incredible feeling after having seen so many gripping one-day battles in Sydney beamed to our television sets in the early 1980s. You were glued to the screen as Lance Cairns came out to bat or Hadlee took the ball to begin his spell. You wanted to be there too. It was such a boom time in the 1980s, late 1970s. We couldn't get enough cricket – that's why we started playing indoor as well. It was an incredibly exciting time – and Australia was the centre of the action.

The razzmatazz, the heat that fired you up under the towering lights, the thunderous noise and heckling from the crowd, the whole circus was a performer's dream. It was a real stage. The stage on which Dennis Lillee, my idol, had played.

The New Zealand team always quite enjoyed going back to Australia. It was the place where there were seldom any hassles with life on the road. Everything's there at your fingertips. Simple things like eating or shopping or finding something to watch on TV weren't a problem; you could switch off the way you really needed to between games. In Melbourne one time I went to the art gallery with Tony Blain and Shane Thomson; saw a bit of Van Gogh in Victoria there, the cultural centre of Australia. In Perth we'd hit the beaches. In Hobart you took it easy. There was a casino there, where the social committee within the team would organise team functions. I've never played a test match in Sydney, but I passed through for a few one-dayers and it was the full metropolis. You'd just shop, or eat at the great seafood restaurants at The Rocks. We had a great time in Brisbane in 1987, too, when our liaison officer was Shaun McDonald – Ginette McDonald's brother. Kiwi Lager was big at the time and he drove us down to Surfers Paradise to do a team promotion for Dominion Breweries, where we took in the famous sandy beach.

Because everyone kept in generally good spirits on tour there, we had a lot of fun as a team unit in Australia. Before our Boxing Day test in 1987, the social committee – Wrighty, Smithy and Braces – had decided that everyone had to get a present for each member of the team. Hadlee got this little matchbox car, which was very tongue-in-cheek; this was only a couple of years after controversy about him wanting to keep a car he'd won as a prize, going against the team protocol of selling it and divvying up the spoils among all the players. He took it in good spirits. Braces got a dummy, because he spat his out all the time. I got a poster of a cheeky chimpanzee – I was nicknamed "Judy", as in the chimp from *Daktari*. You'd hear the call in Auckland, "Come on Jude, you mad chimp!"

But team spirits weren't always thick and fast. On one occasion in Australia Willie Watson had met a Canadian girl and, being the shy type, was taking his own time getting to know her. He brought her into the hotel where we were having a bit of a team drink together. But Tony Blain took a shine to Willie's lady friend and furnished her with his room number. She darted off up there. Willie was gutted.

The next day Willie and Blainy went down in the hotel lift together, both stone silent. While Blainy was downstairs saying goodbye to this Canadian girl, Ken Rutherford rifled through Blainy's toilet bag in the room upstairs and found the soapbox. He took the soap out and popped the box neatly back in his toiletries bag – after defecating in it – for "Captain Morganning" a mate.

It was always good catching up with the Aussie guys again. I got on quite well with Steve Waugh over my career. Merv Hughes was quite a full-on sight to behold for most of us, a noisy big Aussie bloke and a tireless prankster off the field – they used to call Merv the fruitfly; Australia's biggest pest. But as much as you enjoyed the Aussies' company, there was always that feeling that you were inferior to them. They were the generals and you guys were just the captains, because their country was bigger and so much more successful. They had a lot of star status, much more than us. You couldn't help but notice Shane Warne's media profile with all his endorsements, the state-of-the-art Nike ads. No wonder his nickname's Hollywood.

Some of the Australian players are on about $A850,000 a year, with endorsements and so forth added in. Most of our guys in a full 12 months would earn between $60,000 and $100,000 – and that's in a good year with endorsements thrown in and no time out with injuries. We came from a different world, and a different mindset.

You saw so much more money ploughed into the sport itself, as well – I think every test ground in Australia has lights now, except for Adelaide, which is putting in hugely expensive retractable towers so they don't detract from the charm. It made me sad that we didn't have day/night cricket at all in New Zealand for so long. It was brilliant dynamics as entertainment. You couldn't help but feel the one-day series at home were a little flat and humble after experiencing the Australian way. I felt the New Zealand administrators missed the boat after the 1992 World Cup, when cricket captured so many New Zealanders' imaginations. We needed to borrow more from the Australian style of entertaining people to help maintain that high.

But the harsh reality is that it's a bigger pond over there, a bigger economy and everything about cricket in Australia is on a grander scale. The fact that the Australians have been winning virtually since 1989 has only fuelled the machine. They play a hell of a lot more than us, sometimes going away on five-month tours, such as the Ashes. We'd go away for 12 weeks. I don't think our guys would know how to handle that, and my wife certainly wouldn't want to be married to me if I played for Australia.

Besides the bright lights and rivalry, my other great emotional connection to Australia was my father. I've been really grateful for the chance to tour there so often through cricket, starting with the youth side in 1984, and see him.

Dad's a hard shot. He had become a rough diamond – life's been hard on him. The crash in 1987 pulled the rug out from under the building trade and he was in and out of work for a while, and it was tough. There were times when I felt very emotional thinking about his life. He'd split up from Mum when I was seven, but after seven years he split from another great lady, Heather, when my half-sister, Shea, was also seven. It was as if he'd blown a second chance.

John Wright always liked a few poles and I had a bit of a fall-out with him in 1990 when he caught me carting off eight cartons of the sponsor's cigarettes that the team had been given free – he knew I didn't smoke. When I went back for more, he hauled me up about it. I explained they were for my Dad; he was out of work at the time and cigarettes were getting quite expensive over there. And Wrighty understood.

Whenever we were in town I'd get Dad to come along to the team hotel and party up large in the house bar with the lads. The guys really enjoyed his hard case character on tour. He'd bring along a couple of workmates to help him lighten the load of free beer at the Hilton; they looked like they'd walked straight out of ZZ Top. Then at the end of the night I'd give them $50 to take them home safely in a taxi to the Dandenongs.

They loved us coming to town. It was a great bonus for my father that the key sponsors of Australian cricket were always cigarettes and booze.

YOU'RE THE
BEST THING

My life changed the day a gruff old room attendant with the full Whitecoat syndrome opened the door to the visitors' dressing room at the WACA and said stiffly, "Is Danny Morrison here? Where's Danny? Danny Morrison, there's a couple of *blonde females* looking for you . . ."

It was the middle of November, 1987, in Perth, where we were playing a couple of warm-ups against Western Australia. Elizabeth Langford was a friend; back in Devonport she was flatting with some of my mates, round the corner from my mother's house where I lived. I'd see her at parties. Lizzie had been working as a travel agent for ASB Travel, but the business was folding after the stockmarket crash. She'd earned a free first-class flight to Perth and back for her work for British Airways and had a friend and workmate that she was travelling with. So there was mad Lizzie the blonde standing outside the WACA, having talked her reluctant friend into going along to see the day-nighter at the WACA because she knew one of the guys who was playing and could get a couple of free tickets. That's how I first met a beautiful woman named Kimberley Talbot.

The New Zealand team was based in Perth for the first 10 days of the tour, perfectly timed to coincide with Lizzie and Kim's holiday. It was a whirlwind romance. When the day came that they had to fly back, I went out to the airport and saw them off. I said to Kim that I'd call her, but she just thought, "Yeah right"; not thinking I really meant to get back in touch. But when we got to Adelaide I rang her. Kim was at a bit of crossroads between jobs and ended up coming back over to Australia for the Boxing Day test at the MCG. We really hit it off from there and she travelled around with me for a few weeks on tour.

It was quite bizarre. I was only 21, coming up 22, very much the junior in the side, yet here I had a girlfriend charging around with me, flying with the team – on my first major tour. Smithy used to give me a hard time about my blonde. Even now, when there's little left of the old school in the New Zealand environment, it's not the done thing for younger guys to bring a partner on tour when they're trying to gain acceptance in the side (and the protocol generally is that wives and girlfriends should only join a tour towards its conclusion). Albie Duckmanton was our team manager and I remember him coming and saying to me, in a kindly way, "Dan, I'm not putting my foot down here, but I think you should be concentrating on your cricket. Kim's a lovely person – but don't forget there's a home series against England coming up, then Sharjah, and you could be there. Remember your career."

Kim had plans to do the big OE in England with Lizzie at the same time that my tour of Australia was ending. We both knew we had to part ways to get on with our lives, and so left it at that. But instead of getting to England, Kim never got out of the blocks! For the next three years she stayed in Melbourne, meeting another man who led her into the remedial massage and aromatherapy business.

Meanwhile, I came home, played cricket and eventually started another relationship. It lasted almost three years, but it was volatile at times, because of the time I had to spend away with cricket. In the end, parting when we did turned out to be the best thing that could have happened to Kim and I, because we both grew. Maybe it was meant to be.

But we kept in touch. I sent postcards on tour. In 1989 Kim came back to New Zealand briefly for her 21st, and my girlfriend and I went along. By this stage I'd also met Annie Talbot in Harefield, so I'd keep in touch with Kim's mother, too.

Then, at the end of 1990, New Zealand had a one-day series in Australia. By now I was 25. My other relationship had hit the rocks and as I returned to tour Australia again the memories of Kim welled up in my mind. When we were playing in Melbourne, I went along to her clinic for a massage. We had a big talk. I had to decide what I really wanted. If Kim was to come back to New Zealand for me, it was for keeps.

She arrived in February 1991, when I was playing Sri Lanka at home. At the end of the season we went back to Melbourne for a week to collect her gear from her old boyfriend's place. We had a rental car and had to climb in the back window of the house to get in, loading Kim's stuff into the car as quick as we could, in case he decided to come home for lunch! I was a bit scared of the full-on scene, you know.

Back in New Zealand Kim got a job as a remedial therapist at the practice of David Abercrombie, the All Black physio who I'd been seeing for my pubis symphosis problem. Kim had a sports background – she'd been right into marathon and ultramarathon running in Melbourne – and appreciated what it took out of me to achieve in cricket and to train. That's where our relationship really worked. I was lucky that she was able to have flexible working hours and could travel with me in cricket, but she understood that tours were work for me and that the only times she might see me would be in the mornings or at the end of the day, and that by then I'd be exhausted and probably not much fun. Kim would run a bath and throw in some oils, then give me a massage on my sore points. I was blessed.

International cricket is such an intense environment that relationships sadly just haven't worked for a lot of players. You can't blame the wives for wanting to see more of their husbands, because it's an unnatural lifestyle, in a sense. You're living in hotels instead of a home, and though cricket opens some amazing doors for you, you miss the normalcy. The nomadic nature of the sport really affected some of my relationships when I was younger, and with the increase in itineraries and travel this decade, the situation for a lot of players has only got tougher. Even when I was in my last year of school, girlfriends would get fed up with me and my cricket. You were never available for the beach, for going camping, for a normal life.

That's where I was lucky in that Kim was very giving. Kim was very tolerant of the shuffle from hotel to hotel, training to training, match to match. Being an Aries, the full fire sign, she was very independent and I really enjoyed having her around.

Getting together with her again was the start of a much more stable time in my life. I was 25 now. Starting to feel much more confident in the national side and in myself. New Zealand Cricket had started bringing in annual contracts, retainers for the players which made you feel much more secure. I finally stopped being a nomad, in the sense that 1994 was the end of me wanting to go back to England in the off-season. Instead we did our house up, and Kim started her own aromatherapy business.

For the Christmas of 1991 Kim and I were at my Aunt Lorna's in Mairangi Bay, with my mother's family. Uncle Rube had brought some fabulous Christmas crackers back from Hong Kong and when I pulled mine, a little yellow plastic ring popped out. I grabbed it, stood up, popped the plastic ring on the Kim's finger (it fitted!) and asked her to marry me.

The ceremony took place on April 4, 1993. "You're the best thing" played as we walked up the aisle. Martin Snedden was beaming. He obviously thought we'd look great together with kids.

When Kim and I got married, my old Harefield clubmate, Dave Singleton, flew out from England – in my London days we'd always said we'd be each other's best man. By that time my sister Zhara was on her own with her daughter, my niece Aasha, and before we knew it more romance was in the air – all that love energy at the wedding, you understand. We think it was the lilo that clinched it.

I come from a very close family, but, because of cricket, my sis and I have often lived very different lives; Zhara having her first child when she was quite young. Back after the bomb thwarted my first international tour in Sri Lanka, I went to England to continue the romance with Harefield, but I cut short the trip in early July to come home to see Zhara compete in the national Rose of Tralee, the Irish festival competition, as she'd won the Auckland regional round. It was the real pull of being drawn back home, the essence of family; when I could otherwise have stayed a couple of months more in England – the lads gave me quite a bit of stick for going home early.

The Rose of Tralee final was held at the Irish Society in Great North Road. A few celebrity faces, like Phillip Sherry with his eyebrows, were there, beautiful Irish music whirling in the background. Whoever won would be going on a trip to Ireland. I desperately wanted Zhara to win so she could go overseas, like I had done, and experience it all, too. The whole family went to watch, and when Zhara didn't win, I got very emotional. I'd had quite a few Club 99 champagnes sitting there at a rough, long table with a paper napkin-type tablecloth, squashed in with my aunts and uncles. I was in tears, overwhelmed with emotion and Club 99, and because I had a bit of a cold at the time and couldn't squeeze out of the table I finished the night by blowing my nose into the tablecloth. All my family looked at me in utter dismay!

In 1993 Zhara and Dave Singleton discovered they were expecting a baby. That's how Singy became not only my best man, but my brother-in-law as well. The day Myles was born in January 1994, I had got in from a tour of Australia after being flown home early with an injury. Zhara had chosen a home birth and when I got there the family was sitting around cheering her on – "Come on Sis, *push!*" We thought we should put up a scaffold and sell tickets. But that's how close the family is. I wouldn't be without any of them.

We always stuck together. Through my cricket profile Kim, Zhara, Singy and I ended up doing a story in a women's magazine about their meeting at our wedding, for which we were paid a good sum. We gave it to Zhara and Sing to help them buy a car. The Wattie's baked beans ad I did with Mum in 1991 similarly built the deck on Mum's house. It's been very much a family concern of helping each other out, and it's been nice being able to give back to them. They'd already given so much to me.

ROCK AND A
HARD PLACE

In the late eighties New Zealand wasn't playing a lot of cricket compared with countries like India, England or Australia. I was therefore very fortunate to stand at close range watching some extraordinary things happen in New Zealand cricket – like Braces taking 6-51 in Bombay to win us only our second test victory in India; Smithy blasting that incredible 173 at Eden Park against the Indians, Mark Greatbatch's epic 146 not out in Perth, in partnership with Sneds; and Richard Hadlee simply dominating. Being part of that was really a special time.

Very early on in my career, I remember Wrighty leaning across and saying, "You're quickly forgotten, mate. It's the way it is." You always knew one day it would end. But I never quite expected that whole generation to be forgotten so quickly, for the foundations to shift as much as they did in New Zealand cricket this decade.

It really has been a climate of change throughout the 1990s. There are times, in latter seasons, when I've even felt left behind, as if I belonged to a different era, caught between a rock and a hard place, just like the old Stones song I sometimes listen to. Brought on by the explosion of one-day cricket around the world, the game is becoming so much more intense, hyped up and fast – just look at the introduction of Cricket Max. Perhaps it's simply become a young man's game. Hadlee's generation came through in a time when there wasn't nearly as much cricket played, as many tours as there are today. Once we played only three tests at home in a calendar year, and perhaps three away; now we tend to average nine a year, with a truckload of one-dayers in between. I believe it takes its toll on your longevity and as a result we're missing out on so much talent maturing the way it once did.

There isn't a nucleus of older generation-type players within the team anymore and the whole environment has changed. Younger guys own the culture now, and I can't imagine a man like Chats or Paddles wanting to carry on in that environment, to the age they did. It's gone. And I've felt it going. I was down at Chris and Ruth Cairns' wedding after the 1996/97 season when John Bracewell mentioned to me that he felt I hadn't really been enjoying my cricket for the last two seasons, ever since New Zealand toured South Africa in 1995.

It's not just the culture within the team that's changed. It happened that as the great success of our side in the 1980s fell away, the hype and marketing forces around the team were increasing. The profile of the sport blossomed when we suddenly weren't performing. It was very bad timing, but nothing anyone could prevent.

I think players have always slipped off to have a night on the town, even among the old generation. I can think of times that I did, too. But you were discreet about it, and you made sure you fronted up in the morning. But then you were also more anonymous, in a way. You certainly didn't think your late night would be in the papers the next day, or that the taxi driver or barman would call the press. You didn't feel that people would take a potshot at you for it.

That changed when the new band of young guys in the 1990s, hyped up sky-high as "The Young Guns", failed to fire. Some of them struggled to cope with the new pressure, the team culture, but trying to release it, escape it with a night out backfired badly, because the public was so much more focused on you – and disappointed that you weren't winning anymore. In the 1990s New Zealand series victories became as scarce as hen's teeth.

Over the last few summers, especially, New Zealand cricketers have suffered some biting comparisons with our new and blazingly successful rugby professionals, but I believe the winter fraternity doesn't really know what it's like. Having played winter sport and been on soccer tours in my youth, I know how much of a shorter, sharper game football is. In the Super 12, players are only away for two or three games in South Africa; they tend to be brief trips, two weeks max, then they're home again. Even an All Black tour might be only six weeks. But cricketers go away for two or three months.

Until you've been in it, I don't think you know what it's really like. Cricket's such a long, demanding game. You're out there standing in the field for two whole days sometimes. It's never longer than when you're on tour. That's when it's tough mentally, when you're away from your family, from your life. Every time you go away on tour for another two and a half or three months, you realise you can't have that time back again. You inevitably miss things happening with your friends, your family, your kids, your partner and can't do much else with your life, except with your cricket, in that time. The game demands your total attention. Of course there are pluses and minuses to anything in life, and you are away in another culture doing something you love. But it's a narrow time. To struggle with it sometimes is a normal human reaction.

You can look at professional golfers, who spend most of their lives on tour, playing a game that's basically as long as a test match week after week, and ask why it should be so hard for cricketers. But the key difference is that golf's an individual pursuit; bringing their partner with them on tour isn't going to create an issue with the team dynamics.

In cricket, some guys find it harder than others to be away for a length of time with a bunch of individuals trying to be a team. You have to imagine that, although you make friends with these guys, they're really workmates and you don't really spend a lot of time seeing them outside the game. You sleep in the same room as them, you eat with them, you work with them on the field every day. Imagine if you lived with your workmates 24 hours a day. You spend a hell of a lot of time together if you're in the side for 10 years, and if you don't like certain things about people, there's no option but to put up with it and get on because you're in each other's pockets almost every day. And there's always been guys not getting on with each other towards the end of a tour, upsets as guys get on each other's nerves. The public can't really get a taste of the whole touring culture, not even from reading about it.

But it was less of an issue when international itineraries and tours were so much more leisurely than today. The travel experience, the sheer enjoyment of being away, was a greater part of life in cricket. Now a tour is a procession of dressing rooms, hotel rooms and airports. Once more one-day series developed, there was so much more travelling to be accommodated. And within the modern itineraries, everyone's wanted their pound of flesh from you. The four trips I've made to India, I've still not had time to see the Taj Mahal.

I could see why often relationships haven't worked for cricketers during these times. Those sorts of things really started to catch up with a few team-mates on tour. My generation's been the first to experience that intensity in international cricket, and there were times when it really got you down.

That's where the pranksters like Wrighty were good; one silly moment could defuse all the tension. We did have some great times as a team on the road, particularly when those older guys were still around. They imparted a sense of tradition, a sense of what touring was all about, after cricket.

Usually a social committee of three players within the team organises and runs team events on tour. When you've got a good social committee, and people are in a good team group, you seem to get a happier team. We had some great times when Wrighty and the gang were still playing. These were guys who'd grown up in a culture where, if guys wanted to go out for a beer after the game, they had to remember the pubs shut at 10! I think they had more simple pleasures in life, like going to a restaurant with good company. I notice guys in the team would dine in quite large social groups back then, as opposed to now when you tend to stick with your mate inside the team.

On my early tours to Australia, the team would make a point of taking a couple of minibuses out to the Barossa Valley in South Australia, to the Yalumba Vineyards where there would be grapevines for miles, good wine and banter as we dined in the sun, Wrighty taking the piss and telling a few old stories about days with David Steele and Derbyshire. You'd give your right arm to be there in that company. Then Wrighty would throw a grape at someone across the table and it would be all on. It was time out, fun and so healthy for the team.

It was on tour in Australia that I had my first taste of another great team tradition – the first tour speech. Andrew Jones and I had to make ours in 1987. The social committee guys would come up with a topic for you to speak about. Jonesy was not too gweat at pwonouncing the letter "r" so Wrighty decided that he would stand up and explain to the team how to play a skill game that we often used in training called Rats, Rabbits and Rastas, and also to perform the poem that goes "The ragged rascal round the rocks . . ." It was so funny. Jonesy tried to do it, but because the rest of us had had a few beers and were quite relaxed, we were having a really good laugh at him. Wrighty kept jibing him. "So was that wascals, or was that wastas, Jonesy? Could you just go through that part again?" Jonesy got fed up with trying to explain it and ended up by making us all demonstrate it. "You jerks on that side of the table stand up, and you other jerks over here get in a line and . . ." It was hilarious.

Because I'm such a gnome I had to do my speech on "My Little Yellow Stilts"; how I was one of the big boys in the team photo because I had my little yellow stilts on, how I could run in like a big fast bowler with my little yellow stilts, and so on. Braces was sitting next to me at the table and said, "Now look Dan, when you get up and do your speech, you've got to get up on your chair really quickly, because otherwise you'll get smartarses like Martin Snedden calling, 'Stand up, stand up!'" I remember Sneds opening his mouth just as I was getting up, but he had to choke back his words – I was already up on that chair! He was dribbling at this stage. We used to give Sneds a hard time because when he gets excited that big bottom lip starts trembling. We'd offer him a bib.

Ten years on I still have vivid memories of that whole team dinner, all the innocent fun, and I feel sad because we don't do that enough anymore in New Zealand teams. Sure, we still have the odd team event. We all dressed up for Christmas on tour in South Africa – the theme was sex, drugs & rock'n'roll which turned out to be horribly ironic; while we had a great time in Bangalore in 1995, when we had a traditional garb night where we each had to spend no more than 500 rupees on an outfit. Adam Parore was saving his pocketmoney for sending faxes to his girl back home so he grabbed one of the bellboy's one-piece outfits with a turban. There were nice moments, like when we presented Roger Twose with his cap, accepting him into the group, things like that. But a lot of the tradition has died. Steve Rixon has tried to establish more of the old team sense, with group outings and meals, sticking together before the start of a series or a match. But it really has changed.

It was a great shame that towards the end of Wrighty's era, a lot of the young guys on tour in Australia didn't want to make the effort to come out to Barossa Valley. Braces called them the cultural cripples: they just wanted to go shopping or crash by the pool instead of getting involved with organised, team-orientated things.

But by now the world was changing. Our sponsors were organising many more official events and commitments and maybe team-orientated functions had become a bit of a drag, too much like a daily job to interest some players. The increased commercial demand had really started back in the late eighties, when Rothmans sponsored the home series and DB, the team sponsor, would organise a lot of official appearances in their pubs. Now the guys go to shopping malls on

Testing my lungs on test debut at The Gabba, 1987.

I cherished Allan Border's wicket. This is the second of eight 'AB' dismissals I achieved – Perth, 1989.

Getting close to a taste of victory against Australia at the Basin Reserve, 1990.

The second sweet taste (few and far between) of victory against Australia at Eden Park, 1993.

Happiness is . . . getting 'Deano' with a slow 'pie'.

This classic action shot helped make Andrew Cornaga 1993 cricket photographer for the year.

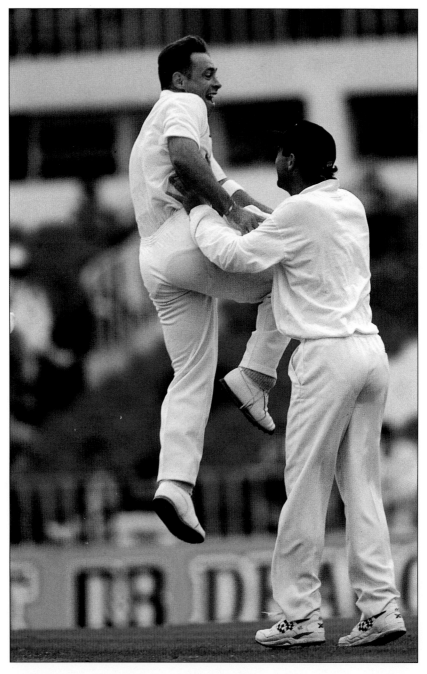

Celebrating my hundredth test wicket with skipper Martin Crowe – I.Healy, c Jones, b Morrison.

Above: Nayan Mongia – victim No. 3 of hat-trick versus India, McLean Park, Napier, 1994. Below: Celebrating the historic moment with the lads.

Catch it . . . jeez-ass! Another one shelled against Australia.

The last stand . . . who'd have thought 'Duckman Dan' would one day share in a test-saving partnership? About to break open the champers with Nathan Astle after our 2hr, 45min vigil at Eden Park against the Poms in January, 1997.

A crowning moment. The two lineups for my Crown Danny Morrison testimonial match at Ericsson Stadium, January 7, 1997.

practice days for Bank of New Zealand promotions and simply have more functions to attend than they used to.

Change wasn't just happening in the New Zealand side, either. I remember Ian Botham saying that right at the end of his career he was struggling to enjoy it, because there was less time, more cricket and you couldn't have a mental break and explore new things anymore. There's no doubt the increased marketing of the players, and therefore the game, is great for building public awareness and corporate support around the game, but it came at a price. You used to get to know players a lot better on tour, it was more like an extended family. Culturally, that's how we always were as a national team – we were different from the Aussies in that even when we got a good side together we still had to work like brothers on the field to cover our weaknesses; we just didn't have their depth. We had a family culture in cricket anyway – there have been so many actual brothers involved, like the Hadlees, Bracewells, Crowes and Howarths to name a few, and many father-son-uncle-nephew involvements, too. It was the same in New Zealand league, rugby, netball: it's part of our background. And when you had 15 different individuals on a tour and might not get on with everyone, but could accept it was like a family on the park, all going down that same road together – it was our strength.

When we were in Pakistan and India at the World Cup in 1987, guys like Braces and Stephen Boock would be really interested in getting out for walks and exploring. That was the first time Willie and I were away on tour together and as the younger guys we'd tend to form a little group. But the social committee, led by Wrighty, was onto it immediately and got us out with them to make sure we interacted as a group. It was too easy to disperse and hang out in your room. We just wanted to be lounge lizards by the pool, but guys like Braces and Boocky wouldn't put up with that and dragged us off on their adventures. Then, in the evenings, we'd have rooms all on the same floor, or in a wing, and everyone would just fling open their doors and we'd all wander in and out.

It was a sense of togetherness. Wally Lees tried to instil that feeling in the side, reinforce it, when he took over as coach in the early 1990s, but these other forces were pulling against it. By then it had actually become harder touring at home than when you were away, because you'd started to see so little of friends and family that they became distractions from the unit. Often guys wouldn't stay at the team hotel if they were in their home city. And, because the culture had become so saturating, some guys were wanting to escape it more often.

The sadness is that this decade guys have found the wrong ways to escape. Sure, you can say the individual should take responsibility for himself, but it also comes back to the team environment. It is such an artificial life in which you're so engrossed that you need safety catches, a reality check. Instead the same scenario has happened over and over again where a player freaks out, wants to get away from the team environment, goes out to 4am trying to escape the problems and then gets sprung so there's even more pressure on him off the field. You don't need that. There should be someone you can talk to, but this is where I have a big gripe with New Zealand Cricket. They haven't had the human resources or mechanisms in place to help address the changing cricket lifestyle. They always say to us that you can always talk to the team manager, but the reality for some time has been that you can't. Not without shooting yourself in the foot.

When I began my international years, Graham Dowling was the chief executive at what was then called the New Zealand Cricket Council. 'Dowls' was the heart and soul of New Zealand cricket, a great servant of the game and a past captain in the 1960s and early 1970s, who'd for years had the task of organising and running the national sport from a very small office in Christchurch. Basically he was a secretary reporting to the New Zealand Cricket Council Board. He was a mild-mannered man, a true gentleman, but an accountant-type lacking the hard nose for business. I felt he didn't see cricket and sport as an entertainment industry enough, that he was a little out of step with the development of the game that took place after he'd finished playing – the impact of Packerball and the one-day cricket phenomenon, for instance. It was like the last of the great amateurs trying to run a professional sport. But then, the administrative structure in which he had to operate was one that embraced the mindset of the amateur game anyway – the board was really a bunch of old players, lawyers and the like, doing their best to give back to the sport, without necessarily having the corporate or marketing skills to do the job justice.

For too long, as the composition of our side and the game itself quickly mutated in the critical period after men like Hadlee and Chatfield retired, our players were trapped by this set-up. There were innumerable frustrations about simple things, times we were made to feel like semi-professionals at best. The marketing of the game in the new era caused its fair share of grief. Our marketing manager in the early 1990s was Mike Dolden, a Christchurch club player who had an advertising business to run and other interests: I don't believe he had enough time for the role cricket required.

Cricket missed the boat badly after our great roll in the World Cup in 1992. The chance to study the Australian way from our joint hosts in that tournament and the interest and support that flowed into the sport was squandered.

Even in quite recent seasons, we'd go down to Christchurch for a test or one-dayer and see billboards of the "Canterbury Bombers" all over town; the provincial side had more exposure and was better marketed than the national side. You used to question what was going on. It peeved you. Why weren't they promoting us as heroes for the young, role models in the sport?

The amateur feel about New Zealand cricket lasted an age. It took forever to even get the drinks trolley sponsored. It's only now, for example, that we're seeing New Zealand cricket razzed up into entertainment, with lights, a long time coming, and modern marketing – chiefly through the introduction of Christopher Doig and Neil Maxwell, who've both studied and borrowed from the way cricket's managed in New South Wales. Hearts were always in the right place, but for a long time our administrators weren't skilled enough to keep up to speed – and it impacted on us, the players.

There are still key areas of the structure that need to be tidied up. Selectors have a thankless task at any level, but at national level, although they're flown and accommodated around the country to watch players, they're teachers and company directors for a living and are not really paid in the professional sense. I think that has to happen if they're truly to be accountable for their decisions and procedures, and so that you can then expect to have the right person in the job. For too long, particularly with regard to communicating with players, it's been a bad case of history repeating itself.

The reason it's so important that the structural aspects of cricket be professional in every sense is simply because for a player, realistically cricket can no longer be a part-time job. You almost have to put your life on hold to play cricket, to give it a fair crack in these times. You give it your heart and soul. You need to have a good administrative and marketing structure so that you can afford to.

The Australians have a superannuation scheme for players that means not only are they well paid, but when they leave service for their country, a payment is made appropriate to their impact in cricket, and cricket's impact on their life. When Martin Crowe tried, beginning in the late eighties, to get that moving here, the Board looked at him as if it was just these greedy players wanting more money yet again. But I think it makes a lot of sense and I can't see why some of the money currently earmarked as bonus payments couldn't be used for a fund along those lines.

Prizemoney has improved immensely for us in the last two years, but I think that playing international cricket for a living generally hasn't been as hugely glamorous as people in the public make out. In the late eighties, a lot of the players still relied on another job for a living; back then, before New Zealand Cricket contracts had developed, if you didn't play, you didn't get paid. Braces worked as a coach for Auckland Cricket, Smithy at Countrywide Bank. I worked for FADE – the Foundation for Alcohol and Drug Education – with Murray Deaker, touring schools. Willie Watson and Dipak Patel worked selling stereos at Sound Plus; Chats was a courier. Cricket is a little bit more glamorous now, and guys like Steve Fleming live by their Nike contracts as well as their salaries from New Zealand Cricket, making appearances for their sponsors. The lifestyle of cricket is finally working for the players economically. I can't imagine Flem leaning over the counter of the local Noel Leeming store to make ends meet now. But it was only recent history, when too many amateurs were running the game, that that wouldn't have been the slightest bit unusual.

Even so, professional sport has remained, and always will remain, an insecure lifestyle. Personally, I've never really grossed above $100,000 for a year, and that's with endorsements and other personal efforts thrown in with the money I've been paid to actually play the game. But I think the public has a perception that that kind of figure is just your starting salary. The reality is that cricket's a poor cousin when you compare the money stakes with the $250,000-plus riches of top professional rugby and league. It's nice, but it's not that huge.

In the seven years of this decade, I would have averaged between $50,000 and $80,000 a year in income. But for a long time before then you got around $30,000 a summer – and were pretty stoked with that at the time. Fringe players would be getting a lot less, and didn't train any less. The top pros were on separate deals and they got handouts, grants from the Sports Foundation as well. But generally the incentive in terms of playing for your country wasn't money.

The eighties greats had the misfortune to play through an era when there was no bonus money for individual performances or team wins, as there is now (if there had been, it might have sent New Zealand Cricket broke!) While you were away on tour you relied on a weekly payment – that hasn't changed too much over the years. The difference in earnings has come from the win bonuses, performance bonuses, BNZ prizemoney and the U-Bix MVP money that goes into a pool for the players – and your contracts.

But, as I said, though the bucks are bigger, the nature of the game is insecure; you know the job won't last a lifetime. It's the risk you take. But the recompense is better. Last summer, missing out on the team cost me about $50,000 in earnings both directly, through playing, and indirectly, through endorsements. Some of the guys would have done very well in 1996/97, winning two tests back to back and the test series – for which there's another bonus – against Sri Lanka. It is a long way from the personal insecurity I felt in my first three years trying to establish myself in the team.

The place where there's a real problem with money in cricket now is in our domestic cricket. There, too, itineraries and demands on players have escalated – but the professional structure has, in most parts of the country, scarcely kept pace. That's impacted negatively on the demographics of the sport in New Zealand, and it will end up impacting on the national side. It's already started.

New Zealand didn't have much in the way of "youth tours" when I was young, but I remember when I toured Zimbabwe in 1988 with the "Young" New Zealand side, Bert Vance, our captain, was 32. Mark Priest was 27, Trevor Franklin 26 and quite a few more around the mid-20s mark. Yet, at just 31, last season I found myself one of the oldest players left in New Zealand cricket, and at that age, it seems, I'm just about finished. But when I started playing cricket a decade ago, there were plenty of players older than that both domestically and in our national side. They were the experienced, dependable heads, and often great characters, the life of a team, but the best thing about them was that they were able to lessen the pressure on raw, immature young guys who were really still learning as they entered a new level of cricket.

It seemed to happen that while the demographics were changing at home, the New Zealand side was also playing more tours and therefore not mixing as much with the young things coming through on the domestic circuit. You'd really only play a bit of Shell Cup. You rarely play Shell Trophy anymore if you're an international player, with rugby sandwiching the cricket schedules into midsummer. That was a shame, because, like the older heads domestically, you weren't around to pass on knowledge to the next generation anymore, either.

I look at young bowlers brought in now to our international side: they're expected to perform right away on tour, sometimes in very difficult conditions against in-form international batsmen, with no old bowling heads around or even moderately more senior bowlers to show the way. It seems the luxury I had of learning my craft from its masters is gone.

Your typical first-class player today is in his early to mid-twenties, without a mortgage or family. Once those come along, it's usually just too difficult, economically, to keep playing. I played a lot with Steve Brown in the Auckland side, we were quite close in the team. Brownie's a classic achiever and also genuinely loved playing the game, but had to fit it around his regular job for Marathon Industries because Auckland only paid about $50 a day when you played, and on tour, that really didn't go far. Brownie would take all of his holiday and sickness days off from work to play cricket. I remember we'd fly into the airport from a game down country and he'd get into his car, coffin and bags loaded in the back, and head straight to work for the day. When he retired at the age of 31, he calculated that playing for Auckland had cost him about $10,000 a year and a managerial position. That's the sort of maths that's going to cost our cricket many more in the way of talented achievers.

Even at international level, Bryan Young, who scored that mammoth 267 in a test against Sri Lanka last summer, just a year beforehand had had to go on the dole and sell his house in Whangarei because he hadn't been picked for the 1996 tour to the West Indies and hadn't had the opportunity to get any other sort of employment. He was always away playing cricket trying to perform for or to get back into the national side, didn't have a contract with New Zealand Cricket and obviously wasn't making a living playing for Northern Districts. Why should it have to come to selling the roof over your daughter's head when you make such sacrifices to play the game?

The age demographics have already started drastically changing in the New Zealand side, too. Look at Stephen Fleming: our captain, the youngest ever in New Zealand history, at just 24. They are mainly guys in their early to mid-twenties in there. Adam's been around for a while, but he started when he was very young. Cairnsie is getting into his late twenties, but he's wild at heart. There's really only Gavin Larsen and Dipak left to represent an older age-group, both of whom are in and out of the side because of their specialty positions and, in Dip's case, because of injury. Youngie is in his thirties too, but was a late starter and is really still establishing himself. There just aren't enough of the old crew around. I notice, too, that Dip and Gav tend to hang out with Peter Wills, the breweries' rep, and Mark Plummer, the physio, on tour because there is a real age difference showing in the team now and, like myself, those older guys have sometimes found continually bridging the generation gap on the interrelating side hard work. I also mainly hung out with Plums, Crowey when he was there, Greatbatch, Blainy and Jonesy after 1992.

I still really enjoyed the opportunities I had to be the old hand and room with the new boy, as Hadlee had done for me so many summers before, rooming with young pace guys like Heath Davis in England last time we toured there. But there's less and less opportunity for that to happen now.

Coinciding with the loss of senior players, for the young players coming through in the changed New Zealand side there was (up until the Sri Lankan series in 1997) a shattering low after almost every good performance, wild inconsistency that led to some media-bashing, pressure from all quarters and young guys feeling increasingly that they had to escape. I look back and realise that syndrome was most noticeable after two of the older batting heads, Martin Crowe and Mark Greatbatch, were no longer on the scene. Crowe's knee injury was a tragedy; without it I'm sure he would have easily played through to at least the 1999 World Cup – and been a great stabilising factor in the team, a "great" in the side that would give many of those young players more confidence. He would also have been the last link to that fantastic eighties era.

It was such bad luck after 1992, when Crowey's knee was keeping him out of cricket a lot, I was also in and out of the New Zealand team with groin problems and 'Paddy' Greatbatch was in and out with form. There was no stability. None of us older ones were around enough to help if we could, a senior nucleus wasn't around enough to contribute to the tradition and knowledge of the team. Gav Larsen has a tremendous heart as a senior player. He's a "100 per cent man" and leads by example, giving so much to the team. But too often it was too much to ask that he should have to carry that weight alone. If young guys couldn't follow that example, it was their loss.

For a long time I've had the feeling that guys coming through in the national side didn't have the total respect for me that I had had when I was 20 and looking up to Paddles, Chats and Sneds. I'd think about it often. Maybe it's the physical stature – most of them couldn't look up to me, literally! But also I think perhaps because I'm fairly liberal and extroverted, with a mad sense of humour, the younger guys didn't take me seriously when I did try to be serious at times. I'm also sure a lot of it comes down to the drugs issue in South Africa in 1995, but we'll get to that later. The only person from the next generation that I really connected with was Cairnsie, and I seem to have lost touch with him at times, too, since South Africa.

So much seemed to go wrong during my last years in the side. From 1993 until 1997, when results on the park were poor and there was often controversy off it, there were so many occasions on tour when dinnertime would roll around and you'd pick your restaurants on the basis of where you were least likely to get hassled by a couple of sports-talking blokes who'd had a few drinks at the bar. Without a doubt, you get a harder time in public when the side's losing. People will pass comment, poke the finger at you, though generally New Zealanders aren't nasty. You know it goes with the territory, but some players have sometimes got into a confrontational situation after a friendly discussion has got heated at the bar.

I never saw being public property as a downside – it's part and parcel of the life. I was lucky to live in Devonport, where people were quite low-key and pretty good around you, but so many times, when I listened to members of the public get stuck into the side, I really felt sad. The magic I'd felt as I'd watched the New Zealand stars just a decade before had vanished.

DESPERADO

Over my career, almost every coach I've played under in the New Zealand team has turned out to be a vastly different personality to his immediate predecessor. Sometimes that's worked against the continuity of the side, and sometimes it's been a breath of fresh air. Bob Cunis and Wally Lees were in the latter category.

Bob Cunis was my third coach in the New Zealand side and the last of the great old guard. Cuni took over from Gren Alabaster, who'd been in Australia with us at the tail of 1987, for that summer's home series against England and coached us through to the end of the England tour of 1990.

Cuni was a hard old warhorse who'd been quite a gutsy pace bowler for his country in his time, taking just over 50 test wickets although he wasn't built for the job. I think he saw that I was a similar, short, stocky guy like he was, and we got on well from the beginning.

Cuni was big on team spirit and getting guys to gel together as a group and feel part of it. He was also very grounded, a no-nonsense Northland school principal who didn't let you get carried away with yourself or swollen-headed. But he also never let you feel down, and I enjoyed his sense of humour. He was the sort of coach you could take the piss out of and the team had some great laughs with Cuni.

He wasn't the most relaxed guy getting out the old wallet for a shout, so one time when we were batting in England Wrighty and Smithy superglued down a fat little pound coin on the walkway near our showers and lavatories. Then we just sat back and waited for the inevitable. It was hilarious – the boys got all the cameras ready. Finally Cuni came in to the team area to make his way to the lavatories and, as he went by, just quietly half-noticed the coin on the floor. The boys kept straight faces and there was a pregnant silence while we waited a few minutes. When Cuni returned from the lavatories, he quietly looked down at the coin, tried to kick it, then bent over and tried to pick it up – at which point the boys turned around in their chairs and sprung him with their cameras! Everyone was in hysterics – and Cuni gave us heaps back, telling us we were all very clever sons born out of wedlock (or words to that effect).

Cuni was great for us younger guys. He'd often sit in my corner of the dressing room, fagging away on his cigarettes talking to Willie and me about bowling and getting into different batsmen. Even though he was from a different generation, you could relate on a normal wavelength to him. He was always giving me a hard time about eating fennel and not enough red meat. "You don't want to go eating fennel, son. That's the stuff cats and dogs piss on."

It's commonly held that bowlers are more unselfish, giving types than batsmen because they rely on other team members to perform, to take their catches and work in tandem with them; whereas batsmen play their own game, relying pretty much on their own ability. Braces was always adamant that batsmen were intense and strange men – and then you'd look across the dressing room and sure enough you'd see Wrighty going through all sorts of states over his game. He even glued his gloves straight on to his bat handle once, to get his grip right as soon as he picked up his bat! Certainly whenever I've had a coach who's been a batsman, it hasn't really worked out. On the other hand, having a coach like Cuni, who was a bowler first and foremost, worked well. Wally Lees, meanwhile, was a keeper, that in-between animal, and he turned out to be a good bridge in the side.

Cuni was lucky as a coach in that he struck a very balanced New Zealand team. He had a side where the senior players looked after themselves and interacted well together as pros, were sensible about things and fronted up for work when they needed to. He never had to worry unduly about the team culture, about what guys did in between playing. Meanwhile the batting and bowling more or less ran itself, so it was much easier for Cuni to run the show. Paddles was left to his own devices, because he did his own thing, and both Cuni and Paddles were happy with that. It was a really nice equilibrium, because Cuni would still crack the whip on the young charges like myself and Willie in Aussie in 1989 and India in 1988. He'd growl at us in the nets, "Shut up! I don't want you chatting. You're here to practise! I want you to get back to your mark and be lonely like me!" It was the schoolteacher thing, but he was hard case with it. The one area in which Cuni did irritate some of the players was that he wasn't a great watcher – he'd often go and have a sleep in the dressing room or on the physio's table when we were batting, but that was him. Because he'd had to battle against his physique as a bowler for so long, with the advancing years he needed a hip replacement and could get quite uncomfortable with all the travelling and practice. He was going to get it done in 1989, but put it off because he would be coaching us instead. His knees have been operated on, too.

I was sad when Cuni finished up, which happened to be at the same time as Hadlee and Sneds, the last of the old seamers playing around me. He was good for me, just by being around, cracking the whip and talking about little bowling things. Little exercises to get your wrist going, working on different techniques, keeping your shoulder round more, using your front arm more and following through: those were things I did by myself more when Wally Lees took over as coach. I was on my own after that.

Wally Lees ushered in the new era after we'd lost Hadlee, Sneds and Braces in one fell swoop of retirement in England in 1990. It was strange at first, because time flies in cricket and you felt you'd only just been playing against Wally in Otago in 1986/87. Some of the others felt that, as a coach, he was too much like a player, too close to the players. But personally, I didn't feel that at all and there wasn't a problem. For Wal, you wanted to give it your all. He was great. He was there for people, there for you. That was him in a nutshell. He was the perfect coach for the new brigade of post-Hadlee guys like Chris Harris who were coming into the team environment so young, because he made a point of getting round everyone, making everyone feel comfortable. He made that transition easier. You'd always feel comfortable popping into his room for a coffee on tour when you couldn't sleep or you needed to talk something out. He had a cheeky sense of humour and a nice nature and you could sit around and just enjoy his company, but also you'd know to get on with the job at hand. He created a good environment within the team.

Martin Crowe started to run the technical side of our cricket

SIMPLY THE BEST

There's a lot you could say about Martin Crowe, but a few simple words say it all: he's the best batsman we've ever produced.

He's also the best captain I've ever played under. Without a doubt, he got the best out of me and I relished the series I played alongside him in the team. The cricket world really saw his ability as one of cricket's thinkers on display in our 1992 World Cup. He knew the idiosyncrasies within that New Zealand team better than anyone – and could piece the whole jigsaw puzzle together better than most. Considering the armoury he had compared with that which Wright, Coney and Howarth had had in the 1980s, I think he was the best captain we'd produced for a very long time.

But, for all the great contribution Crowey made to New Zealand cricket as a player, I can't help but look back over his time with a sense of frustration. Some of the press really had a go at him over the suggestion that he was gay, at a time when, as captain of our national team, he had problems with Howarth as coach, when he was losing valuable senior players to retirement and others, including himself at times, were struggling with untimely injuries in the middle of hectic summers. I thought he handled all the ridiculous speculation over his sexuality and marriage very well given everything that was going on, but it was made unnecessarily uncomfortable for him. It was like the Chinese water torture, tapping away on the forehead all the time. There were a couple of times he just didn't want to go to press conferences, because he felt some of the press were ganging to have another go at him, rather than to talk cricket. You saw that and you just felt angry. We didn't need any of those issues affecting such an inspirational leader and world class player. It was a critical time in New Zealand cricket, but too much media focus on Martin was personal. There wasn't much understanding, or even sympathy, for his position.

But the real tragedy was that injury cut short his brilliant career. He's been the Michael Jones of cricket with his knee.

Crowey had major surgery at the end of 1993 and I look back on that summer as the crossroads not just of his own career, but of stability in the side. We played Pakistan without our master player and marshal as Martin targeted the tour of England later that year for his return to the crease. It couldn't help but shake you around a bit, as much as you tried to carry on and band together for Ruds. Some people thought Martin's knee was just a good excuse not to tour with Howarth, whom he clashed with. That was very unfair.

Towards the end of his career, he'd been battling against his knee for some two years and there was a feeling of inevitability in the team, that it was coming, the day we'd have to go on without him. So when he retired in January 1996, in a way, it was quite a comfortable transition, because we'd semi-adapted to it. But also I felt that Glenn Turner, the coach and convenor of selectors then, didn't give Crowey enough time to prove his fitness. It would have been right to take Crowe to the World Cup or the West Indies: he deserved a good send-off. I think Turner thought you couldn't have two rules – one for Crowe and one for everyone else – about being fit at selection time. Then again, Glenn also used to say too many "soups" – as in superstars – in your side was detrimental to the team culture. I didn't agree. We needed him so desperately in the Caribbean; he would have been the only one there who'd played there before, the last link to the powerful side of the 1980s.

Crowey loved playing cricket and was deservedly earning a good living from his talent. It's a tragedy the way it ended so prematurely, and also that so many things went against him in the last years of his career.

In the West Indies, the locals remembered his blistering centuries in 1985 and all wanted to talk about him. Whenever we were at a function, no matter which island, you'd look up on the walls and there would be a photo of Martin smashing runs like a young god.

more, and when Crowey found tough times, Wal would act as a sponge for that, absorb all the hassles and bad energies. It was a great balance. Crowey had wanted the captaincy a great deal, wanted to succeed at it and really relished having a greater input – he's a very good thinker about the game, as our strategies in the World Cup in 1992 illustrated. But it was hard for him. Of the side he'd grown up in, only Wrighty and Smithy stayed for his era; he'd lost all that artillery, all those great players. All of a sudden I was our most experienced bowler with 50 test wickets – a little way behind Hadlee's 431! Joining me in the bowling ranks were Chris Pringle, who was only 22, and Willie Watson, who'd be in and out on tour. Then you'd look around the dressing room and see Mark Priest, who was drafted in when it was suddenly realised we didn't have a John Bracewell anymore, Grant Bradburn, David White . . . it was a sea of untried, new faces. Test matches weren't the even contests they'd often been in previous years. We got a hiding in Pakistan in 1990, but even despite all the ball-tampering business, it was clear Pakistan was such a far superior side. They had experienced batters and a balanced attack; we were in a monumental rebuilding stage. Yet Wal made people feel comfortable in that environment, that the task wasn't beyond us.

The 1992 World Cup was Wally's finest hour. As we charged unbeaten into the semi-finals, we experienced the most amazing feelings in cricket, touring round our own country beating the world. For me it was the closest I ever came to a taste of the heady days of the 1980s, the Coney and Howarth era when people used to watch New Zealand cricket with a real sense of excitement and expectation. I was so proud to be part of it.

It was also one of the few occasions that everything was working well behind the scenes, and perhaps that says it all. We had a good coach in Wal and a focused captain in Crowey. Don Neely was the convenor of the selectors and while there are a lot of theorists in cricket, he had quite a balanced view. The players generally felt comfortable within that framework and some, like Batchy, simply blossomed. He was on fire throughout that tournament, blitzing the opposition attacks from his position at the top of the order. Everyone wanted to know what he was having for breakfast. I was sharing a playing berth with Cairnsie and, personally, it was tough missing some games, especially the opener against Australia, but your emotions quickly picked up watching those magic team and individual performances.

But I'll never forget the feeling I had after the first innings of our semi-final against Pakistan on Eden Park. I just had that feeling that

262 wasn't enough; I was quite nervous. The Pakis had had their backs to the wall the whole tournament and were like caged tigers. When Crowey injured his hammie, meaning John Wright had to captain that do-or-die last innings, Wrighty was visibly stressed and hugely under pressure. You felt for him – no one loved playing for his country more than Wrighty, but he had a different style from Crowey and was simply out of practice when it came to shuffling the field and the bowlers. Poor Chris Harris, who'd been our bowler of the tournament, suddenly went for 72 off ten overs while Wrighty bowled me too long. The bubble burst: we were beaten.

We were stunned. Gav Larsen and Rod Latham were really emotional, as was Wally. Willie was very down. And I remember Cairnsie hugging me as we walked around the boundary for the crowd.

The nice thing was Peter McDermott, the New Zealand Cricket Board's chairman at that time, allowed everyone in the team to go and watch the final in Australia, and some did – even though the Pakis were on the same flight. I went. Our accommodation and travel was all paid, and despite the disappointment, I remember sitting back and reflecting that it felt good. Things were going well for me. I'd consolidated my position in the team, I felt secure and had just been asked to go to Lancashire to play county cricket. I had a niggly groin, but this was still before my hernia nightmares. It really was the peak moment of my career.

Late in 1992, New Zealand toured Zimbabwe and Sri Lanka. It was the first time New Zealand had been back to Colombo to play cricket since my very first tour in 1986/87 had been shattered by a bomb. Sure enough, the same thing happened this time. There'd been two tours in five years and bombs had gone off both times. I didn't go on that second tour, but I understood completely why Wally and five of the older guys came back. Wally had been through the trauma of losing his first wife in a car accident and couldn't abide the thought that his wife, Jude, might have to go through that same tragedy because he was in the wrong place at the wrong time. There was an anarchic edge in Sri Lanka and it just played on your mind that you couldn't control that. It was like playing percentages, and that just wasn't good enough. I would have come home if I'd been faced with that choice a second time, no longer the carefree, self-absorbed youth. There was more to life than taking a chance that another might go off in front of you.

I think everyone understood that over in Sri Lanka and that a lot more players really wanted to come home, but instead of deciding action as a team as we had in 1986/87, Peter McDermott flew over to Sri Lanka and influenced a number of the players into changing their

DESPERADO

minds and staying. To some he promised contracts, which, more than money, meant security in the squad. That swung quite a few players, but unfortunately for some of the younger guys, the promises weren't kept. Later, some of them were quite upset at their treatment.

At no point was Wally ever ostracised for coming home from the tour early by the players. Nothing was held against him, and when we then had a good home series and close-fought contest against Pakistan and Australia it seemed the train was back on the rails. Because we'd done quite well, although there was plenty of talk in the media about the possibility that Wally would be made to pay for "bailing out" of Sri Lanka when it came time to appoint a coach for the following season, there was no feeling in the team itself that Wally would be or should be axed at the end of the season. Geoff Howarth was hanging around in the background, being touted as a potential replacement, but none of us took that seriously, because a lot of us had toured under him as players when he'd coached the 1989 New Zealand Youth side in England and the 1988 Young New Zealand side in Zimbabwe. We thought it was well known that there were some concerns about his social habits – and we'd seen those for ourselves. At the end of the summer, when it was time to disband, I remember Wally saying he was looking forward to 1994.

So it was a real surprise when Murray Deaker rang me up from New Zealand one day during the English summer later that year, when I was playing league cricket in Rochdale, and told me the news. Wally had got the sack, Howarth was in.

I felt really sad. We'd done so well that season and Wally was keen to keep doing a good job. There was no reason to suddenly cut him adrift; it wasn't logical. It simply seemed that New Zealand Cricket wanted to make him pay a price for coming home from Sri Lanka after the bomb. I believe it came down to personalities: McDermott and Wally didn't get on. Wally was adamant he had to follow his integrit and McDermott's authority was affronted.

Looking back, that single decision set the team development back, perhaps by years. Wally's axing was tragic timing. We lost continuity. Wally had wanted to get us all going down that same road together – that was his chorus during the World Cup, and it worked. Inside the team during that tournament we'd just started to get a good thing going. Then we had a hiccup in Sri Lanka, but got back down to business in 1993. Wally was a great balancing influence for Martin and it was just so frustrating that team culture was sawn off.

Wally always used to sing that song "Desperado" on the team bus. It turned out to be prescient, and that was a great shame.

SEX & DRUGS
& ROCK 'N' ROLL

When I next saw Geoff Howarth, at the New Zealand squad training camp in October 1993 at the Christchurch Football Club, he looked terrible. He'd been living there in the latter stages of the winter, and he seemed washed out, tired, like he was really roughing it.

Geoff's whole life had been cricket, and the dangerous side of the lifestyle was evident in him. Sometimes you just had to smile. In Sharjah one time I remember Geoffrey highlighting his hair like Rod Stewart, strutting around poolside with a gold chain round his neck, a silky shirt open to the navel and speedos – you can see why All Blacks get this image of cricketers as rock stars following the sun around. He'd lived in London for years, rubbing shoulders with the Rolling Stones, who were members of the Surrey County Cricket Club for which he'd played. He enjoyed the glamour of English, and international, cricket. But he also had an infamous reputation for overindulging in the lifestyle, and I believe everyone in the side in 1993 had doubts about whether he'd work out as coach because of it. It was sad to see, because those doubts overshone his great reputation as an astute captain and fine batsman for his country.

Howarth's first summer as coach was really the beginning of the demise of the New Zealand side. The 1993/94 season was also my last full tour to Australia. Personally I'll miss playing there, it was a hell of an experience. It would have been nice to have had a swansong in 1997/98 – because 1993 wasn't at all a pleasant way to farewell the place I'd adored playing.

I started out that summer feeling quite good about things, personally, because Kim and I had just got married that year and I was coming off my best season at home, against the Pakistanis and Australians. I was looking forward to the tour, but this Australian trip turned out to be my worst tour anywhere.

There was a lot of expectation, but our unit didn't field as well as we should have (we had quite a few new personnel in the side, the slip cordon kept changing, catches kept going down – things weren't happening for me at all there) and the energy within the team was down. I don't know if it was because we'd lost Wally and there had been so much change so quickly, but there was certainly a sour feeling left about the way it had happened. We all felt Wally had lost his job because he'd come back early from Sri Lanka, and now, on a tough tour, we missed him. I felt that it was then that we really broke off into little groups of players, instead of trying to stick together and keep the circle strong. That wasn't Howarth's focus.

We suffered badly over there. A lot of the newer guys got a rude awakening as to how tough it was against the Aussies in front of those large crowds in a big arena. Their media put you under the microscope. And there were frustrations off the park. Murphy Su'a wasn't playing as much as he would have liked, competing with Cairns, Doull, myself and Willie, who tore his hamstring after Perth. It was one of my first real times as a senior player, but I got no joy. I was trying to stay focused, look after the bowlers and help Murph, but it was such a fragmented time that we just weren't going down that same road together.

Geoff was trying to create more accountability in us individually and wanted us to be more proactive as players – to be more self-sufficient and not have your hand held. But his method came at the cost of things like working out fielding drills together as a group, the fun team things that might have buoyed the spirits more on a hard tour. Instead they fell away, and his practices became long and stale instead of short, sharp and quality. Because it's so hot and demanding in Australia, you'd quickly get tired. We never had enough net bowlers and Geoff didn't demand them. You started to hate training. We told Howarth practices were going on too long, but because our performances had been so up and down, it was as if we lost the authority to say we needed less practice. So lots of little things weren't addressed and that snowballed into one great frustration.

We hung in at Perth for a draw. Chris Cairns had suffered the tragedy of losing his sister in a train smash earlier that year and you could see he couldn't help but have that on his mind. He said he got his four wickets in the first innings for Louise; I think it was her birthday. Crowds would get into him there at the WACA but he showed what he's made of.

Crowey aggravated his knee in Perth and returned to New Zealand for surgery. It was a devastating blow so early on tour: we'd lost our best player, our captain and the driving force of the team. It was the moment his involvement in the team changed, the start of Crowe "losing" the captaincy for good. Ken Rutherford took over as captain in his absence. We lost the tests badly, going down two-nil in the series, and missed out on the World Series finals. The last two tests, we weren't batting well at all. We were bowling reasonably, but chances behind the wicket were being dropped with monotonous regularity. We weren't switched on in the field at all. Everything just went from bad to worse and it was a very soul-destroying time for a lot of guys.

The tour had started off well enough, but later, when it became a long haul, you could tell how the previous day's play had gone by just looking at Geoff the next morning. If we hadn't performed, his eyes would be hanging out, red like road maps. He'd be grumpy. You knew that practice wouldn't be run well and that he was going to take it out on us. You could see that Geoff liked to socialise and have a night out. That's the way he was after stumps: meals, wines, beers at the bar. But there were a lot of times he'd be slurring his words in front of us as a result – and that was a quick way to lose respect. It was a very difficult situation; there seemed to be a lot of denial going on that there was a problem . . .

We struggled on through a tough home series against Pakistan, without Martin, and then, at the end of March, drew a sole test against India in Hamilton, where Crowey officially resigned as New Zealand skipper. The saddest aspect of that summer was the way we seemed to just meander through it. A lot of that time is just a blur. Nothing seemed new or innovative; it just rolled on. Ruds was having to run the show, and some of the senior players were helping, but you could feel it on the park; we had no real direction.

We won the last test against Pakistan with Youngie and Tommo getting very good hundreds together in Christchurch, but usually, rather than concentrating on cricket, the team would get into a whole emotional state of negativity. We spent too much time thinking how much we disliked the Pakistanis for their attitude, for the way they mucked about with the ball and the fact that they weren't particularly social. There was a lot of nastiness going on.

India wasn't as good a bowling side as the Pakis, but the Hamilton test was a good match. It was a spark in the gloom as we watched the tall, slight figure of a very young Stephen Fleming go out and hit 92 runs on his test debut, getting his career off with a hiss and a roar in the twilight of a long summer. Greatbatch got a new lease of life, and Dion Nash came in. Flem's performance and a few fresh faces gave the side a lift. But next we went to Sharjah and England, and the chance of things looking up was dashed: the team culture wasn't strong enough for that tough tour.

Martin Crowe was back as a batsman and you could sense that Ruds felt threatened as captain with Crowey there. I think Ruds always thought he was captain by default, and the pressure of that thought was exacerbated by Howarth's behaviour as coach.

I enjoyed playing under Ken. He was the classic down-to-earth Kiwi guy who loved nothing more than playing for his country. It was very hard for him to take when his batting form on the job started to go and a lot of his resources were lacking, particularly with guys getting injured in the bowling department – his artillery was continually weakened. Thankfully there weren't so many injuries in the batting, but there was pressure on Ruds to lead from the front the way Crowe had, and it was so frustrating for him that his form didn't coincide with that need. He had problems with his family life, too, which you would notice. He just started to struggle. You understood why, but it didn't change it.

Impersonations of Geoff Howarth had become a stock joke in the team, and Ruds was one of the great impersonators, taking the mickey out of him. We were all guilty of it as senior pros: it was a standing joke at the bar or at a restaurant table to look into an empty wine bottle laughing, "Who am I?" It was funny at the time, but those sorts of energy shifts start to filter down through the team. The young guys picked up on it quickly.

On paper, Howarth had a good record. He'd been coaching Northern Districts and it was a very good side, playing very well and winning the Shell Trophy for two years in a row under Howarth. The public would look at that and say he was the obvious contender to take the mantle from Wally Lees. But ND had a good balance of youth and experience in their side, talent as well as middle-of-the-road players who performed for them. Howarth struck it lucky.

That season the nucleus of the ND side was playing for New Zealand, guys like Matt Hart, Richard de Groen, Blair Pocock,

Shane Thomson, Bryan Young and Simon Doull. I think they had a greater insight into what Howarth had achieved with them, and there were a lot of the ND guys in that New Zealand circle saying that, while Howarth's trainings and ideas worked for ND, it just wasn't working the next step up.

In England, off-field confrontations were starting to take place; there was an uncomfortable energy between Ruds, Crowe and Howarth. Ruds felt undermined by Crowe, Crowe felt frustrated with Howarth, Howarth felt he had no respect. And after that England tour, he certainly didn't have respect of either of those guys.

It was a bad time for Ruds, because just as there was the discomfort off field, the on field injuries had started hitting us. Chris Cairns had already been unavailable to tour, and now I had hamstring problems and left, Simon Doull broke down with his shoulder (he went home even earlier than I did), Blair Pocock didn't finish the tour with his shoulder, also – there were lots of little hiccups to go with this overall picture of muddiness. Plums, our physio, was under huge stress and exhausted. And practice was always the same – there was not a lot of variety. It all added up to a long tour. We were scattered, physically and emotionally.

It was at this point that guys were starting to get away from the team culture. We were often based in London, a mecca of bars and entertainment, and guys were escaping to the nightlife or had other distractions through old club connections there. I'd go out with some of the younger guys to the Cuba Club in Kensington. I remember drinking more than I usually would – being out late, drinking and eating late was a bad combination for me and not something I normally did. But you felt the unease and it was getting to me, too. It was amazing how it enveloped you, that trap of too much nocturnal activity, every time we came back to London. At 5.30 one morning the fire alarm went off in our hotel; men had to bash on our doors to make us get up and out of our rooms. Standing in the cold street outside the hotel, I looked around and you could see us, the New Zealand cricket team, in the middle of the tour, looking bloody rough. You could tell half of us were hung over. That's where it started to go off beam, where we lost the balance: you can play hard, but you've got to work hard, too. When I left that tour after our game in Gloucester, it was with a feeling of relief.

One time in 1993, in Sydney, the team had gone down for a meal at The Rocks, there by the harbour bridge. Geoff drank a lot of wine there and got into a relatively good-humoured slanging match with Crowey across the table. Food was splatting out of his mouth: he was spitting crayfish across the tablecloth. Mike Sandlant, a very pleasant, tolerant man, a pharmacist in Tauranga who was also a great servant to the game and a member of the New Zealand Cricket Board, was our team manager. I'll never forget looking across at Mike, who was sitting diagonally from me, as he looked at Geoff Howarth in absolute disgust. It was simply not becoming of a New Zealand cricket coach, a role model to the guys in the side coming through. I knew Mike could see that for himself at that moment. But 'Sandy' was also a friend of Howarth's. They'd worked closely together over the years for Northern Districts cricket and I felt that compromised the situation. I understand that Geoff won't see or speak with Mike now, when he comes back to New Zealand, but in Australia, and again in England, the harsh reality was that Mike would give Geoff another chance, time and again, after unhealthy episodes like at The Rocks.

Though no fault of Mike's, part of the problem was the system that usually saw board members given the tour manager's position. We were pretty lucky, in all, with our managers, they were good people; but their human resources skills were sometimes stretched in a very demanding job. With Howarth and Sandy, it was painful to watch – and what made me angry was that it was allowed to continue from tour to tour, because it clearly wasn't working with the team. We did think that, after England, Howarth would at least get the hard word on his habits, but it didn't happen. A situation had developed where his personal issues off the park needed to be confronted, but if you tried to talk to him about it, geez, he'd go off! He'd be very defensive and there would be denial. It would be, "I've got my life son, worry about your own . . ."

Mark Greatbatch told a story in his book about Howarth actually looking into an empty wine bottle for the last drop. There were numerous instances like that and it was embarrassing. If no one was out having a quiet drink with him, he'd go to his room. I'd go in there to get something from him occasionally, if I needed the rooming list that I was in charge of, for instance. The room always smelt of cigarettes and wine. They'd be empty bottles lying around. It was depressing, sad.

That first year under Howarth, we'd lost the test series to Australia 2-0, lost against the Pakis 2-1, then lost to England 1-0. Dion Nash had a great test match at Lord's, becoming the first player to score a 50 and take 10 wickets in a match there, which earned him a lot of prestige amongst the English and earned us a draw. It looked there as though we were coming right, but it was a false illusion, the wavering oasis in the desert. Because our next tour was South Africa.

I didn't fly out with the rest of the team that toured South Africa after a quick trip to India for an international one-day tournament. Instead I was recovering from my second hernia operation, which I'd had in August 1994. I'd had it done laproscopically, because that gave me a chance of a quicker recovery time, which meant I could possibly get to South Africa – this was the first New Zealand tour there in 30 years and it was quite exciting. But the recovery took longer than I thought and initially I didn't pass the fitness tests required to go. I had to stay and bowl in the Shell series instead, to prove my fitness. So I watched New Zealand's victory in the first test at Johannesburg on TV. I sat there in the lounge at night feeling their happiness and relief, the pride that everyone had chipped in and achieved something quite special. I was sad to have missed it, but pleased for them.

But not long after, the convenor of selectors, Ross Dykes, rang me. Dion Nash had injured his intercostals. With depleted bowling, the side had struggled to contain Pakistan, Sri Lanka and South Africa in the Mandela Trophy, a one-day series wedged between the first and second tests, so it was the big SOS call and I could hear Dykes' huge sigh of relief when I said I'm raring to go. I wasn't quite ready, but I'd bowled enough overs to rebuild some strength. It was a nice novelty to be called over as a replacement. Usually it was the other way around.

The long flight ended at Jan Smuts airport in Johannesburg. I was in the gift shop there, waiting to be picked up, when I glanced up and saw Nelson Mandela. He was about to go into the executive lounge, and had some bodyguards with him but he was just talking to some people and looked quite relaxed and normal, just standing around in an airport. Five minutes in South Africa and I'd seen its most famous identity. First Cliff, now Nelson! Another time I'd gone to Heathrow to pick up a mate from the airport and there was Lance Cairns getting off the plane behind him. They followed me around.

I turned up for just the last three weeks of the tour. Personally it was a very significant time for me in South Africa. It was nearly 40 degrees when I arrived, but I walked around and drank it in, because I felt a huge connection in that my mother had been born in this country. She'd lived in Johannesburg and Cape Town (where we would play the third test) until she was 12, before the family came out on the boat to New Zealand. In Durban later on I caught up with my great-aunt Geri, who comes out to New Zealand occasionally, and met some other relatives for the first time.

I caught up with the guys as they were about to head to Paarl for a first-class game against Boland, a provincial side on the western shoulder of the republic. You could see the colonial influence in Paarl through the graceful, curling Cape Dutch architecture. We stayed in a lovely guesthouse owned by a Dutch woman brought up there. It was really nice, traditionally furnished and with grapevines overhanging the pool. But behind the beauty lay the first signs of trouble.

Some of the guys kicked back at the guesthouse and had a bit of an unruly night. Some players on tour come to take it for granted that other people will take responsibility for them, that others will clean their hotel rooms, provide their meals, pick up their clothes and empty their ashtrays, and that's what happened at Paarl. The lovely Dutch woman was in tears the next morning. There were port stains and cigar ash on the furniture, glasses left half full. I hadn't been there that night myself, because I was so jetlagged I'd crashed out. But I saw the troops when Mike Sandlant gave them a dressing down in the team room. They got the discipline call, but what upset me was that Sandlant had ended up having to stress quite a few times that the side was to respect our hosts and remember we were ambassadors for our country – especially as we were the first New Zealand side there in three decades. He'd done the same thing in England. But the privilege was abused again and again.

I remember that, when I arrived, the guys had seemed tired, having come off an arduous string of one-dayers that involved a lot of travelling and a lot of losing. I was rooming with Youngie and he said it had just been a long and tiring tour, that things weren't working on the field and guys were jaded. Coming in as an outsider into the tour, I definitely felt distanced from them, though quite unintentionally.

Soon after, the team went off to the Nederburg vineyards, the breathtaking centre of one of South Africa's most elite wineries, where we would be wined and dined. There'd already been the hassle with the spilt port, so Mike Sandlant was standing on the bus repeating his speech, saying he couldn't stress enough that we were ambassadors and we must act like it. But at Nederburg guys once again got out of control. I couldn't believe the nonchalant cheek that was there, and the silly, immature things that happened that were just rude to our hosts. A few of the team helped themselves to a couple of bottles of the host's alcohol. It was embarrassing.

The actual game in Paarl, a three-dayer, was abandoned after one over of the second day because the pitch at Boland Park was a shocker. The umpires declared it dangerous. It was a shame we couldn't play, because some of the guys could really have done with a bit of longer match practice after the Mandela Trophy, but it really was a minefield, the ball scudding into guys' grills. So we ended up with even more time to kick back in this beautiful belt of wine country. One of the guys in the Boland side took us out to some more vineyards for an afternoon. The vineyard was very quiet at that time of day – the Boland player knew a girl who worked there. I think the rest is history.

I simply could not believe that four days out from a test match some of our players wanted to light up and smoke marijuana. It was very open. Guys would come back giggling to a braii there. Ruds was extremely upset to see it, understandably. He knew something was up and was very frustrated. I'd still been in South Africa only a couple of days at this stage, still feeling quite distanced from the tour unit. I sat there and thought, well, what do I say here? In the end I was trapped, unable to do anything about it.

We came back from the vineyard that day for an evening banquet in our hotel courtyard. Before long, seven players were going back and forwards between the courtyard and their rooms, coming back down with that unmistakable sweet smell of marijuana around them. I couldn't believe how naive they were. It was blatant, in full view of a lot of people. It was hard not to realise what was going on. I also thought the team was out of control. Some guys were doing their thing and it didn't seem to matter anymore.

It was their blatancy that led to a management inquiry: that's how Ruds, our captain, and team management realised what was happening. When practice was rained out the next day, Sandlant and Howarth interviewed each player separately. They intended to keep it in-house, but it was poorly organised – the interviews weren't conducted in the privacy of a hotel room, but in a lounge area of a local cricket club where guys played table tennis and pool. I was sitting there with Ruds when Crowey came over, feeling very uncomfortable about the way the interviews were being conducted – the touring media knew something was up and were hanging around. He said, "This is uncool. Peter Williams [part of the media contingent] is going to want to know what's going on here . . ."

My turn came and they asked me if I'd been smoking marijuana. I said, "Excuse me, I pride myself on being a professional and I work for FADE. That means being a role model. If you think that sounds like a righteous prick, too bad. That's where I stand."

After the interviews, in which some of the players involved had been honest and some dishonest, Howarth left it to Sandlant to be the disciplinarian. It was hard for Mike, because he's not that type of personality. He's a well-organised guy who expects guys to act like adults and things to run smoothly through good planning. He was put in a very awkward position by everyone.

And so the tour rolled on. We didn't bat very well at all in Durban and lost it by eight wickets – it really was a sad occasion for Crowey to finally become New Zealand's highest runscorer in test cricket. Then, on New Year's Eve, we flew to Cape Town for the final match.

With Cape Town in the full swing of holiday season there were more distractions around than ever. Big blonde topless South African women would be flaunting themselves on the magnificent white sand beaches, while at night there was an ocean of bars and clubs buzzing with revellers. A group of us went to this place called 50 Orange Road, a wine bar/brasserie. James Small, the Springbok winger who'd just toured New Zealand that winter, was in there. François Pienaar was partying in another bar. It was still seven months until their Rugby World Cup, but you could see at a glance that the rugby stars were treated like gods in South Africa.

Cape Town was one big party scene. You'd go to catch up with a couple of the younger guys, have a nightcap with them in their rooms later on, and it would still be rolling. I'll never forget going in and instead of a team-mate there was a naked woman standing in the room. She'd been at one of the wine bars. She reminded me of Barbra Streisand and was just so confident, standing there talking to you with no clothes on! It was bizarre and full on, that holiday time – a very tough time to be thinking about your cricket.

The test series was now one-all, Cape Town being the crucial one, the decider. Before the match began on the second day of the new year, Howarth stood up and addressed us at a team meeting. He reeked of alcohol and was slurring his words. He'd been out at Robin Jackman's, a South African who'd played for England and who'd played at Surrey with him. It was New Year's Day and there was no way Howarth wasn't going to enjoy his celebrations.

That was the writing on the wall for a lot of guys. It made me so angry, because it was our first tour there in so long. Our New Zealand fans deserved to see us compete – and, personally, I had such a huge connection with South Africa, my mother's birthplace, that I wanted the guys to really fire in and celebrate. But that test was off the rails before it had even started.

Again, South Africa beat us by seven wickets. A lot of decisions went against us. I had a caught behind against Hansie Cronje turned down – it was a shocker – while Ruds was fined for his outburst when he was given out lbw, and that decision was even worse. I'll never forget the umpire, Barry Lambson, later saying that he was sorry, that he wished he could go back in time and have that moment all over again. Great. Thanks Barry. He really went off the international circuit after that; I think that test match shattered him.

In rugby league we've seen clear cases where, if a linesman or ref has made a blatantly wrong call – for instance, by not awarding a try – their career at that level of the game is on the line and they may drop down a grade. In cricket, we're too soft. As an aside (and I'm not at all suggesting this was the case with Barry Lambson), there have even been instances, well known to our players, when overseas umpires have been literally handed a pouch of gold for their "performance" the night before – needless to say against New Zealand's favour. There are people in the world who want subcontinent sides to win at all cost and that's sometimes how you get shocking lbws in one-day tournaments in certain parts of the globe. It happened in a situation where we had a "neutral" umpire – yet he was still bought off. That's why I think umpires should be accountable. The harsh reality of the game is you're going to get bad decisions here and there and everyone accepts that. What's not acceptable is that there is no immediate accountability. Even to have umpires rated on an independent and public points system would be an improvement on the current whatever-you-do-don't-criticise-the-umpires scene. If that happened, an umpire would risk sacrificing the chance to stand in international fixtures if he was bought off. Why not?

Anyway, from being one up in a test series in South Africa we'd crashed to a 2-1 series defeat. It was unbelievable, and heartbreaking to see the team in real disarray. If you look at it, Howarth had had three chances to really sort it out: Australia in 1993, England 1994 and the South Africa tour in 1994/95. It was a long life, but in the end, all that development time was wasted.

But in the face of defeat, Geoff was smug. He stepped off the plane back in New Zealand and told the media how confident he was of keeping his job, of continuing to coach the side, that the wolves were all out for him but he was contracted for another year, to the end of the 1996 World Cup.

When I saw his attitude I could scarcely believe it. Howarth had cards up his sleeve when he got off that plane. The players all thought that the marijuana issue had been dealt with in-house on tour, but it seemed to me that Howarth was in a position to say to New Zealand Cricket "if you don't honour my contract, this is what's going to hit the fan". I was also getting feedback from sections of the media where it had been put to me, "What the hell's happening with Howarth? He's so confident of keeping his job after that cock-up of a tour. What's going on?" I did a lot of thinking about it, but felt I really couldn't let a guy hold us to ransom like that. Knowing the way the team had been run, the whole negative spiral – it was tragic.

The media continued probing why Howarth was so smug. He wasn't on a performance based contract, but it could have been paid out, with some damage to his reputation. So, I thought I could see the game he was playing and decided to meet the chairman of New Zealand Cricket, Peter McDermott. It was a confidential meeting and I took my solicitor, Martin Snedden, with me.

I said to McDermott that Howarth obviously knew what had gone on in South Africa and was putting pressure on the board to keep him as coach – or he'd tell the media. I told him I wasn't prepared to have Howarth hold the team to ransom like that, particularly when I felt our cricket had already gone off the rails so badly under him. I wasn't prepared to be part of it if that continued. It was my dream and goal to be a professional cricketer and play for New Zealand. I'd worked so hard – and this was the environment I was supposed to work in? It wasn't good enough. Cricket was the best way I knew to earn my living and I really cared about it. They say your staff reflects your management, and the team's performance over the last year and a half had been an enormous downward spiral. For Geoff to be so confident of keeping his job in those circumstances was unacceptable to me.

I don't know how the story about the smokers got out, I just left the ball in McDermott's court – and I never named names. Mike Sandlant had to make a report to the board, and a number of people were starting to find out what had happened at that level. Then New Zealand Cricket had to make a media statement, holding a press conference at which Steve Fleming, Matt Hart and Dion Nash were identified as the smokers in Paarl.

They were three younger guys who'd tripped up over in South Africa and got suspended at home. I think Flem was outstanding in the way he handled it. He came out and said he'd made a mistake. It was the best way to handle the situation and you saw his maturity. But he, Harty and Nashy really were made scapegoats, because there were some guys, older guys, smoking in Paarl who never got suspended. They were more street smart, that's the way they wanted to play it in the interviews. They'll have to live with that.

But what really gutted me more than anything else is that I soon realised that Ruds believed that I had gone to McDermott to sing like a canary and dob my mates in.

Ruds didn't name me in his book, but he described a player called "the rat" and that was directed at me. For years Ruds and I had got along well, hanging out together, going to restaurants together. He should have known me better than that, and it upset me that he didn't come to talk to a guy that had played with him for

10 years on the circuit to ask what the story was. He has never personally asked me what I had said, and ended up with a different scenario. Frankly, he got it badly wrong. I believe now that whatever Ruds made out of his book, the bottom line is that he sold his soul, because he never came to the horse's mouth to find out why I'd gone to see McDermott with my lawyer before he wrote about it. It's possible Ruds may have taken it as gospel from McDermott that I'd come to see him and blabbed. It's a shame, because in 20 years' time when we're a couple of former players in a room together, I probably won't want to have a beer with him.

Because other guys who'd smoked in Paarl hadn't come clean at all, the dressing room was uncomfortable for some time afterwards. I really felt for the three players who'd been suspended, they were all young players really wanting to fit in with the team and do well for the country, just as I once had, but they were put in the most difficult of positions. But the bottom line is, who screwed up? Those guys all know they shouldn't have been doing that in the first place. Representing your country is too important.

I hoped that the guys would all know me well enough to know that there is no way I'd dob my mates in, but it became clear that wasn't the case. Dion confronted me about it in Christchurch, after he'd come back from suspension.

He said, "How could you?"

I said, "Mate, I know what I said and I didn't dob you in."

He said, "Well, you've lost a lot of respect as a player."

I said, "Look, you can think that if you want, at least you've said that to my face. But I only went down to open it up about the management situation and to say that New Zealand cricket was going down the gurgler because of the way management was running the show."

I was made vice-captain after the suspensions. It wasn't my idea, or even something I was looking for; I was simply the only senior player around to do it that series. To be honest, I don't know that you even need a designated vice-captain. But because of the timing, some of the players thought Dan had a hidden agenda. They thought I was feathering my own nest. Cricket's a gossipy environment at the best of times, but that whole scene got so political, with different information and sources moving about the team, that I think some players let the rumour-mongering lead their opinion instead of confronting me about it. Ruds thought I was the whistleblower and the other players seemed to follow his lead. Some of them may still hold it against me that I went to see McDermott in the first place, but I wouldn't change anything in retrospect. It was a dangerous situation and they deserved better as players. My intention was to sort out what Howarth was up to; then the story got out anyway and he lost his job.

To the credit of Glenn Turner (who took over as coach after John Reid stepped in to see that summer out), he sat everyone down in Darwin, at a camp early the following season, to have it out. But by then a lot of feelings had sunk in. It should have happened when those three suspended guys first came back into the side. I can understand why those guys had some doubt as to why I went to McDermott, but I can still look in the mirror and know I went into that meeting and didn't mention any names. If I had, as they all should know, more than three guys would have been hauled into the spotlight – because more than three guys were involved.

My ultimate feeling about the incident at Paarl is that it's too easy on tour for guys to start feeling bulletproof and just follow the lead of other guys in a group situation, whether they're into drugs, alcohol or whatever, when the tour or environment is getting them down. There is a lot of baggage that goes with playing for your country, with being an ambassador and a professional, but I believe it goes with the territory – and to run away from it is a lack of maturity and respect for representing your country. I've got into arguments with team-mates about this. Some of them think I'm righteous. And some don't quite accept it, don't quite accept the media hassles that come with your place in the spotlight, or having to do charity-type appearances and fulfil other demands on your time, all because you represent your country. But to me, a responsibility to the New Zealand public comes with it.

When I look back on the Howarth era now, my overriding thought is that it was just such a shame. After the whole debacle of Wally Lees' axing, the team structure wasn't stable. Ever since, the personnel and ideas have chopped and changed so much that players always felt they were trying to get a foothold on shifting sands.

As for Howarth, despite everything that happened, you couldn't doubt what cricket meant to his life, and it was sad for him, too. Just over a year after South Africa, when the team was about to head from Bombay to Calcutta for the opening of the 1996 World Cup, Geoff was booked on the same flight. We spotted him with Mike Gatting in a bar near us. He obviously felt uncomfortable with me there, but he'd also been invited to the opening ceremony as a noted former captain. He wore his New Zealand blazer.

TALKING 'BOUT MY GENERATION

It was from 1987 to 1993 that I played my best cricket. It was also the time in my career that I played in a climate of stability. It was no coincidence.

John Wright retired in 1993 and he was really the last link to the elder generation of players I'd looked up to in my youth. Of course, things had started to change before he hung up his boots. All of us had struggled in the home series against England in 1992, just before the World Cup. That was our first home test series loss since 1978/79, a long time in cricket. It was a record we'd been proud of – and so wanted to preserve. We lost both the first two tests. The last day of the second, at my home ground of Eden Park, happened to be my birthday. I was emotional. I felt like we'd let down all those teams from the 1980s. Let down Chats, Hadlee, Sneds, Braces . . . To go down two-nil, to lose it so drastically; it was as if something had died.

I was a blubbering mess back in the dressing room. Willie Watson couldn't believe it; I put a towel over my head and was just sobbing into my hands. It was just as well I didn't know what was still to come. The following summer at home we managed a draw, but then lost another home series, to Pakistan, 2-1; lost to the West Indies and a one-off test against South Africa in the centenary summer of 1995; then to Sri Lanka 1-0. It was the start of the nightmare.

England 1990 had been the last dance for Hadlee, Bracewell, Snedden, Jeff Crowe; only Smithy and Wrighty hung on for the 1992 World Cup, and then Smithy retired as well. After that it was a really tough time for Wrighty – not just because the fortunes on the park were changing, but because the new breed of New Zealand cricketer was very different from a Paddles or Chats.

My biggest single memory of the changing environment within the New Zealand team occurred one day at the start of June 1990 on the team coach in England. We were leaving Birmingham after a three-day Warwickshire game. Shane Thomson was 21 on that tour. Mad Shane was always interested in the darker side of life (I'd roomed with him throughout our Young New Zealand tour of Zimbabwe in 1988 where he was right into collecting knives and spears) and Tommo had bought a video on body art containing quite explicit film of piercing, tattooing, male genitalia and the entire bit. Tommo actually had a whole book about the stuff as well. There was a video deck on our team coach so Tommo got up and put on this video.

Richard Hadlee was also a big video man. He had his own western collection on tour, a Clint Eastwood man. Paddles took one look at the pierced nipple up on screen and jumped up and shrieked, "That's enough! Turn this rubbish off!" We all thought it was quite funny, but Paddles' reaction said it all. He turned the video off and put on a family movie.

It was really when Martin Crowe took over as captain from Wrighty that the new generation's era officially began. Crowe was from a sort of in-between generation of cricketers, one of the few of his age-group who'd really been able to force a way into the strong New Zealand side of the 1980s, because he was a special case, a world class player. People respected him for that. But he also glided in well to that next generation. He was a bridge; he could relate well to the younger players. He's quite an emotional character anyway and wanted to "give" a lot to the team, and I think he adapted to the change as well as anyone could. He liked to go out with the new guys, and so did I. They were exciting young players – and the difference between myself and them wasn't that noticeable. The only real distinction was that I'd played so much more in the late 80s with a lot of the old culture. The transition to playing with a younger age group wasn't hard for me then, in the early nineties. It's been harder since.

It wasn't just the team, but the world that was changing around us at that time. We had a far more heightened profile with aggressive marketing and hype pitched around the game now – specifically, around the international players. I remember seeing Martin and Annie Snedden on the cover of the *New Zealand Woman's Weekly* when they got married in 1983. In those days, it had to be an event of that scale to get a cricketer's face in any popular magazine like that. People were more interested in what we did on the park, if they were interested at all. Now we're standard celebrity fodder – we've had stories like "Simone Crowe's psychic omen" and "Greer and Adam's wild romance" popping up in women's magazines fairly regularly. Adam Parore's always been into looking like a Calvin Klein model and even did a photo shoot for *Cleo* half-naked strutting around in a waterfall, while Danny and Kim's "baby secret!" is yet to be revealed (we still haven't got one past the goalie!)

Far more attention is paid now to players' lives away from cricket because we're local celebs as much as we're sportsmen. Adam has said that there's been more written by papers and magazines about his love life and off the field activities than his actual playing ability. Part of that stems from agreeing to do women's magazine stories in the first place, but it also underlines the fact we're living in quite a different era and a culture. It's really moved in the last five years, from about the time in 1992 when we were pumped up on TV and billboards as "The Young Guns". Imagine seeing Chats half-stripped and reclining in a waterfall to have his picture taken! People would have laughed their heads off at that back in the eighties.

Most of us have been paid to appear on game shows like Wheel of Fortune and Celebrity Squares and some of us have had exclusive contracts with women's magazines, which means supplying a certain number of personal stories a year for money, but it's interesting that a few guys have moved away from doing the women's magazines now. There's a certain amount of baggage that goes with it. But what I found interesting was that in the nineties you started to see players come into the side almost expecting those trappings. When I started, I thought that getting a sponsored car just because I played cricket to international level was great; now, if you're in the New Zealand side, you almost expect it. You expect to get a sponsored mobile phone, a footwear contract, a sunglasses contract, a women's magazine contract offered to you; and it's all worth a lot of money. If you haven't got it, you'll stand on someone else's feet to get it, to be on the way up. They're like badges of success. The old guys didn't need badges, but it seems you need them now.

To get those kinds of deals in the eighties you had to be one of the best players. I remember Braces and Sneds *bought* their cars. It seemed it was up to you as to how far you pushed for those perks – now a lot of it is standard, taken for granted. Paddles and Crowey had the most contracts and were the guys with managers. And Lance Cairns was still very popular. I remember Lance popping up in a commercial for Nissan. He'd say, "I'll buy that!" It was so dated that it was hilarious. But in those days the marketing of your profile was on a smaller scale.

They were living in simpler times, and so was I. I wanted to get into the national team because it would mean I'd be playing with these heroes who'd been through such a successful era, who'd made me want to live and breathe cricket. It just seemed a neat thing to do. Now, there seem to be different aspirations mixing with that basic desire in the players coming through. The money, the glamour status, all the little intricacies that now go with the cricket scene motivates people more to play international cricket in the nineties. That's not being derogatory to the guys in this era. There are just so many other things that have come into the picture. It's a reflection on society as much as anything else.

To be honest, in retrospect I don't think guys who have come into the side in recent years have seemed as awe-struck as I recall having been. It's more like they'd *expected* to get there, and some enjoy quite a high profile before they actually cement a place in the team. And it may sound harsh, but nowadays it seems guys are worried about losing their endorsements if they don't get picked, worried about their own dealings off the park, extraneous things. When I came in, anything else paled into insignificance. Cricket was the passion, playing alongside the likes of Hadlee and Wrighty the be all and end all, something you wanted to do at all cost . . .

I remember very early in my career talking with Wrighty over in India. He said, "This is a hell of a place for you to come and experience so young, especially being a quick bowler in these conditions." He was trying to explain to me that I needed to get it into my head how intense test cricket could be. Wrighty was a pretty relaxed guy as a person, but very intense when he was on the field. He just lived and breathed it. That was the team culture. For me, it was like an osmosis thing where you just absorbed all their energies, the way they wanted to be there. Nothing but cricket mattered when you were away with those guys. It was such an incredible feeling.

The intensity of the game for me means that there hasn't been a single day in the last 12 years when cricket hasn't gone through my mind. It always comes into your thoughts, even now. You're thinking about playing it, coaching it, being absorbed in it. You can be walking down a hotel corridor, or standing in your lounge, and you'll just gently go through your bowling action or visualise seeing yourself running in smooth, thinking of those Dennis Lillee coaching videos . . . thinking of being out there doing it, because your heart and soul is in it.

Last summer Heath Davis showed how the medium of television can make a cricket personality capture the public imagination so quickly these days. But then, compared to cricketers, how many other New Zealanders spend so much time live on TV? It was really after the Aussie series in 1987 and 1988, that our level of exposure at home was visible. In 1989, when I was getting around a lot of secondary schools doing some speaking for FADE with Murray Deaker, I really noticed my face was recognised a lot more. I'm sure it wasn't just happening to me, and today players enter the side and almost instantly become well known and get on a game show. Once, I think, you actually had to perform well before the public showed much interest in you.

The increased marketing has had an effect on the team culture itself, without a doubt. John Bracewell famously called us "the Gucci cricketers" in a newspaper column in 1992. We'd been so hyped up by our sponsors and television, doing commercials as a team, having a higher profile, that a few of the players tried to look the part with a bit more style awareness!

But the changes haven't just been superficial. Off the field, it used to be more of a quiet restaurant scene or a good old, down-to-earth Kiwi night out for the guys where you were at a pub, people would recognise you, say gidday, maybe slap you on the back and say "Good on ya". I didn't really go out too much at home as a young player, because Devonport people tend to dine out a lot around Devonport there squirrelled away on the end of the peninsula, but I used to sometimes catch the ferry over to the city. In the winter of 1989 Willie was working for Sound Plus on Queen Street. I'd meet him in town and we'd walk up to the Globe and drink Swan Light – there wasn't a DB light in those days – on a Wednesday night. We did get recognised a bit, but we weren't ogled as if we were in the goldfish bowl. We were pretty much left to ourselves like normal people. But, back then, we weren't seen as the guys who had it really easy, on fat contracts to play cricket and getting up to mischief off the park. Today guys tend to seclude themselves away more. Apart from sponsor's functions, it's more of a wine bar scene. Guys seem to grab a quick meal and then escape.

I notice guys tend to go out with friends outside cricket more, too, and perhaps that's a symptom of playing so much that the life is too unbalanced now, too claustrophobic. Guys also tend to stick in bunches of three or four, whereas in the past at least half the team would head for a restaurant together. It sounds like a strange thing to comment on, but I think it shows a difference in the way players see the environment. The culture's that much more intense off the field; the old days were a lot slower and more normalised. It's led sometimes to the pressure building up and guys wanting to escape it. That's where you've seen guys sprung for being out late. The papers and other media sensationalise it, as in Wellington in 1997, but they don't comment on the reasons.

Fame was an interesting experience at times. People you didn't know could send you some really weird stuff. Willie and I were in the dressing room one time in 1991 during a one-dayer against Sri Lanka when a package from Sydney was delivered to me – this was just after we'd been playing in Australia. Willie was urging me to open it because it was obvious from the scrawl around the packaging that it was from an enthusiastic woman. It contained a letter and a pair of red, g-string undies. Willie had great delight in whipping them out of my hands and swinging around the room. It was hilarious. This mad woman had drawn a picture illustrating her desire to see me chained naked in a dungeon with a snake twining its way up my leg! Willie sat down and proceeded to construct a letter back, because it was so bizarre he decided we had to get some more info!

Some of the guys got seriously weird stuff, including tracts from fervent strangers telling us that if we beat the "heathen Muslim Pakistanis" that God would reward us. One woman said she'd had a vision from God telling her to tell us that if we thanked Him publicly on television after our victories we'd get more of them.

Then you got the really scathing mail. A grumpy old man from Christchurch wrote one that really chewed into us all for thinking we were "movie stars and glamour boys". He said that Smithy thought he was just so suave, that Danny Morrison thought he was Tom Jones with his tight pants on. Obviously the marketing campaign that year didn't go down too well!

There was also a recurrent correspondence in lovely, old-fashioned handwriting on notepaper from a rest home in Christchurch. They really got stuck into me. You had to laugh – perhaps they had nothing better to do.

You got some great hate mail. After bowling Inzamam-Ul-Haq in our World Cup round robin match against Pakistan in 1992 and giving him a bit of a nod as I sent him on his way, I got letters saying how disgusting they thought my behaviour was. I was a pussycat compared to a lot of bowlers from other countries; they must have got sackloads. Then there was the time I got Dean Jones lbw in the one-off test against Australia in 1990. I'd hit him right on top of the flap, the low thighpad really. As I said to the umpire, Steve Dunne, "It was just taking the bail on its way up!" It was a little high. But Dunney momentarily lost the plot and gave it out. I got a lot of hate mail about that one. I got letters asking how I could even appeal for that, how disgusting I was. The Aussies had lost that one-off test and it was obvious some of their fans were gutted. Were it not for cricket I would never have realised people like that were out there, getting so wound up. You learned a lot about the human world.

But I still always enjoyed meeting people. I went into schools a lot through my career, popped into clubs. When it was discovered I only had one kidney, I got quite involved with kidney foundation events. Once I met another young guy who had only one kidney – and his name was Danny Morrison as well. You needed to make time to do those things, but I think it's part and parcel of being in public life. I was happy to do that. It's nice to give back and to be able to make people's days.

I'm glad that I was able to experience New Zealand cricket in a simpler era. But beyond all the hype and marketing issues, the thing that was really different about being in the team back then was that, in the 1980s, the people who were actually responsible for the direction, behaviour and standards of the team were the players themselves – not the CEO, the coach, the captain, the manager or the chairman. The players were the people who set the rules, the standards.

The senior pros ran that team. Wrighty, Chats, Sneds, Braces, Smithy, Paddles. They were the ones you were answerable to and if they gave you a bit of stick, you obviously had to belt up and take it, get on. You felt an incredible respect for them and for their traditions. And things seemed to work smoother. Sure, there were ups and downs. Wrighty and Cuni had their moments with each other, for instance, mainly because Cuni was sleeping while Wrighty was batting. But there was never anything major, that the team couldn't deal with.

Today, there's just no way you can get through to a young player the way the senior pros got through to me. The respect thing just isn't the same.

We had no idea it was going to change so much – and it's very hard to get back. I think it may come back, that sense of standards, when the current players finally get older. In another couple of years, there'll be a group of them around 30 or over. Some of them have already started getting married and are in a settling-down phase of their lives. It will be interesting how they come up.

But I won't be there. I can really only look back at what's happened over the course of my career and contemplate the things I had to deal with. I look at the three World Cups I played in, the first at the very beginning of my career, the second in the middle of it, in the transition phase, and the last towards the end of my time in the team. Those four-yearly tournaments really encapsulated the changes in and around us.

In 1987 we didn't do too well in the tournament over in India and Pakistan, but I was just the new kid on the block, searching for my way into the team, and it was enough for me to look around me and see how a bunch of gifted, hardened, experienced players got along and worked together. Away from our own country and in a place where, though there was plenty of local passion for the sport, marketing and television wasn't a great influence, it was relatively low-key for us and the side ran smoothly. They just seemed like simpler times. And there was always a sense that we could do it.

Four and a half years later at home, that eighties side had been pretty much gutted. The younger guys came through in a sudden brigade. They hadn't had many of those old pros around to respect and it just wasn't there anymore. Smithy struggled with that; it was hard work for him. At the end of that 1992 tournament, even the guy who'd always been most determined to uphold the standard had had enough.

Yet it was a great campaign, that World Cup. After the bad England series, you were so lifted by the hype and excitement of it. For the first time we had quality coloured clothing, Australian marketing, and everyone played each other once, which was more fun and fairer than two pools. It was a time when we had a real sense of excitement and promise, excited by the new and fresh beginning, sensational results with a young team.

By 1996, when the World Cup was back on the Indian subcontinent, I'd matured in cricket, become a senior player. But of the promising side of 1992, only five players had survived. Mark Greatbatch, our sensation in 1992, wasn't selected – he should have been; the tracks over there would have suited him and he was confident in his game at the time. It was only four years on, but those four years had been such turbulent times.

All the essentials seemed to go wrong, and that was symptomatic. The uniforms were terribly done, hopelessly uncomfortable – you sweated like a pig in them. Some guys ended up having uniforms made and painted with the right colours while we were in Faisalabad. None of the ones we were given even fitted. Even shortarse Dan had to have pieces sewn onto the bottom of his trousers. And what really annoyed us was the words on the front were "N. Zealand".

There was expectation from New Zealand that we'd do well, because we'd shown a bit of form as a side at home. The country was really just waiting for us to get on the train tracks again. But after a buoyant start, winning three out of our first five matches, we went off the rails again. Then we rallied against Australia; whoever won would go through, but despite a gutsy century by Chris Harris, it wasn't to be us. We were frustrated in a very intense environment. But that, in a nutshell, had been the problem for years. And if only you could, you would have given anything to avoid the disappointment that came with them.

HOW BIZARRE!

Y ou get to meet a lot of very interesting people in cricket and sometimes you don't even need to step outside your own team. That was the case as the new generation of New Zealand cricket talent came pouring through in the nineties.

I go back quite a way with Shane Thomson, who shared my passion for running in and bowling fast in our early days. We've often roomed together on tour.

Tommo always makes for quite entertaining company. He's very flamboyant but also the full lounge lizard type, heavily into movies, videos, books – and he'd read everything from quite depraved material to the Hollywood gossip rags to bodybuilding magazines. He has his Chinese birth sign and a couple of theatrical symbols (the masks of comedy and tragedy) tattooed on his arm – his "tough stickers", as Craig McDermott called them. We roomed together quite a bit at the 1996 World Cup, cooped up for a good three weeks together in Faisalabad when the team had to wait almost a week between a few one-day games. Tommo's quite a big coffee drinker and would tend to stay up at night, so we jacked up a video in our room and watched a few movies – he's a bit of a connoisseur. Then the cabin fever would get to us and we'd just wrestle each other around the room. Tommo's always fancied himself as a bit of a singer, too, and likes to do the full Guns and Roses or Bon Jovi number. It used to crack me up, but then he'd put on the Stones and we'd both lose it.

Shane and Bryan Young are as thick as thieves, the two Northern Districts boys in the side who got their maiden test hundreds – 120 not out and 120 – together at Lancaster Park against Pakistan in 1994. Next to Tommo's flamboyant, blond and quite cocky presence, Youngie seemed much more dour and dark, so we used to call them "the Glimmer twins"; our very own Jagger and Richards in the band. Youngie has immense powers of concentration and showed it in that match, as he did again when he scored his double hundred in 1997.

Chris Pringle is an irrepressible character. Pring was once listed as "B.G. Pringle" on the Auckland scoreboard; the initials were short for "Balloon Guts". He often seems like a cricketer from another time, or possibly planet. He has enormous energy and heart, but the training lifestyle wasn't really him. He would sneak off during the game into the toilet to have a quick ciggie on the throne. Given his fitness habits, he really was an amazing performer.

Pring was a great bowler at the death. There was no better illustration of that than at Hobart in December 1990, where we were playing Australia in the Benson & Hedges world series with England that summer. We'd made 194/6 off our 50 overs, and with one over left in the second innings Australia needed only one to tie and two to win the match. Pring was having a *Boys' Own* summer. Crowey tossed him the ball; he'd be bowling against their last man, Bruce Reid. Bruce was never much of a batsman at the best of times, but with six chances and only a couple to get you'd think the odds would favour him.

The stadium was charged with tension as Pring loped in. Reido couldn't lay a bat on it. He kept playing and missing, looking as if his feet were nailed to the ground. Pring played him like a piano. Then he slipped one down the leg-side that was very close to being a wide – but it wasn't called. It was definitely Pring's day. He coolly bowled six dot balls, with Youngie running out Bruce Reid in the end, a great over that got us into the finals that year.

Pring was the happy-go-lucky golden arm. He just had that knack of picking up wickets and was great fun to have around the team. He was a bit like Merv Hughes; he couldn't help himself from talking about off-the-wall theories about cricket and life in general, a great punching bag for the rest of us in the dressing room. He was full of hot air and crazy, Freudian theories. He also had this reverse psychology theory going that he'd feed a guy a couple on the legs if they liked it there, then bowl a slower ball. We all thought it was mad, but he would often get a wicket with it.

I'll never forget a North versus South Island game where Pring was raving on about players he did and didn't rate in the dressing room. He was saying he didn't rate Mark Douglas, from Nelson, because he had a few weaknesses and was too easy to tie up – you'd come round the wicket and nick him out. Dougie was sitting listening to all this round the corner of the dressing room; he was playing on our side!

Stephen Fleming is a much more sedate character and a player far more in the classical mould. Flem was born on April Fool's Day, like David Gower, whom he's often compared to as a batsman. He was very nervous at Hamilton on his New Zealand debut in 1994. He came in with so many expectations, having been the captain of the New Zealand Youth side that beat the Australian Youth side the season before. But he just oozed class and has these big bucket hands that can be lethal for batsmen in the slips.

The New Zealand side was playing so much international cricket by that stage that I'd hardly seen Flem play at first-class level. He was almost quite timid at the start, a very shy-looking, gentle giant, a bit like Willie Watson. But he was a nice, approachable kid, wanting to experience and be around the culture and get on and do his job. He was intent on learning and absorbing, not one of these bolshy, cocky young guys.

If anyone had said this kid would be captain in three years' time, I would have laughed, but also, it didn't surprise me, because you knew he would be captain one day. It just happened very early. He's a natural leader in that he's a class player who can lead through his own, flamboyant style in both forms of the game – long and short.

Even when Lee Germon was appointed captain after Ruds' demise, people within the team culture were already talking about Flem being "the next captain". There was a sense of who else was there? But I think we thought Flem would take over really from about the end of 1998 – that would have been ideal in terms of the programme and his development. As it is, it sits comfortably with him. Though outwardly relaxed, he's a driven guy. It took him three years of hard work to reach his maiden test hundred and I think that will be the making of him.

One thing that struck me about Flem in India at the Independence Cup recently was that, before a match, he'd talk to the media about "looking to win" and "getting a win under our belts". That's the kind of statement New Zealand captains and coaches have often made over the last few seasons, particularly when there's been a few losses and the pressure's come right on to reverse the trend. But, although every time you run onto the park you obviously want to win, I think making that kind of statement puts the wrong emphasis on the real intention – and only backfires if you should happen to lose, which happens to the best of teams every now and then, after all. If you look at the All Blacks, you never hear John Hart or Sean Fitzpatrick say the team's looking to win a match. They don't use the word at all. Their emphasis, publicly and privately, is on the *quality* of the gameplan and the standards of play. They focus on their professionalism in all quarters and on creating the right environment and formula that they believe is most likely to help the side attain the goal of playing to the best of its ability. Winning may then be a consequence of that. I think that psychological tack is so much healthier, for both the players and the public.

Flem's great friend in the side is Nathan Astle. I first met Nath in 1989 at Shirley Boys' High School, when I was working for FADE and he was in his last year of school. Then I played a bit of first-class cricket against him in 1994 and thought he was a talented kid, though a bit of a Flat-track Bully. But he really blossomed and has been quite thrilling to watch at international level on a number of occasions since. He's become a dominating batsman who likes to go after his shots and entertain. He actually reminds me more of an Australian player than a New Zealander. But Nath's quite quiet and reserved off the park. He struggles a bit within the group, not really an extrovert. Such a pugnacious butcher of the ball out at the wicket, it's almost like he has a split personality.

It was a great asset to Nath's development that he played a lot of his early cricket on Lancaster Park, one of the few tracks around New Zealand that really comes on, where the ball goes through with pace and has good carry. McLean Park in Napier does sometimes, too. As batsmen, Crowey and Greatbatch moved to CD to lap that up. Jonesy played on a lot of tracks like that, too. Guys who do seem to be more confident in taking on their shots. Nath's back to back hundreds in the West Indies were a great achievement in difficult conditions, especially in the first one. It was remarkable to see that so early in his international career – they were only his third and fourth tests. It was no mean feat, even though the deck was placid in Antigua. The bowlers were still intimidating. He was taking them on, playing brilliant shots off the back foot square of the wicket, not scared to poke them over cover and played that little short-armed swivel where he gets up on one leg and pulls it. Then a bouncer would nearly rip his ear off; he'd shake his helmet out and away he'd go again.

His third test century came at Eden Park in 1997, when I was batting with him. It meant that he had three test hundreds from seven tests, and he already has four one-day hundreds, equalling Martin Crowe's New Zealand record. He's going to absolutely shatter it.

I first met Chris Cairns in Zimbabwe in 1988, when he came over late, after Shane Thomson broke his hand. He was only 18, but when he strode into our hotel in Harare it was as if he already had a reputation. We all knew who his father was, and he even looked

INTO THE GROOVE

I always relished performing in my own backyard. A lot of cricketers do play their best in their own conditions and that's certainly been true of me; I've taken 10 five-wicket hauls in test cricket and only one of them has been overseas, in the Caribbean. But in my book, taking a one-day international hat-trick in Napier was one of my greatest achievements.

It was a huge blast. No New Zealand man had actually taken one in limited overs international before, so that held special pride for me – and no one's matched it yet.

I'd taken only one hat-trick before in cricket and that was in an Under-19 trial at the end of 1993. It probably helped me get into the Auckland Under-19 side, but I had to wait just over 10 years for another one; they don't come often and you relishd them when they do.

I'd come back to bowl at the death, a challenge I really enjoyed in the short form of the game – and it was perfect conditions for reversing the ball at Napier that day. There are certain tracks around New Zealand that do it for you; Christchurch is one, because it eats the ball; Napier is another if it's brown, flat and hard. It depends whether there's been a good period of dry weather. This time there had been. The ball was nice, shiny on one side and rough on the other, and it started to hoop around sweetly.

The first to go was the great Indian allrounder Kapil Dev, chopping on a full delivery that I was trying to get up in the blockhole. He hit his off-stump. Prasad strode out to replace him. You could tell he'd come out for a slog. I was looking for the inswinging yorker, coming wider off the crease, all hunched and charging in with my eyes beaming on the target. I got the length perfect, right on the button and it hit the base of middle stump. Two in a row; you little beauty!

quite a bit like him, a big and athletic guy with a bright smile on his face and real gregarious energy about him. People often harp on about how difficult it is being a son-of, but it does hold truth. I remember in Perth, where Christopher made his test debut just a year later, Wrighty pumped up the emotions in the team meeting beforehand, saying he'd had an incredible time playing through the 1980s with Chris' father and now here was the next generation coming through. There were always going to be those comparisons, people couldn't help but compare them. But Christopher was such a

Those were the fifth and sixth balls of my eighth over and I started the ninth over realising I was on a hat-trick. Nayan Mongia, the wicketkeeper, was in; he was a capable batter who'd opened in tests for his country. I'd jogged back in from fine leg, where I'd had a drink and the crowd was pumping me up. We were dominating, victory was foreseeable and the spectators were delighted, because it was a break in the weather for us. I charged in at full steam. You can see how hyped I was on video. My eyes are like headlights. I was conscious of good rhythm, intent on not bowling a no-ball (I'd been on a hat-trick against India in a test in 1990, had Tendulkar out and then bowled a no-ball, stretching too hard to make it happen), coming wide of the crease and looking for that perfect yorker length. I was trying to take a leaf out of Waqar Younis' book and to bowl inswinging yorkers at the death, especially to righthanders where you're tucking them up, and if they miss, you hit – and it's hard to get underneath the ball and hit it over the fence. It hit the base of off-stump.

I remember jumping sideways to the public and seeing them all leaping out of their seats. The sound of the whole crowd going up was deafening. The guys were swarming in. Pringo was bounding in from third man. The big Galah, as we call him, has been one of our best one-day bowlers ever. He came up and hooted, "Aw Jesus mate, I'm due for a couple of those in my career!"

Venkatapathy Raju came out next and I almost got four wickets in four balls, but he dug it out at the last minute.

That's been one of the best feelings I've had in cricket. The Hawke's Bay Cricket Association made a little trophy for me with the ball, which was presented to me at the airport the next morning. They'd had it done overnight and it was a lovely way to farewell the scene of my only international hat-trick.

young man at the time and it was a piece of baggage he just didn't need. I think he, more than any other individual, always felt the pressure of trying to uphold the success that his father had helped create that decade – it was personal.

I was away playing for Auckland in the Shell Trophy when Cairnsie blasted his 120, his first test hundred, against Zimbabwe at Eden Park, but I saw bits of it on TV and was stoked for him. There had always been so much to live up to, that image of his father swiping sixes, and that innings in a way put that expectation to rest.

Cairnsie was thrown in at the deep end in Perth back in 1989. He'd really only played a little first-class cricket and it was going to be tough for anyone to walk onto that stage at 19 and mix it with the Aussies. But he tried so hard. Off the field he was a little reserved, and nervous. I think he was a bit in awe, much like I had been two years before. He got 28 in the second innings, after having been dismissed for just one in the first, and I remember he came back into the dressing room and just collapsed on the floor. He flopped down, wanting to dig a hole and just dive into it; he was so embarrassed that he'd been set for a good score, about the way he'd got out playing for New Zealand.

He tried so hard in that test match that as a bowler he ended up breaking down with stress fractures in his back, which is a nasty injury. The most frustrating thing for him, and also for the rest of us, is that injury has troubled him from the very beginning of his cricket, from such a young age. Every injury has put his cricket back a square. It's been so frustrating for him. He obviously knows he can perform well and feels a need and desire to show it, but whenever he gets on a roll something seems to stop it. You sense his real frustration at being on the world stage, but unable to make his mark on it.

I always liked Cairnsie and we became quite close after New Year's Eve 1989 when we caught up with 'uncle John', as we called "John Bracewell", and went out to the Palladium nightclub to see the new year in, bopping away on the dance floor in Christchurch. We'd often go shopping together on tour, go to see *Batman* together in Adelaide at the movies. So I really felt for him, particularly as a fellow strike bowler in the side, as he struggled to get his career moving. Chris missed a tour in 1990, came back and did well against Sri Lanka in 1991, then was out again after playing the 1992 county season when he needed his kidney operated on. He missed tours in 1994 with his patella tendon, a knee operation; then I hit him unintentionlly with a skiddy bouncer in the spleen during a Shell match between Auckland and Canterbury which caused internal bleeding. He ended up missing most of the centenary summer, and when he did play he was having injections of local anaesthetic to get by. For someone so young, that's a lot of scars. But he keeps coming back for more.

I remember having a discussion with Cairnsie in England, where he was playing for Nottinghamshire. He wanted to be one of the best allrounders in the world and was saying that he knew being in that county environment had helped Hadlee, Wright, Crowe and Turner become class acts and that he was trying to learn to be professional too, learn his craft like they did. But for Christopher it was very frustrating that times had changed and playing county cricket caused him to sacrifice playing for New Zealand sometimes, because there's only so much pounding a body can take. Unfortunately, guys with long spines like Cairns, Simon Doull and Angus Fraser suffer during their careers. Cricket is so unnatural to the spinal column; you must contort yourself as you move through the bowling crease. We can't be solid-as-a-rock front row types, you need to have some fluidity in your frame to complete the action, and it can lead to weaknesses, imbalances between the muscle groups. Some guys suffer more than others and Cairnsie's been unlucky.

Christopher performed well in Nottingham and had an especially good season there in 1995. The public find it hard to accept that he hasn't performed to the same degree for his country. They see this guy with an immense talent and flair for cricket who should be a really class act for New Zealand, but has mostly just thrown up sparks and glimpses here and there. But Christopher would like nothing better than to be injury-free and able to get into the consistent form that Richard Hadlee used to show in both facets of the game, batting and bowling. You only had to look at his body language last summer, when he was playing just as a batsman because he'd injured himself again, to see how frustrated he was.

It's irritated him, too, that he's played England's summers while missing so much of ours, but no one plans that. And Notts has been important to him. More than money, Notts actually gave him security; they offered him a contract. Everyone needs personal security. He didn't have a contract with New Zealand, after all, for some time.

I've very much enjoyed going back to Trent Bridge, the Nottingham county cricket ground, over the years to catch up with Cairnsie. It's always reminded me of the first time I stood there at the foot of the spiral staircase, nervously waiting to meet Richard Hadlee for the first time. Now, having played a bit of county cricket, I just stroll up sometimes – the Whitecoats are still there, but they recognise you. It was nice to go back there when I was 30, married and an international player of some 10 years' standing, going up to see another young bowler who wants to make an impact for his country's cricket.

Kim and I had a great time one August afternoon at Cairnsie and Ruth's in Nottingham, a good Kiwi barbecue. He was in really good spirits, it seemed things were getting on track for him at last. The next day we found out his sister had been killed in a train crash back in Canterbury. They'd had a hell night, coping with the shock and arranging to fly home. It knocked Cairnsie for six, naturally it was traumatic for him. But he flew back, after the funeral, to complete his commitments that summer to Notts. Later that year, in Australia, his body was suffering and people were ridiculing him for it; especially when he pulled out of a test match very late. I really don't think they knew how much he was giving of himself.

As much as being a son-of itself, it's sometimes been hard for Cairnsie as he's become caught in the middle of old personality conflicts between his father and other players of Lance's era. It was hard with Lance making comments in his column in the *Sunday News* about some of our coaches, like Geoff Howarth and Glenn Turner. Lance and Glenn particularly had not got on throughout their respective careers and I think that did pressure Chris.

In Bombay once we were next door to Turner's room when we heard all this yelling, doors slamming and a player storming out. It turned out Turner had questioned Chris' loyalty to the team.

The TV crew travelling with us had put on a barbecue function by the pool of our hotel that Friday when it was balmy, warm and the players just wanted a break. Guys had a few drinks, but they didn't go overboard. They were just doing light-hearted things like throwing CDs into the pool so that people had to dive in after them. It was two days before the deciding match in a one-day series, an important game – but the players felt that there was nothing wrong with having time out with a day still to come before the match. But Glenn didn't agree, and singled out the guys he thought had overdone the partying and decided to punish them with an extra training session in the afternoon. It was bad enough to split the camp like that, but Cairnsie's hamstring was also giving him trouble and so he simply refused to be pulled into this extra training carry-on. So Turner hauled Chris into his room for a meeting with the management committee – Turner, Gren Alabaster (the manager) and I think Lee Germon, our captain. It didn't sound like there was much management going on to us.

Cairnsie will always have an independent streak, a wild heart,

Humping on tour! Camel riding in Sharjah desert, 1994.

Seriously stressed out on the Caribbean tour, 1996.

Zimbabwe youth tour, 1988. Team manager Ken Deas telling more 'pork pies' at the snake farm . . .

. . . more wind and antics on the set of the famous baked beans commercial.

On tour for FADE (Foundation for Alcohol and Drug Education) – signing autographs at Westlake Boys' High School in 1989.

Out for a dip, or was that a duck? Winter training at Narrow Neck Beach, Auckland, 1989.

Calm before the storm. New Zealand takes the field at Nagpur, 1995. A section of the top tier of the stand collapsed, killing nine people.

Touring the subcontinent was always fascinating. Here's an example of local street industry.

D.K. Lillee and R.J. Hadlee – no greater inspiration for aspiring fast bowlers.

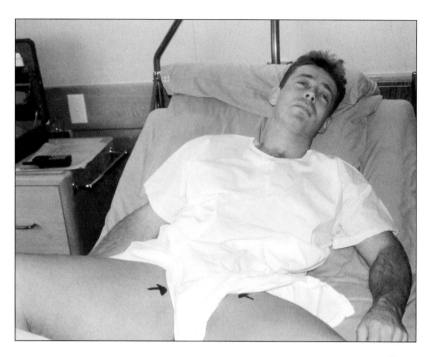

Operation Groin, Mk III, June 1996. Right: Nurse Nightingale, aka Kimberley Morrison, getting me through it.

Takapuna Grammar buddies helping me to celebrate my thirtieth birthday party at the North Shore Cricket Club, February 1996 . . .

. . . Birthday parties in the summer can be a bummer. Thank heavens for the rain!

My testimonial season was a challenging, but wonderful, time. Above: Dean Jones is merely signing a shirt! Below: Top testimonial team – a player couldn't have asked for more support.

but that's part of his make-up and it works for him. He's started to grow as he's got older. He's a key figure in the side now and I think he'll respond well to the responsibility. But there'll probably always be extra pressure on him to star for the team every time he plays, because he's such a big character, a big man, often having bowled with that wild hair bouncing everywhere. It's like he's physically on top of the batsman, in your face and with a lot to say as well. He thrives on the confrontation, a real showman and competitor, winding up especially the Australians if he can.

Because of that strong image, a lot of people wouldn't realise that it's not all fun and full on with Christopher. He's actually very thoughtful and when things aren't going well for him I've found it hard to communicate with him. He can go quiet on you, go into his shell. Sometimes he just feels the need to escape – even by reading a book. In a way it balances his energy.

He's aware, I think, that this merry-go-round of international cricket just isn't a real life in a way. He's also projected as a star and, aside from other people's expectations, he's the sort that really puts a lot of pressure on himself. Christopher needs to escape the new culture more than most. He's just got to realise you can, but you have to watch the timing.

It's hard to escape by yourself when you're on tour. You go out anywhere and you stand out like a sore thumb, because you have such a public profile. That applies to Christopher more than most. I was away playing Northern Districts last summer when Cairnsie was caught out late during the Wellington test match against England. I rang him to see how he was feeling and what was going on and it turned out he just needed to get away from it all for a bit, the frustrations of the lifestyle were getting to him. It was genuinely embarrassing to him after New Zealand Cricket had backed the players after problems with the Turner regime in the West Indies and it was embarrassing in the greater picture, with the game's sponsors speaking out about it. Without them, cricket doesn't survive. He was hurting. But I hope that will pass, that he'll get his chance to dominate as a true allrounder in world cricket. And that he shines.

MY WAY

Whenever there's been change during my career, be it in the team culture or the personnel, it's been drastic change. And usually it hasn't been handled well.

After the debacle of South Africa, Glenn Turner was appointed as New Zealand coach for the following season. As a personality and coach, Glenn was the south pole to Geoff Howarth's north. He was an intense, organised and disciplined person who actually seemed to be a bit of a control freak. Because of the perception that the side was full of out-of-control young players, he was seen as the antidote. But the change didn't stop there. Glenn was appointed not only as coach, but as convenor of selectors – he wasn't interested in the job otherwise, because he liked to have authority over which people he would be coaching in the side. Christopher Doig had also just taken over as New Zealand Cricket's executive director, Graham Dowling having retired after the centenary season. It was felt Glenn would have a lot of say in the new Doig era as to which players received contracts; he suddenly had a lot of power and for obvious reasons a lot of the players felt uncomfortable with the lack of balance in the set-up.

Completing the new world order, overnight Lee Germon had been elevated to the New Zealand captaincy. He'd been a world away that winter, playing club cricket in Haarlem, Holland, when

Turner was named coach. Turner wasn't a great admirer of Ken Rutherford, and Ken had chosen to accept a contract playing in South Africa the following southern summer rather than be dropped as captain or otherwise humiliated by Turner. While Martin Crowe didn't want to come back and captain because he couldn't guarantee his fitness with his knee. Germon had toured South Africa the season before as wicketkeeping back-up to Adam Parore, but he'd hardly played and had yet to play a test. He was the laundry boy on tour. It must have been quite a surprise to him to get a long distance phone call saying that not only was he replacing Adam as the New Zealand wicketkeeper, but Ruds as the New Zealand captain.

So a lot of roles had suddenly changed and it was a strange time when the band met up again for the first of Glenn's squad training camps near the end of winter. Everyone was finding their feet again and there was an added edge in that, as Glenn had been commentating on television for the last few years, some players couldn't help feeling uncomfortable because of the public, analytical criticisms he had made about them in the recent past.

Glenn had been my first experience of a New Zealand team coach back in 1987. The idea of national coaches was still pretty new then. It had been introduced around 1985. Until then, the captain and manager had always run the show. Being the junior on a steep learning curve I didn't interact with him a lot in 1987 and wasn't really in a position to get a sense of how it really worked with the guys, but I knew Glenn was very methodical and good at running practices. He did a lot of preparation, left little to chance. By the time of his next reign I had become much more involved within the side and was better placed to assess a coach's impact. It turned out that Glenn was still methodical and prepared, but the downside was he couldn't compromise.

Glenn's player management/people skills have already been publicly criticised. Certainly I found it hard to relate to him. Sometimes it was little things, like his sense of humour, and sometimes it was bigger issues. Usually I just felt he was quite remote, different and distanced from the team. But that was part of the way he liked to operate as coach. He wasn't big on patting someone on the back or using superlatives to say well done and he acknowledges that himself. If people thought Wally Lees was too emotionally attached and family-orientated within the team structure, Turner was the opposite. Personally I didn't think Wally deserved criticism for that; it was about making guys feel wanted and welcome, not "massaging egos". Glenn was more of a technical advisor, taking that role rather than helping guys emotionally.

But then again, Glenn, like the newly appointed team manager, Gren Alabaster (who'd taken the side to Australia in 1987 as our manager/coach), now came from a very different generation to the young players in the New Zealand side and maybe he found it hard to relate to us, too. It was a very different environment from the first time he'd coached the side in 1985/86. I think he felt the world had changed and that he couldn't sit down and have more of a personal, relaxed discussion with guys. But for us to approach him always felt like going to see the seventh form dean.

Cricket's such a hard, long game that it's difficult enough to get a happy balance in a side in normal circumstances, but with intransigent management the problem becomes an issue. Glenn was always quite defensive; the culture had changed so much since he'd played, yet he was uncompromising, inflexible on certain human emotion issues. I really don't think he could adapt well enough to the situation and at times the way Glenn talked to us was as if we were 15-year-olds at high school. We felt talked down to. He was the headmaster and I think he didn't know any other way.

Turns' theory was that he wanted us "to be more self-sufficient and accountable, not having to nurse us along". That was at the expense of nurturing the team, pumping the guys up. It was too unemotional. There was so much cricket played now that you needed that help to get the best out of yourself. But that was the way he wanted things to happen and it fitted with the big call for more discipline to be seen from the players.

Glenn wanted, and got, a disciplinary structure set up where the management team had the power to discipline and fine players for perceived misbehaviour. He had himself, the captain, Gren and Mark Plummer, the physio, on the management team. Plums hated it, being involved in that scenario – he was always a players' man, but he was seen by Turns as a longtime member of the squad and therefore senior. There were no senior pros holding it all together anymore, so it was really desperate measures trying to recreate that. I could see Glenn's intentions were good, but he went about it the wrong way, or at least the wrong way for that group of guys. They didn't react the way he intended.

Some of Glenn's changes verged on the ridiculous. When we toured at home, Glenn had us staying in smaller hotels than normal, for example out in a motel at Greenlane in Auckland instead of the usual, bigger hotel in the city. The feeling was that would make us focus more on our cricket, because it would be harder to cruise out to the restaurants and bars downtown in the evenings. He could keep a better eye on us. But it was too much of a change, with guys and all their gear suddenly cramped into small rooms. All that happened was that guys started feeling more disgruntled about life on the road than ever.

The same mindset entered our training environment. At the World Cup in 1996 Turns noticed the South Africans' militaristic approach to cricket, the way the whole team would get up early and assemble for breakfast quite early in the morning, the way they were always well drilled and regimented. His eyes lit up and he decided that we would be well drilled, too. He set a team policy that meant we all had to come down to breakfast at 7am, because that was the time you needed to be up on matchdays. But these weren't matchdays and guys wanted to sleep in. Shane Thomson hated it, he's not a morning person and didn't like going down to breakfast at all. His routine was to have room service and that worked for him. Some other guys like to make up their own breakfasts with tonic drinks and powerbars and so on. It didn't suit a lot of the players, so it became an aggravation you didn't really need in the middle of an overseas campaign. But if anyone was late, you got the full fine. Adam Parore was 25 minutes late one morning because he'd been on the phone to New Zealand. He had to report to Glenn and Gren. It was real school dormitory stuff.

Gav Larsen is a mild-mannered, very nice guy, but at that World Cup we saw even Gav get really angry. We usually trained at 9.30am, but because Turns didn't like us lying around in the morning after breakfast, he decided we would train earlier, at 8am. At that time of morning the ground, even in India and Pakistan, would often be greasy with dew. Glenn had us doing shuttle runs and drills one such morning; Gav slipped and pulled his calf muscle badly. He was fuming. We were training twice a day at this stage, in the afternoons as well; why the hell couldn't we have done the shuttles in the afternoon session, when the grounds were dry? It cost Gav the chance to play in three matches, including our last, the big quarter-final against Australia.

The more things change, the more things stay the same. Just as Howarth hadn't changed his style from tour to tour, by the time we got to the West Indies at the end of that summer, the discipline call was like a stuck record. Even before the test series began, in Grenada, where we'd been stuffed by a President's XI, losing a four-dayer in two and a half days, the tensions were surfacing. It had been a long summer, almost non-stop touring from Darwin in September – and now it was nearly May. A lot of the players were mentally and physically tired and really wanted a break.

Because the match was over early, Roger Twose had an

opportunity to go on a diving course with his partner there in the Caribbean the following day, but Turns would have none of it. Because we'd lost the match badly, he ordered a compulsory – and long – open wicket training session for that day instead. Twosey actually asked him if it was possible to alter the time of the session to allow guys to have a break as well and the answer was a flat "no."

That time in the Grenadines was really the point of no return in terms of the team spirit on that tour. Better man management would have been to step back and identify the tensions – we'd been a long time on the road, away from home and guys were nitpicking, getting a bit short with each other. We'd already won a few games, after all, before the loss. Even when you love it, you can get too saturated with cricket. We'd also just bowled last in the game and our bodies could have done with the time off, recovery time. But moreover, mentally, if you can go away and freshen up, you come back with more desire to play hard. Regardless of Twosey wanting to do his dive class with his lady, it would have been beneficial if we'd all just had a day relaxing, doing our own thing. We needed a compromise, flexibility, a release. But we got the opposite. Tired players were being made to practise and it was supposed to be good for us. As it was, Dion Nash, who'd already struggled physically through the previous tour match at St Vincent, practised and broke down. All he'd needed was a rest. He ended up unable to play for the rest of the tour.

It's interesting to note that John Hart makes a point of sending the All Blacks home from camp after a match during their long test seasons now, for some time out and normalcy. He also has a central policy of player consultation – he believes that if players take ownership of a game, have input themselves into the decisions about how the rugby is run or how a tour is run, then they will have a vested interest in taking personal responsibility to see their gameplan work. I think he's right. It's also smart management and I wish we'd had it in the West Indies, because the tour was turning into a nightmare in paradise.

We'd done reasonably well in the one-day phase of the tour by that stage, the West Indies taking the series only narrowly, 3-2. But in Trinidad, after what was our first ever international victory in the Caribbean, it had been decided not to organise a celebratory gathering and put drinks on for the team. Management had to give the team's social committee the OK to do something like that. When permission wasn't granted, the guys felt quite sad. It was a missed opportunity for togetherness. Now, in Grenada, after our military open wicket training exercise, a team meeting was held and it got quite unpleasant.

A lot of the guys were by now really feeling uncomfortable and quite stressed on tour and put it to the tour management group that they felt they were getting a bit stale – and just wanted to have more input into the daily organisation of team things. But Turner was unrelenting. He seemed to impress that we were questioning his authority by wanting to have an open forum and input in the first place. Instead we were supposed to follow his instinct. Lee Germon was a big Frank Sinatra man on tour and we had no trouble picking out the theme song for Glenn . . .

Cairnsie was very outspoken. He's got a thick streak of bravery in him and wanted to stand up not just for himself, but for the team, because he felt the success of the tour was being jeopardised. But it didn't earn him any respect from Glenn. His frustration only grew. After he was sidelined from the first test with injury, he left the tour, flying to England. He ended up in action for Nottinghamshire while we were playing the second test, which earned him a lot of public censure back home. But the atmosphere had degenerated so much in the Caribbean that, had he stayed, Glenn and Lee would have been unlikely to have got the best out of him. Christopher knew the way he'd handled it wasn't wise, but it was the stress at work. He couldn't tolerate that sort of environment and that's what he was saying. At least he had the security of county cricket and it was a better place to be right then.

Cairnsie was an outspoken example of what most of the team was feeling. There really was an unhealthy energy around. The hard thing was that you could see that, unlike Cairnsie, most of the guys were scared of shooting themselves in the foot if they disagreed with Glenn. The management team, particularly Glenn, had too much power, too much say back home over their careers, their contracts. Younger guys felt the management had them by the balls and didn't want to say anything, especially after seeing how Cairnsie had been treated. So instead guys were talking amongst themselves, getting grumpy, disgruntled and disillusioned with what was going on, hating the fact they were on tour. We'd left New Zealand on Waitangi Day to go to the World Cup, it would be a total of three and a half months until we got home – the longest time most of these guys had ever spent on the road together – and there was a truckload of travelling to be done across the scattered islands of the Caribbean. The West Indies sounds like a glamorous place to be, but there were times when no one wanted to be on that tour. We felt trapped there.

When Lee had been drafted in as New Zealand captain, it was said that he, like Glenn, would have the right personality to improve the discipline in the team ranks. But, to be honest, while I think the side did need more discipline, the obsession with it took precedence over the balance of the side and putting the best players on the park.

With Lee, the bottom line was he wasn't good enough as a player. He tried, but he wasn't. Adam Parore was our best keeper and a good batsman, as he'd already shown at New Zealand level. Adam's strengths were sacrificed in the name of order, but it didn't work.

I could appreciate the dilemma the selectors were in trying to find someone who could lead the side for two or three years. Someone like Mark Greatbatch could have done it well, but wasn't a guaranteed selection for both test and one-day cricket. Flem was too young, he needed more confidence and experience. And the rest were also too young or couldn't guarantee our physical fitness to be there to do the job, which is the case with a lot of bowlers. We didn't have a natural leader to step in and take over and it's disappointing when someone gets that role by default.

Lee had an undeniably good record with Canterbury, they were unparalleled in domestic cricket; but for New Zealand he had to be the best player, as well as the best captain, available in his position. Regardless of your first-class record, international cricket's a huge mental step up, for all of us. We're brought up on a workbench of slow, indifferent surfaces, quite different to most around the world, in a country where cricket is not the number one sport and there is a lot of competition from other codes. You get many guys performing well at first-class level here, but those are the reasons they're often inconsistent at international level. Look at Chris Harris and Dipak Patel; they've dominated our first-class cricket, but overseas they've struggled. They're not alone, by any means. It's partly mental, it's partly experience and it's the harsh reality. Not enough great players come through to counter that tendency. That's why the 1980s were so great; for once, they did.

You just know when people take the ball well at the top level and I think Lee's keeping just wasn't up to the highest standard. It's very easy to be critical, but as I believe Howarth couldn't make the step up to his role in the international set-up as coach, nor could Lee. You have to be the best to make it work when you get there.

Lee's appointment was also a dramatic change because it upset the balance of the batting order with him batting seven or eight. Because he wasn't as good a batsman as Adam, it put pressure on the middle order and also on the bowlers. If we'd had Adam keeping and batting higher up, we could have played two spinners and three seamers, including Cairnsie as the allrounder. But with Lee, usually we had one spinner and, say, myself, Nash and Cairns. It made life just that little bit more difficult. Lee was promoted to three in the World Cup. A couple of times it came off; he played well in the quarter-final against the Australians, and got a 50 in the West Indies. But, particularly when Rixon later took over the side, the feeling that he was upsetting the balance lingered. Chris Harris, for example, could have played a lot more tests as an allrounder this last season had Adam been able to keep and bat six or seven. We lost that edge and again you got that frustrated energy throughout the team.

The other tragedy about it all was that you have to have a captain who can command respect from the players, who has that certain mana, and to do that you really have to have been around and performed, become worldly. That's the hard cold fact. Whether it's sport or business, you have to come up through the ranks. This was like a clerk being promoted to CEO overnight.

It was hard for Lee having no experience at that level, other than as a tourist in South Africa. Because of it, he would end up clashing with some of us older guys – and it wasn't just me. It was a difficult situation for everyone. When I look back at it, I can only sympathise with him. It's a big ask to debut as captain and it was particularly tough going for Lee to have to start with a rain-affected series and things not going well for us in the harsh climate of India. He was up against it from the beginning.

Perhaps because he'd never really cemented his place in the team structure, as captain Lee would spend a lot of time with the management crew rather than with the players. That was unfortunate, because it created an "us and them" feeling. It was like Upstairs, Downstairs; players felt separate from the management team. You'd often see Turner and Lee and Lee's finacée Toni dining together. You could see that Gren tried to redress that situation more with the players, but he'd been drained by the cricket season's length. The manager's job was heavy enough and there were times when you could see he was so tired. He'd fall asleep at the ground, sometimes, during match days.

Overall I felt the management team's style was too dictatorial rather than consultative. You'd find out what was happening after decisions had been made – and weren't asked whether you agreed with them or could cope with them. You'd get instructions under your door instead of in a meeting which weren't necessarily the best or wisest decisions. You seemed to be finding out everything second-hand and that would reinforce the aloofness, the separateness. In

Pakistan on one occasion one of the guys had mistakenly been given a confidential fax for Lee from New Zealand Cricket. It discussed details critical about some guys' behaviour at a time when contracts were being negotiated, and happened to mention a job possibility for Lee through their contacts. That really underlined the "us and them" situation.

We felt that Lee was Glenn's right-hand man. At the same time, you understood the difficult position Lee was in; Glenn had put him in that job, changed Lee's career overnight. I'm sure that because Glenn had given Lee the opportunity, he felt obligated to Glenn in that regard. But for the rest of us, it only added to the concerns we had about the imbalance of power.

In Grenada, Cairnsie had approached Lee, whom he'd known for years in Canterbury. Cairnsie tried to explain why the players felt they needed to have a forum with the management committee and said to Lee that it was an opportunity for him to back the guys, to make them feel he was part of the team. But in the meeting, Lee stuck with the management. People were forced to take sides.

It was frustrating that Lee had no say on behalf on the players, and that was the case not only off the field, but on it. There were numerous run-in situations where our opinions conflicted with the coach's, but it was made clear his philosophy wasn't going to change. Glenn was calling the shots and strategies and Lee had to follow them. Glenn was such a strong character that he was holding it over Lee, whose place without him was insecure. No matter how often Lee said he "wasn't Glenn's puppet", that was the impression we got. The most positive thing about Lee was that he always gave 100 per cent of himself. He did feel the honour of leading his country deeply and always believed he could change the team culture for the benefit of the team. He was continually trying, but his efforts would be stunted by Glenn. I could see Glenn pulling him in, giving him little freedom. I felt sorry for him.

Far too many times over the Turner era, when we wanted to bat first, Glenn said we had to bowl. It was particularly frustrating when we were playing a day-nighter. A lot of the guys told Glenn that it was hard to see the ball batting second under lights, when it was swinging around, but he wanted us to bowl first because then we'd have two bites at the cherry; if you bowl first and it doesn't go too well, you still have a chance to dominate with your batting. If, on the other hand, it does go well, you can put the guys under pressure. It was supposed to be good for our confidence after a bad few seasons, but we'd be crying inside when we'd see these beautiful, flat wickets – whether we were playing Zimbabwe at home or over at the World Cup or in the West Indies – knowing we would have to bowl first even if we won the toss, surrendering the natural advantage.

As a strategist, Turns could be quite defensive, protective against failure instead of attacking for the win. Perhaps that was a sign of the times, or just the opening batsman in him, always looking to defend his wicket. I remember one particular moment during our first game at the World Cup that seemed to sum him up. England had won the toss and we'd been put in to bat. Later, when we were fielding, I was sweating like a pig and had to come off to change my trousers and shirt. I remember jogging past Turns; he was freaking out, very uneasy that we didn't have enough runs on the board (we'd got 239/6 after Nath made a hundred). As it was, we dug deep and won the game.

The defensive mentality had been there all along. Years before, at the previous World Cup in the subcontinent, Turns' theory then as coach was that we would bowl leg-stump yorkers to cramp the batsmen. He was asking the bowlers (without Hadlee) to do something that was very difficult, to deliver a classic line of middle and leg yorkers. If you got it slightly wrong, straying outside off-stump, or if it was even slightly overpitched, in India it would often be a six. You'd be drop-kicked out of the park or through the gap. Turner knew that, because he used to do it himself as a batsman.

Our guys weren't Waqar Younises, even then. Chats bowls length. When Chats tried to bowl at the death against the Australians in Chandigarh, doing what he was told and trying to tuck it into them, it was like a fish out of water and he was belted out of the park. Then I remember the Indians going inside Willie and putting him over cover, because there would be no man on the fence there, hardly anyone on the off-side – just third man, point and mid-off. The Asians were such good, wristy players that Turns' theory didn't stand a chance. It was embarrassing to watch, actually, all these fielders standing helplessly on the leg side. But Turner was inflexible about the gameplan and Jeff Crowe, the captain, had had to accept it.

Lee was a *déjà vu* of all that. Under him, I don't think the bowlers were utilised well. I felt Lee didn't get the best out of me at all – and that was frustrating. Worse, you felt you couldn't talk to anyone about it, couldn't talk to the manager or coach. He tried to get the best out of Cairnsie, the attacking weapon who'd just come off a great season at Notts in 1995, and that worked at times. But in the West Indies Cairnsie, you could see, was becoming a spent force, with his exasperation at the inflexibility of the regime before the test series, the fact we couldn't sit around and openly discuss how we should play the conditions coming up because we had to follow the dictatorial pattern.

The situation drained Lee as much as it did the team. You could almost see it wasn't Lee on the park there – the Canterbury guys in our team all felt that, too. Lee would try to communicate with the players on the park, but you could see from his body language that it just got to him at times. If the action plan failed, he wasn't allowed to change mid-stream. All of us felt like a piece of machinery, a cog in the machine rather than a human with thoughts, ideas and emotional reactions.

Unfortunately, Lee also had a particular smug giggle and a smile that made him look like an arrogant, smartarse schoolboy. It sent out the wrong message and, with all the frustration, a few of us couldn't help bouncing him in the nets. Guys wanted you to hit him. At times it got to you and you did. You'd vent your spleen in the nets. It was sad and it was nasty.

The funny thing was that in our first-class game at St Vincent against a West Indian Board XI, which Justin Vaughan captained when a few players, including Lee, were given a rest, everything went a lot better. Turner had decided before the match that we would bowl first, because we'd get a better workout if it did something early on. The locals had all told us that if we won the toss we should bat, because the pitch assistance was negligible – and we would get a workout anyway, no matter when we bowled. But the decision was made and there was to be no consultation.

Justin Vaughan, who was my captain for Auckland, had come over as a late reinforcement on tour during the one-day series and so, as an outsider, hadn't been affected by the confrontations and the history that had been brewing within the team. When Glenn said he wanted us to bowl first, Justin just said no. He said our best chance of winning was by using the wicket at its best and bowling them out second. Justin won the toss, we batted first – and won by 156 runs, bowling them out for 209 in the second innings. But Glenn gave Justin a hard time, accepting it only after we'd won the game.

It was the same scenario when we went to Grenada for our next match; we wanted to bat first because the locals had all told us the pitch did a little bit for the first hour and then panned right out – it actually got like plasticine, quite sticky. But now Germon was the captain and he had to follow Turns' gameplan. Turns said we were to use it as a practice situation as he felt the pitch was denting. He believed we should bowl first. We won the toss and we bowled. The locals couldn't believe it. We got one wicket early, then they smashed 454. That was the match we lost in two and a half days.

Throughout his time as captain Lee shouldered a lot of blame in the media and from the public, for supposedly calling the wrong gameplan time and again. But my criticism is not so much of Lee as of Glenn. You can still feel in the side today the "us and them" situation that he created with the management structure. It eroded a lot of trust. Funnily enough, I found out afterwards that when Glenn won the coaching position in the first place, beating out Jeff Hammond, the Australian, John Hart had been on a subcommittee making the appointment. Hart had recommended that if Glenn were to be picked, then it was important that a different personality type, someone more like Wally Lees in character, be placed on the tour management structure to balance his severe personality. It wasn't followed through.

BODY AND SOUL

I was built to be a wicketkeeper or a batsman in cricket, not to open the bowling. When I was 18 years old, I went to see a physiotherapist in Birkenhead and she told me that because of my build and short spine, if I really wanted to be a fast bowler I was going to be on the table a lot. Sure enough, my whole career I've been on and off physio tables and chopping boards.

What I was trying to achieve with my body was so demanding that I learned to go through the pain barrier early. I'd read my Bible – Dennis Lillee's *The Art of Fast Bowling*, which showed pictures of his back and described the pain he was sometimes in. He said it's up to you how much pain you can take and that you have to put in hard yards to keep your body as strong and balanced as possible to hold off injury.

I first seriously injured myself in 1984 when I was still a teenager, but those early, frustrating years of struggling with it actually put me in good stead for the future. I learned how to deal with injury and look after my body. I bought and slept in a thermal back brace to keep the injured area warm. It's like a wetsuit material, with a velcro fastening. My wife calls it my contraceptive suit. Sometimes I've slept with a couple of thigh ones and an ankle brace, too, because the best time for the body to heal is when you're asleep. After my dear grandmother customised it for me I also wore the back brace bowling all day, and even practising.

Maintenance and recovery have been a large part of my life as a cricketer and with it comes the need to train relentlessly. Generally as I built up to a season I'd train six days a week, with both gym and aerobic work, and recuperate on Sunday. Sometimes that meant putting on a wetsuit and hitting the ocean with a cut-down board and flippers in the middle of winter to help strengthen key areas of my frame. But, like Jim Blair used to say to us at the Institute of Sport in Auckland, "It's tough enough getting to the top, it's even harder staying there."

As a fast bowler your action is really cast in stone in your teenage days. After that it's all fine tuning. My delivery stride is quite demanding on a short body; I have a high leap and long, dragging delivery stride. Chris Cairns laughs that my style is a 1950s action, the dragging foot like Fred Trueman's, Harold Larwood's, Frank Tyson's or Ray Lindwall's. But if you think about it, most of those with the slugger actions weren't big men, either. It would have been better for me to have bowled like Malcolm Marshall, who is of similar stature but ran through the crease more, but when I tried that, it was like trying to teach an old dog new tricks. I'd built up a biomechanical pattern that was difficult to remould. I experimented with it in 1990 in some county games and in a test match at Edgbaston – Martin Crowe called me "Malcolm Morrison". But I wasn't getting my ultimate rhythm and pace working. It was also bleak, quite cold, and as I tried to push my body through, I felt my groin go on me.

I'm sure the public get sick of hearing about injuries and how often our bowlers break down, but really, it's such an abnormal thing to do to your body, twisting and leaping and contorting and slamming yourself down into the turf, that injury is virtually inevitable. Lillee compared it to being a decathlete in terms of physical strain on your body. That's why bowling injuries are usually unlike rugby injuries, for instance. You often hear of rugby injuries occurring as a result of sudden impact incidents on field. Bowling injuries tend to be the result of what you do, day in, day out, to your body – almost like occupational overuse syndrome. That's the difference. You have to accept that injury is part and parcel of the function you're trying to perform. Merv Hughes and Craig McDermott both wrecked their knees for Australia; they have no cartilage left between the bone, pounding on those hard Aussie decks burned it out. The slighter Bruce Reid had a weaker back, he landed on the scrapheap, too. The harsh reality is that you're just another brick to be used.

I've never had knee problems; my frame is stronger in the quads than taller men. But my groin suffers and as an area where many parts of the body are intertwined, it's very hard to strap it and keep it flexible, hard to put on a warming sleeve. It's frustrating, but I'm not complaining. At least I've had 10 good years of international cricket. I look across to someone like Dion Nash, who's had so much injury to his back and sides so young and doesn't know whether he will be able to come back and contend seriously at the top level again. I think of Dion a lot around this time as I'm finishing up, sad he may not be able to simply run in and bowl fast anymore. I was relatively lucky and I'm grateful for it.

Batsmen, of course, seldom understand. I remember my last game of the season late in March 1997; Auckland beat Otago. I'd run in and bowled 15 overs on the trot, most of the session. Afterwards, Richard Jones and I were having a quiet beer together on the balcony of the Lone Star Cafe in Queenstown. Richard, who's 23 and bats in the top order, said to me, "Why can't you bowl like that all the time for us? Put more in like that?" It was a classic case of a batsman not understanding what you mentally and physically go through as a bowler running in and bowling fast, dealing with the frustration of beating the bat and having catches go down . . .

After you've had three groin operations, two hernias and an adductor tendon release, you certainly realise that what it takes to run in and bowl fast (*and* survive a whole season all on the wrong side of 30) is demanding. The eternal problem is that while there's pressure on you to perform at your best every time you take the ball, there's also pressure on you to manage your body well so that you can play the whole season. Balancing those pressures is a learning curve. I really learned about knowing when to switch on or switch off from my early discussions with Richard Hadlee. He'd talk about bowling "effort balls" when he was going to get more reward, when he had a batsman "on toast" and could go for the jugular; or when the pitch or conditions merited it. But there are other occasions you have to bide your time, think the batter out more and be patient. We don't produce that many express bowlers who can run in and get up people, bounce them and take them on, hurry them up trying to play a hook shot, gloving them off their face; we just haven't got the conditions to warrant guys running in and doing that enough. You're also bowling to the team gameplan. All this at the same time as realising you're only as good as your last performance! It takes a lot of fine-tuning. It's not about being in cruise mode; it's about getting the best out of yourself.

Because so many injuries have hit the New Zealand bowling corps since Hadlee's last summers at the end of the eighties, we've lost our way sometimes in cultivating bowling as a team. The personnel turns over too quickly to develop a reliable scenario where one guy ties up an end and another attacks, the way Chats and Hadlee used to operate. But you only have to look at English cricket to see the reason. England has struggled to maintain a steady attack, because their guys play so much county cricket that they become more liable to injury. They mow through their quicks, a high turnover because the players are ground down on the county circuit. No one English quick's stood out and hung around to dominate this decade. They also have more financial incentive to play for their county than for England because there's more money and security in it – it's a crazy system.

Injury first struck me down after coming back from my first sweet summer at Harefield in 1984 because I didn't have enough warm-up, warm-down and stretching disciplines when I was young, raw, feeling bulletproof and charging in to bowl like Dennis Lillee. When I got the pain checked out, it was quite a common bowling injury (an estimated 80 per cent of international fast bowlers suffer it); spondylolisthesis of the L5 vertebra in the lower back. In other words, a shift in my lower lumbar area, a tilt in the curvature set off by planting my foot down. It put me right out of the 1984/85 summer and I suddenly realised how much fitter, stronger and aware I had to be to survive.

To be injury-free when bowling fast, you need to be front on or side on – anywhere in-between and injuries can occur. My thoracic curvature is more accentuated than normal; it flexes forward slightly from having built up my shoulders through bowling, my spine tending to slump forward over my pelvis. So I've had to build up the lower abdominal muscles to straighten my upper back and incorporate all the muscle groups to help establish a balance. Realistically, with the bowling action I have, this becomes difficult to maintain and hence niggles result.

The first really professional management I received was through Hayhow and Edwards at the Institute of Sport in 1985, which lasted until about 1991, when the arrangement between them and Auckland Cricket petered out. I lost my way a little bit after that as it switched back to players having to organise their own gym training, having to use pretty much their own ideas instead of professional advice. In the early 90s I was having a lot more groin problems. I was also moving into my mid-20s by then; I'd stopped growing, filled out and was getting older. My body was moulded through training, but from 1990 we were also playing and touring so much more that trying to get to the gym in between matches for strength and flexibility workouts was harder to do. So two major forces were happening to me at the same time; age and the effects of the increased itineraries. Now I look back at the 1989 and 1990 summers and see there wasn't enough emphasis on maintaining my work with weights in the gym, even if it was using the facility in the hotel on the road, which you did a bit, but not enough. Usually you were weary and sore from bowling, plus you had your team trainings; after that you were even more fatigued, physically and mentally, and just wanted to chill out. The last thing you wanted was to go and do an hour in the hotel gym. There was little structure and direction for motivation and guidance.

By the 1992 World Cup I was struggling with my right adductor muscle and strained it against the West Indies. You'd get massage, acupuncture and strapping to try to keep on top of it, speed up the healing process, but you were always pushing time so you could get back playing again. There was no time to really normalise the muscle group in question. By the time I was in the thick of county cricket later that year, I'd really started to feel uncomfortable high up in the lower abdomen wall. It would be a sharp pain – it hurt to lean over or sneeze. I struggled through a match against Northampton in July and then consulted a specialist, Dr Ian McLennan, at the Royal Manchester Hospital. My goal was to play the whole season for Lancs and I was hoping he would say it was just another episode of the groin strain. But, after two weeks of physio, it hadn't gone away and he diagnosed the hernia. Builders get a lot of them through heavy lifting and other physical work. For me, it was an accident waiting to happen and a lot of bowlers – McDermott, Hughes, Wasim Akram and a lot of English players – have had hernia operations also.

I didn't want to be cut open, but I had no choice if I wanted to keep playing for New Zealand. It was a really down, emotional time for me. My goal of lasting the season was gone and the thought of being operated on was daunting when I'd worked so hard to fine tune my body. I realised it was a major setback, as it had been with my back when I was 18, and there was tentativeness in my mind as to whether I could come back as soon as I wanted.

The hospital was private, paid for through the Lancashire County Cricket Club's insurance. It was nicely done – you had menus, a television in your own room, like a hotel with doctors and nurses running round, but it still didn't put you quite at ease when you knew you were facing your first surgery. Hernias have tended to be more common in men than in women. It's like a fine mesh of muscle in your abdomen coming apart, tearing and then rolling up into a ball. The open surgery procedure ties it back up. I was stapled up, rather then stitched, and the surgeon placed mesh over it which was to stay on for some time. Just one day after the surgery I had to start physio; you have to get out of bed and walk. I had to go down a flight of stairs and come back up, to keep moving so I didn't get too much scar tissue seizing me up. I felt nauseous, faint, very weak. It was so painful and I was very grumpy with the poor hospital physiotherapist.

That hernia was on my right side; two years later I got one on my left. I'd had a few niggles on the Sharjah and England tour in 1994 and torn my left biceps femoris, which is one of the hamstring muscles. My lower back was having problems, too; it was all connected. So I came home from that tour and had to rest the hamstring, hoping it would heal quickly. An MRI scan revealed a longitudinal tear that seemed to take a long time to heal. Weeks went by and I was still feeling uncomfortable in the left upper groin. I went to a specialist, Dr Robert Fris, who told me my abdominal wall was like a rusty bridge waiting to collapse. If I'd been an accountant or lawyer, Dr Fris said I wouldn't have needed to worry about it. But to be a fast bowler, it was vital to have repairs done. Instead of open surgery he recommended a laparoscopic procedure that Craig McDermott had had.

The operation was at a Southern Cross hospital in Auckland – we didn't have full insurance in those days so New Zealand Cricket paid a third, ACC paid a third and I paid a third myself. They put three holes in me, one inside my belly button. They went in through the bellybutton with an endoscope lens. Then they blew me up like a rugby ball and positioned a piece of fibreglass mesh and stapled it over the hernia through the other two holes. I've got the whole procedure on video. The fibreglass is in there for keeps; it's very flexible, bendy stuff and your own muscle fibres intertwine through it, like the wire mesh in a concrete driveway.

I felt more down and upset about this operation than the first; it came ahead of New Zealand's first tour to South Africa in 30 years and I wanted to make that tour, to go to my mother's birthplace so badly . . . The laparoscopic procedure offered me a quicker recovery, so I still hoped to be fit in time for the tour, but then I came down with a cold the week before the operation and anaesthetists won't proceed when you have a respiratory problem.

So I was feeling altogether frustrated when I was discharged the day after the operation, pain all over my body. You'd absolutely grovel going to the loo.

Unfortunately for me it was the whole 2-4-6 scene because after those operations in 1992 and 1994 two years later the groin went again. It was part three of the trilogy and a real nuisance. In June of 1996 I had a bilateral adductor tendon release operation with Dr Paul Armour in Christchurch. A lot of footy players have that – Justin Marshall, for instance. The adductor tendon inserts into the pelvic bone, running up from the inside of your leg. The operation relieves the area where you become so developed and strong that it's just too tight. They cut the tendon and trim it away: there are two other tendons that take over its role, moving your leg in and out. By clearing out the scar tissue after you've repeatedly strained and torn it, it gives you a greater range of movement.

It's also got a very vigorous rehab and was more sensitive than the hernias; at times I'd be doubled over in pain. I even had a catheter inserted into my bladder at 2am, eight hours after the operation, due to the anaesthetic numbing that region.

I didn't have to have that op. I could have taken the gamble that it would come right. But I wanted to get the groin fixed once and for all and to just get on with it. That was how badly I wanted to keep playing.

But by the time we went to Sharjah and Pakistan at the start of the 1997 summer, I hadn't done enough adductor pulley work with free swinging weights, trying to build myself up again; I just ran out of time. I'd been having a lot of ultrasound to break down the scar tissue to keep on top of it and was doing a lot of exercises with physios to gain enough power to bowl fast, but I underestimated how much strength I needed there. When I look back, I tried to come round the wicket to bounce Saeed Anwar on the slow, lifeless deck in the Sharjah Stadium. That opened me up more in my action and I just felt it go in the adductor area. I was silly. We'd had a very short, limited build-up and I don't normally come around the wicket. I ended up missing the Sharjah final. Then, in Sahiwal in Pakistan, on the very first ball of the match, I leapt into my delivery stride and just felt it click as if one tendon rubbed over another. I was sent home, though personally I felt I would have come right quickly enough to play more of the tour. When I came back home, a nice touch was that a man named Colin White, a pighunter from Wanganui, rang me and suggested hillwalking with a backpack on as part of my rehab, to make my groin and abdominal areas stronger. He said he and his rugby mates never suffered from abdominal injuries because they carried packs and animal carcasses over hilly country on their shoulders! It was genuine concern from a member of the public and it made a lot of sense.

I always felt confident I'd keep coming back. I knew it would be hard work, slogging through my build-up. Wanting to run in and bowl fast, but sometimes having to be patient and hold back. The desire always remained.

I'm very grateful that my wife and family always gave me extra support through the times I'd be very down with injury, was working hard to rehabilitate or was grinding through the training. Kim's experience in remedial massage has been an absolute luxury for me and if Kim was full on with her massage clients, my mother-in-law, Annie Talbot, took over. Annie has done a sports therapy course and has helped me with massage, stretching and programmes for different muscle groups. The family worked as a team.

My mother also introduced me to self-hypnosis after she'd done a course herself. I did my first weekend course with Brian Head in 1990, then Kim and I did a further course a couple of years ago. It was about visualisation, believing in yourself, using key thoughts to help yourself get over injuries, going down to alpha state, getting your body very relaxed and in tune. I found it jarring listening to American voices on the hypnosis tapes, though, so my mother made one up for me in her voice, which was very good. It helped me relax in hectic, stressful times; I'd listen to one before I went to sleep. Feeding myself the right thoughts was like eating the right food, it became part of my self-management, helping me cope.

In more ways than one, playing cricket turned into quite a medical adventure for me. One of the most startling moments came in 1990 when I had a CAT scan on my lower back and Doc Mayhew casually asked, "Dan, you realise you've only got a right kidney?" I was 24 and this was the first I'd heard of it, but it started to make a lot of sense. I'd often felt quite dehydrated playing sport and would get feelings of being run down when I shouldn't have been.

I also have low blood pressure and would sometimes feel quite dizzy during cricket. That came into play at a test match against India at Napier in 1990, though the action was all off the field. It had drizzled the morning of the first day so the test match started late. The team had stood around waiting for lunch for hours and I hadn't had breakfast that morning, either, so when the hot roast meal and salad arrived we all just started troughing in. I ate a piece of potato that had steam pouring off it. It was burning my mouth so I gulped it and it got stuck in my throat – you know that awful feeling of a hard, overcooked edge of a potato in your throat? I grabbed for the orange juice and started feeling nauseous with this hot coal trapped in my gullet.

Ian Smith was sitting opposite me with Martin Crowe and Mark

Plummer behind me in the cramped arrangement of tables. I suddenly dropped forward and nosedived into my food. I ricocheted back up, with surprise I suppose, and my eyes rolled back so Smithy could see just the whites. He thought that was a neat trick, that I was just being silly for Lucy, Martin Snedden's young daughter, who was sitting near us. He said something to that effect, but I didn't hear any of it and rolled backwards, whacking Martin Crowe on the left ear. Crowey looked round with a start and there was Dan slumped backwards on his shoulder with his eyes rolled back. Crowey freaked! Having collapsed off the chair, I woke up some 30 seconds later thinking, geez, this is noisy in bed here . . . Then I could feel a finger in my mouth; it was Plums checking I hadn't swallowed my tongue. The blood was draining back into my brain and I couldn't work out where I was. All I could see was Annie Snedden's legs!

Everyone had scattered; apparently I'd convulsed. The ambulance was called. They laid me out in the women's toilets and checked my blood pressure and everything for half an hour. Then I went to the dressing room. Smithy and the boys were very grumpy with me because everyone had been put off their lunch.

In 1990, during a practice match against a President's XI in Karachi, my thoracic/back area spasmed on me and I couldn't breathe. Crowey looked at me and said, "Dan, you're not going on us again, are you?" The boys thought I was convulsing again, as in Napier. It scared some of them. The doctors call it vasovagal, like people blacking out at the sight of blood. I've mainly blacked out at home.

Like most cricketers, my body's particularly suffered on tour in the Indian subcontinent. The worst I've ever felt was in Bangalore in 1988, when almost the entire team went down with a feverish illness. There was a rest day in the middle of the test there and we all went to a cricket function, put on after Richard Hadlee had broken the world test wicket-taking record that match. Watches were handed out to us all and we had a couple of beers to celebrate the record, some Golden Wing or Thunderbolt. The beer in India isn't great; it says it's "7 to 15 per cent" on the bottles, but if you turn it upside down, you see the glycerine shooting up the top. I remember Bryan Waddle getting a jug full of water and tipping a beer into it: you could see the glycerine float down through it.

So instead we decided to have a couple of scotches for a nightcap. We knew the rules about drinking in India; no ice and watch the lid of the coke bottle being taken off before it's poured in front of you. But the waiter came out with ice in the drinks. We said, "Sorry buddy, we can't have ice." So he took them back and I think he put his fingers in the drinks, took out the ice and just poured them into fresh glasses. He wouldn't have thrown anything away; that didn't happen in India. But we didn't know. We had those nightcaps and then went back to the hotel around midnight.

I was rooming with big Trevor Franklin. I'd won the toss for the double bed and Franko had had to place a chair for his feet that hung over his little bed. Franko was a bit grumpy, because I wasn't even playing and he was!

That night, I started to feel nauseous. Then I threw up in the bath. Before long it was coming out of both ends and I was grovelling with a fever in the middle of the night.

Franko was calling out from his short little bed giving me a hard time: "Bad luck, Dan . . . too much to drink, eh?"

He rung up for some ice and when it arrived I asked the Indian hotel guy to just throw it on me. He thought I was mad, and wouldn't. But the water in India isn't cold – it's tepid – so I got the bucket of ice myself and just writhed naked in it on this cold marble floor with a tepid flannel on my face. I was burning up.

Later that night, Franko had to go to the bathroom. Suddenly he didn't feel too good either and had a long conversation with the big white phone. It turned out that most of the team had, in fact, been struck down in the night. Smithy was one of the very few not to get it and we called him Typhoid Mary. But he had come back early from that function. He'd had a good feed, but he hadn't really had a drink that night.

Poor old Plums was running round marking big crosses on our hotel doors and we were all feeling like death trying to play a test match. The story's well known: Jeremy Coney, there with Radio New Zealand, was in covers, TVNZ's Ken Nicholson at mid-off, Waddle 12th man. I remember being on with Blainy and we were feeling crook as dogs trying to field. Chris Kuggeleijn and Paddles couldn't get out of bed. Chats was on his hands and knees barking at drinks, but kept saying, "No, I'm happy to keep bowling . . ." There were no other seam bowlers. I'll never forget Chats running in to bowl, but instead of stopping he ran straight off the field, grovelling up the staircase, skating on the marble steps with his spikes on and cursing as his whites were turning an unnatural beige. Part of me earning my stripes on that tour was having to then undress him and get him changed.

Two years later the team toured Pakistan and, when we got back, my gut felt terrible. I started bloating and belching a lot and it wouldn't go away. It really started to get me in 1991, when it affected me in Australia. I went to a gastroenterologist who said I had an irritable bowel syndrome and needed a high fibre diet and to drink this stuff that was like liquid sawdust. I did that, but it didn't seem to have an effect. I wasn't happy. Then I went to a naturopath and he put me on a Candida diet, cutting out yeast and sugars to starve it out. Tried that. Didn't work. Then we thought it might be giardia, a parasitic infection. Nope. It still hasn't been identified, but it's thought that it's a parasite that I'd introduced to my gut in Pakistan. I still have it. I've tried lots of things: diets, tonics, herbologists – I went on a Detox diet in 1993 in England. It's calmed down a bit, but if I eat red meat or have fizzy drinks, it really kicks in. Barbecues are a nightmare. I don't eat a lot of red meat now, but when you can't have something, you crave it. I also need to eat before seven in the evening and I can't sleep on my back or I start burping.

It's been frustrating, because you did learn to be careful about what you ate in Pakistan and India. You had to eat only hot food; no ice-cream, salads, unsafe fruit (anything that couldn't be peeled) lest it contained active bacteria. You lived on a boring tour diet of hot breakfasts and curries and you carbo-loaded with rice. You had to like rice! You'd quickly start craving ice-cream, yoghurt, salads, fruit juice, cold milk . . . You couldn't eat these things for two months. In India in 1988 Mum sent me over a rescue pack with Sneds, when I'd already been in Zimbabwe for six weeks. It was great; winegums, muesli bars, jet planes! You always packed your peanut butter and Vegemite and I learned to pack my Nutrigrain, two-minute noodles, tinned fish and muesli bars. In 1995, Bryan Young brought an entire extra suitcase stuffed with canned food and power bars, determined to live off his supplies through the tour. It was always lucky we didn't have to worry about excess baggage.

IT'S A KIND
OF MAGIC

Not many pace bowlers leave a permanent impression on the cricket world with their batting, but I managed to do just that after our match at the WACA in 1989. The Aussies have never forgotten that innings I played. Some even still give me a hard time about it to this day.

It wasn't so much the innings, as the way I played one particular ball from Carl Rackemann. It was towards the end of the third day, after we'd been in the field two days. I was joining Martin Snedden, coming in at 10 with Willie Watson waiting at 11. The pitch was bouncing like a basketball and since I'd bowled a few short ones at Rackemann – I'd had big Carl hopping around – I knew I was due for a few short ones myself. Sure enough, I had to come out and face Rack and big bad Merv. Sneds took me aside, as he had a tendency to do, and said, "Look, the pitch is still pretty true, you'll get some short ones, but just hang in there." So I faced a couple of deliveries and sure enough they were snotting around.

It was getting quite gloomy and I joked to Sneds that they could just turn the lights on and make us stay out there, but Sneds replied very seriously, "Now listen, if you get out here Danny, I'll stick that bat where the sun doesn't shine." We weren't to get out because we could get off for bad light. Sneds, the legal eagle, was already politely pleading his case with the umps between overs. So I faced up to Rack again and he bowled a couple that fizzed by my shoulders, then a couple just short of a length that I left alone, then another one short. I thought there was a good chance of the last ball being right up there, so I decided I'd just have to get into line and go forward to keep it out for the over. I tended to get on the front foot too early anyway and as Rackemann was at the end of his delivery stride I thought to myself, right, going forward here . . . but he dug it in a bit shorter and it really started to take off. I'd already gone forward, so I just leaned my head into the ball to keep it out. The ball hit me on the peak of the helmet and safely dinked off the lid. I'd invented a new technique: the forward headbutt! Mark Taylor's mouth was gaping. I remember Ian Healy asking, "Are you right there Danno?" as if I was quite mad.

I replied, "I'm stunned, an Aussie's actually inquired after my wellbeing!"

Usually you got backchat, but this time words failed them. I shook my dial and carried on. Sneds was just pissing himself at the other end, congratulating me for my survival craft. Apparently Richie Benaud was commentating at the time and deadpanned, "Well, that's one way of playing it." Sure enough, we finally went off for bad light. I was just after a helmet contract.

Because I collected a few ducks in my career I got a bit of stick for being a batting rabbit, but I actually got up to nine in the order on our Aussie tour of 1993. I got into line more than some of our other tailenders, despite being Dan the Duckman. Because of my limited technique, I had to be prepared to take it on the body and I was happy to do that. It meant batting time, rather than swinging at it nervously.

In Pakistan in 1990 I was good enough (or crazy enough) to be designated the side's nightwatchman, a role I enjoyed assuming after Sneds, who'd done the job well for a long time, had retired. In Pakistan it turned out I was going in as nightwatchman on a regular basis because we were getting a bit of a hammering in the tests. In the last match of that series, the infamous match at Faisalabad where Chris Pringle got seven for 52 after carving up the ball, I went in at seven in the first innings after we'd been in trouble at 89/5.

I hadn't slept well the night before because I was rooming with Batchie and as usual he'd snored all night. I was biffing pillows on him to stop it. Bryan Waddle was in the room next door and banged on the wall, then rang us up at one in the morning and growled, "What's going on in there?"

So I hadn't had a good rest, but I said to myself, "This is it Dan, I can go out and do this." It was hot, difficult and guys were falling at the other end. Partners were coming and going, but I was leaving it quite well and grinding it out, facing Waqar, Aaqib Javed, Salim Jaffer and the like on a true pitch with good pace and bounce. I remember getting a short one from Waqar off the thumb; it went to the third man boundary, so luck was obviously with me that day. I took a lot of bruises on the body. I batted with Crowey for some time. Javed Miandad and Saleem Yousef were yappy as hell, winding up Waqar to get the number 11 out, because I'd been there so long. I started to cramp in my forearms after three and a half hours and called for the salt tablets – I'd never batted that long before! I battled to 25 and then everything started to go on me; I was cramping in my hamstrings, I'd lost a lot of fluid, twelfthies were running out at regular intervals. I eventually got out in the last over before tea, having batted four hours. The side had got through to 217, after Pakistan had been done for 102 in their first dig. Waqar had come round the wicket and I nicked it to Shoaib in the slips. I was so frustrated; I'd played at a ball I could have left alone. I was even starting to think like a batsman! Then I came out and tried to bowl, but I only lasted about three overs. I was exhausted. But it's an experience I thoroughly enjoyed, batting for the other guys. I slept well that night, even with Mark Greatbatch in the same room.

One of my first experiences of what it really meant to bat in a test match had come earlier, in Bombay in 1988. I came in at 10, with Chats at his customary number 11 – he was fairly unthreatened there. We were batting first and really up against it, just 158 at the fall of the eighth wicket. John Bracewell, always a gutsy character, was in and he said, "Mate, just watch the ball and leave it if you can. You've got a good temperament and good soft hands, so just hang in there for me."

Braces showed great faith in me and was very good at talking to me and getting me concentrating on every ball. It was amazing how, as you hung in there and then squirted a couple of singles and then pushed it round, your confidence grew. I remember later on I banged a couple of fours over the top and even ran down the wicket in my enthusiasm to get to the other end to get a few more runs! I remember nearly hitting a six over long-off at one stage. I hope someone took a photo.

There'd been a big shout off Kapil Dev early on, but luckily it was a no-ball. The Indians got dispirited then, went through the motions – and relaxed because they just had two to get out. The crowd was getting restless. But Braces and I put on 76 runs, a new ninth wicket New Zealand record against India. Before I'd gone out to bat again after tea that day, I was on about six and my highest score at that stage was still 14 not out. Bob Cunis said to me, "Listen boy, you get to your highest test score and I'll buy you a beer for the rest of your life every time I catch up with you." I just laughed and said that was a safe bet for him. But after I got 27 not out I think he forgot that he said it!

CHAMPAGNE SUPERNOVA

Some individual innings are simply unforgettable and two of them happened against Sri Lanka in our first test of the series at home in the 1990/91 season. We'd been bowled out on the Basin Reserve for 174 when it did a little bit, then it flattened out and the Sri Lankans got away to 497 after we dropped some catches. Aravinda de Silva was dropped and made 267.

So in the second innings we had to bat our way out of trouble. We lost our first wicket at 134, when Trevor Franklin was trapped before the wicket, then Wrighty, who'd played well for his 88, fell at 148. But the next wicket didn't fall until 615! It was the monumental test record partnership in which Martin Crowe made 299 and Andrew Jones, 186. They both played superbly, hitting with the wind, which was great fun for batters in Wellington. It was a shame to see Jed fall short of a double hundred but, right at the end of the day, to see Crowe fall on 299 was, ironically, even more disappointing.

We'd all been ready to clap the masterful performance on the 300. Crowe came off the field drained but, more than that, he was just so angry. He went past the sign that says "Players Only" and gave that a loud bash with his bat, then bashed the doors as he came in, biffing his bat into his coffin. Wrighty happened to be dottering around the corner of the dressing room in his undies having a fag and the rest of the boys came down from the viewing room and were clapping, but it was as if we weren't even there.

Crowey's not really a bat thrower; normally he just sat down and felt a bit depressed. But so much intensity had been compressed inside him out there at the wicket that now he ripped his boards off, the velcro making a loud, ugly sound. Then he smashed one down on the floor and biffed the other across the room at the wall. Wrighty had to duck for cover, holding onto his fag – he reminded me of Andy Capp. We all thought, hell, the volcano's erupted . . .

That test in Bombay was my seventh test match and seven's been a lucky number for me. It was the first test match I'd played in that we won. I've still got one of the cricket stumps.

I've been fortunate over my career to witness some very special afternoons out on a cricket pitch. One was when Andrew Jones and Martin Crowe broke the world test partnership record; another was when Mark Greatbatch and Martin Snedden staved off defeat in

For Crowe it was the ultimate disappointment. No one had made 300 in a test for New Zealand, and he knew Graham Gooch had just made 333 at Lord's. He must have had nightmares over that one shot, trying to run it down to third man. All it came down to was one momentary lapse of reason. But he was in excellent company; the only other batsman to have made 299 in a test was Don Bradman.

Another innings I'll never forget was an incredible afternoon on Eden Park when Smithy smashed 173 against India in 1989/90. The top order had totally collapsed, seven guys going for less than 30 before Hadlee got an 87 and Smithy this blazing hundred. It was a hell of a day to sit and watch. I sat a long time with my thighpad ready – Sneds was next in and I was after him.

It was Smithy's afternoon. He was seeing it like a watermelon and bashing it round the park. He played it like a one-day innings, no holds barred. Manoj Prabhakar couldn't believe how much he was being caned. I remember Prabhakar freaking out when he'd got an outswinger going through the off-side to the slip cordon only to see Smithy play this flamboyant little baseball punch shot, picking him up over midwicket! He'd even upper cut a few off the back foot.

Atul Wasson also had that pace where he came on nicely enough, but Smithy would just make some room and play a swashbuckling one-day shot to square leg – in the middle of a test match where we'd been six down for 85! Dead straight deliveries would be pulled straight back over the bowler's head. It was death-defying stuff. Those are shots, so inventive and improvised, that stay etched in your mind years later. It livened up the game and turned it into a lively afternoon for us. It just goes to show you've always got to expect the unexpected in cricket.

Perth. And even though most oppositions don't generally fancy our chances, I've always felt the ability of our guys to suddenly play great innings like those.

It's frustrating we haven't done it more often. It's frustrating seeing players going through ruts, getting out the same way time after time. Maybe batters feel the same way seeing us picked off by the same batsman. But I've always felt they could do it, and that's part of the magic of the game.

Batsmen are more selfish animals than bowlers and I really don't think they realise how much you want them to do well. They tend to think that you love them to play a long, gutsy innings because it gives you the chance to have a decent kip in the dressing room. Batsmen come in at stumps and say, "So what did you do all day? Read a novel?"

Usually I tell them that I've intensely watched the guys bat all day. Sometimes you get a bit naughty and get trapped into watching the replays on television, but generally I like to be out there on the balcony or in the players' lounge for every delivery they face. I've stood getting quite choked in the throat in emotional team meetings where I've told young batsmen that it's not just the two of them out there, that I believe in a greater energy and that it's important that the rest of the team is willing on and supporting them. I don't think enough of them have understood how much I want to will them on. It's completely lost on some of them. They think we're happy resting back in the hut, but it goes deeper than that for me. On some of those days that we batted through, I'd get so drained that I'd fall asleep in the dressing room at the end of the day because I was exhausted. It's why I don't take my golf clubs on tour.

I really believe that energy worked in Perth in 1989, because the whole team was willing on Batch and Sneds to hang on. Everyone was upstairs except for Brendon Bracewell, Willie Watson and me, who were downstairs with the room attendant in the dressing room. We were sitting there nervously watching it on TV because Willie and I were next in, so we were willing the guys on that way. We sat there for ages, glued to it, practically for the whole last day. Every ball we were on tenterhooks all over again. Geoff Lawson came round the wicket and got Batch to nick it – but the keeper, Ian Healy, left it and the slip, Terry Alderman, was too late to get across instead. Then the same thing happened again and the two Aussies just stared at each other. It was amazing.

The times I've most felt that team willpower is with the Australians. Whenever I've played them in the past, or seen them on television or in photos, I've noticed they group together on the balcony; they've really been there for each other as a team. It was instilled in them especially through the Simpson years. I think it's a strong Australian trait. You're out there so your team-mates batting can see you supporting them.

But for us, it wasn't done enough in sides I played in. It wasn't compulsory, more of an on-off thing. We had too many distractions. Bob Cunis was never a good watcher – there were times when he would sit and watch on the balcony, but really he saw more sense in taking you down to the nets for a bit of a chat and practice. Wally Lees really wanted guys to be watching, though, as does Steve Rixon. Rixon doesn't want any of the guys watching the television in the dressing room while we're batting; he wants the team sitting all together.

That was what happened the day last summer when I batted with Nathan Astle to save the first test against England. This was the last stand. We had no second chance in that situation and everyone sat watching us intently; none of the players were allowed to move from their seats. If anyone had opened a novel, they would have been shot. After the last tea break, they all had to take exactly the same seats. And I believe they willed us on to achieve what our opposition never realistically expected.

That bright January day on my home park was my fondest innings. I didn't know it would also be my last.

Stephen Fleming had finally got his maiden test hundred in the first innings and though we should have got the psychological milestone of 400, we fell short at 390, then let England get 521, none of us bowling well. So in the second innings, we had to hang in there. Doully played quite well after lunch and our spirits were brightening up, but then suddenly Doully got done by Darren Gough reversing the ball. We were only nine runs ahead so I strolled out to the wicket thinking I had nothing to lose. I'd just try to hang in for Nath. The Poms had seen me smack a few in a tour game in Palmerston North and obviously thought I'd just come in and slog it – they had guys on the fence. But I thought that was very negative and said to Nath, "I'm out here to play for you and we'll take it over by over."

Phil Tufnell got more and more frustrated as we played on, swapping ends, then going round the wicket. I was surprised Mike Atherton didn't bring in five or six people round the bat. They still seemed blasé, sure that the match was all but over because the number 11 was in. Goughy was trying to york me. Then they took the new ball and Gough and Cork bowled together, but they bowled too short. The guys in close would say things like, "They're only 40

IT'S A KIND OF MAGIC

ahead, lads," and then, "Only 50 ahead, lads . . ." They didn't try to swing the new ball away from me and get me to nick out. They were content trying to push you back on a deck that was dead as concrete on the fifth day. But the guys could bowl short all day, because as far as I was concerned they could bruise me as much as they liked; that wasn't going to get me out. I was prepared to just piss those guys off. I started cramping after an hour or so and Athers wouldn't let me get a drink – I don't think my old Lancashire buddy believed me. Alec Stewart was barking away, "Don't be soft, Athers . . ." They thought I was just trying to buy time, but it was for real. That made me more determined than ever to stay there.

When Nath realised I was serious about hanging around, his confidence blossomed and the shots came out. We'd been gone for all money until then. When we came in at tea, everyone was still on edge, because of the danger of getting out soon after a break. In a way you almost didn't want to come off, you wanted to keep on a roll. You didn't dare break the spell.

There was almost a feeling of disbelief in the dressing room. I remember Steve Rixon had been practically resigned to defeat at lunchtime and didn't have a lot to say, but a few others were delighted and patted us on the back. I'd cheekily told Blair Pocock before lunch that there were no worries, I'd go out and bat a few hours after everyone else stuffed up; and he came up to me and laughed, "You arrogant little bastard, you said you'd done this before!"

Then the entire team superstitiously went back to their exact same seats as Nath and I headed out for the final session.

Things were on my side; it was a very placid surface now and England had muffed their opportunity with the new ball. But you still had to concentrate on every delivery. You were almost in a trance. I thought of the great match in Perth in 1989 as I was batting. I thought of Batch saying to himself over and over in the middle of the WACA, "Watch the ball, watch the ball." I kept saying it too, now. I remember Nick Knight could overhear a little of what I was saying. Eventually we got into instinct mode – the best feeling I've ever had with the bat. At the other end Nath was smashing away a couple of boundaries per over. I could feel the ball-by-ball attention of the crowd and I had a little luck.

Atherton offered to finish the game as an honourable draw when Nath was on 90, but by then Nath and I were so confident of sticking around that we both chewed into him for that; Nath deserved his hundred. He was so positive that he came down the wicket and smashed two fours to get there. Afterwards we discovered we'd faced exactly the same number of deliveries, 133 – but Nath had got 102 runs and I had managed only 14!

I really enjoyed being able to play an innings like that in my own backyard. It was an amazing partnership to be in. Nath and I had actually never batted together before that day. I'd also batted with Flem for the first time in the first innings. To see the two young stars both get hundreds was very satisfying indeed.

CELEBRATION

I sat in the bathtub so drained and emotional that I was crying. It had been a terrible day. We'd just bowled against the West Indies for two days on the trot, then I'd come back out to bat after the team hadn't got enough on the board and managed only to break the world record for test noughts. But my wife, as usual, was there for me. As she sprinkled some soothing aromatherapy oils into the bath she said, "It's not all bad. We've got a theme for the testimonial now . . ."

When you've played for the same cricket association for 10 years, generally you're granted a testimonial or "benefit" season in which you have the opportunity to stage some official events yourself to make some money – it's a kind of "thank you for your loyal service".

The Auckland Cricket Association granted me a testimonial season in 1996/97. I thoroughly enjoyed the experience, but also, I have to say, it opened my eyes to much that I'd taken for granted about the other side of cricket. I learned the hard way about the enormous effort it takes to put together the logistics of a match and the importance of good marketing and some essential business skills. After getting our fingers burned financially, we very quickly understood the need to have everything in writing and contracts signed! I remain very grateful for the opportunity – thanks, Auckland.

A testimonial season means a lot more to a player than the chance to make some money. To me, it was often a very emotional time, partly because I was looking back over my years in cricket, but also because a number of the wonderful people I'd met in that time through the game came together to help me celebrate and organise the testimonial season's events. Dipak Patel had had his testimonial season for Auckland the summer before. I remember Dipak saying to me that, with the intensity of the workload when it comes to putting together large-scale events, generally the energy of the people who volunteer to be on your organising committee starts off high, but then enthusiasm starts to naturally wane and taper as they plough on through the months. But my testimonial committee just got better and better and I can't thank you all enough.

Barry Sinclair, the former New Zealand test captain, was our chairman, Hilary Jackson our secretary and the working committee consisted of Karen Blenkiron, Andrea Jackson, my wife Kim, mother Sandi Morrison, mother-in-law Anne Talbot, grandmother Hazel Levin and other close family members. We were very lucky in that we were able to attain a major sponsor in Crown Worldwide Movers through Brian Valentine, whose support was generous from the very beginning.

Our two biggest events were the Crown black tie dinner, held at the Sheraton Auckland on January 6, followed by The Crown Danny Morrison Testimonial Match, a day/night cricket max celebrity game at Ericsson Stadium. That was one of the hardest challenges I've ever taken on. For myself and the committee it involved much networking, hard work and mindboggling logistical planning, especially when Allan Border, the captain of one of the teams, broke his finger in Australia before the match and needed surgery on it straight after the game. At a peak time of trans-Tasman travel, all flights back were full and we owe a great debt of thanks both to Air New Zealand and the unknown person who cancelled their own travel arrangements at the last minute, solving our problem and vastly improving our state of mind at the time!

It was a very emotional experience, playing in that game, looking around the crowd at the stadium who had come along to support me and around the faces in the two teams who'd given of their own time and effort to make my day. There was Sir Richard Hadlee, the man who'd been such a role model and inspiration to me all those years ago. Allan Border, my arch foe! Mike Atherton, Alec Stewart from my county days at Lancashire, with Dominic Cork, Andy Caddick, Darren Gough, Nasser Hussain, Ronnie Irani and Chris Silverwood from England also taking time out of their busy tour to play. Dean Jones, the man I'd so cheekily rapped on the helmet all those summers ago in Perth, had flown from Perth to Melbourne on a midnight flight, left Melbourne at 10am, got into Auckland at 4pm, came straight to the game, played, then had to be at the airport at 5.30am the next day to get back to Australia for another commitment. That's a hell itinerary and it just shows the great spirit the Australian cricketers have towards their competitors in the game. Merv Hughes also flew over from Australia, Aravinda de Silva arrived too. Neil Maxwell, New Zealand Cricket's marketing manager and former New South Wales and Australia "A" rep, played, so too did friends from Auckland cricket like Jason Mills, Mark Haslam, Dipak Patel, Emily Drumm and Justin Vaughan. Mark Greatbatch brought his great personality into the team and I was very touched that Dion Nash played for me also. It was fantastic that Marc Ellis, who'd been a very good cricketer in his schooldays, and Junior Tonu'u could be part of the occasion as well. Everyone's support and spirit moved me in a way I won't forget. Special thanks to our team sponsors, Noel Leeming and Milo, to Air New Zealand for providing travel for the players, to Barkers for providing their uniforms, to DB for their constant support and to Lindsay Crocker of Auckland Cricket whose advice and knowledge about the administrative side of the game was invaluable. And, for the record, I just want to remind everyone in that match that, for once in my life, I got 60 and top-scored!

Apart from learning about what it actually took to make a match happen, we also came to appreciate more about the media's task in cricket when we produced our official testimonial publication – it took 85 people to create just one magazine! It cost us $30,000 to produce 6000 copies, which we sold in both Australia and New Zealand, with the costs covered by our generous advertisers and sponsors. Malcolm Evans, the *New Zealand Herald's* cartoonist, is a great talent and designed the magazine, as well as my testimonial "duck tie" and the duck character that formed the logo for the season. It was a lot of hard work and midnight oil but when the first copies rolled off the press we felt so proud and excited.

We capped off the season at home with a testimonial ball and that was also a memorable occasion. Unfortunately I enjoyed it so much that I had to forego a celebrity rally race with Possum Bourne the next day as my constitution was not up to it!

We had so much touching support over the season that it's impossible to thank everyone, but I'd especially like to acknowledge Murray Deaker, Peter Rowley, Mark Hadlow, Martin Snedden, Peter Montgomery, Chuck E. Shearer, Judge Mick Brown and John

Hawkesby for their talent and support, and all those from Takapuna Grammar and the North Shore Cricket Club who reminded me so often of the true meaning of friendship and loyalty.

Of course, I was sad to have been dropped from the New Zealand side during my testimonial summer, but Kim would often still attend New Zealand games, running our official merchandise tent while I was elsewhere in the country playing for Auckland. Kim has told me that many of the public were kind enough not only to support our testimonial season, but also to tell her that "Danny would be back" and that I was a good player. It was really quite humbling to experience that support and it made a long and difficult summer for me far warmer. Thanks for the memories.

Kupe's Incantation
Let the calm be widespread
Let the sea glisten like greenstone;
Let the shimmering warmth of summer
Ever dance across your pathway

(Peter Montgomery, MBE, dedicated the above to Kimberley and Danny Morrison at the Danny Morrison Testimonial Dinner)

ANOTHER BRICK
IN THE WALL

When it was announced that Steve Rixon, the former Australian wicketkeeper who'd coached New South Wales very successfully, would be taking over the New Zealand team from Glenn Turner, some of the public were resistant to the idea of a foreign coach, but I rejected that. We were actually quite eager for some fresh ideas and to get a taste of the Australian style.

I first met Steve down at the winter camps in Christchurch in 1996. We thought his drills were very good and there was a positive feeling around the team. Steve was ideal for Lee's keeping, especially, and Lee worked really hard on it. Adam also worked on his, as back-up. Our first outing together was in Sharjah and though we'd really noticed Lee's form fall away on the wearying tour of the Caribbean, in Sharjah he played well, both behind the stumps and in front of them. It was just frustrating that the top order batting fell away too quickly so that he often had to come in to bat with an impossible task ahead. But full marks to him for getting back up there.

The relationship between players and management was much better in Sharjah. Steve made you feel like it was good fun again and you wanted to get out there and train. He kept variety in our drills and nets, involved the players far more and we were generally more enthused. A better team feeling was developing as a result. We started having "the huddle" whenever a wicket fell, a bit of team bonding. I always seemed to end up between Cairnsie and Flem with my head in their armpits – the pitbull squeezing their ribcages and pecs! Cairnsie used to cry, "I don't want to be next to Dan, he's biting me again!"

We tied a game with Sri Lanka when we could have lost, through total commitment from everyone (though I could have done without bowling two wides). It helped us through to the final. It was great. We were hanging in at the death, making it, and there was more self-belief. Even though we went on to lose the tournament, I thoroughly enjoyed it. I'd really missed that old team spirit.

But from Sharjah we went to Pakistan and there my spirits turned to mud as I felt the tendons clicking over in my groin. A team protocol had been set that if you were injured and couldn't play within a couple of days, that was it; you were on the plane back to New Zealand. I'd trained so hard that it was very frustrating and I had a discussion with Steve Rixon saying I didn't want to leave the tour in Pakistan and was hoping I could stay there as a senior player and be there for the guys, have treatment and see if it would improve enough to play again. But I had to abide by the protocol like everyone else and came home late in November. I missed their test victory over there, though they lost the rest of the tour.

The more injuries you have, the more people seem to write you off. Cameras were at the airport, reporters asking if this was it for Danny Morrison. People made assumptions I just wasn't digging deep enough, taking the soft option out, wrapped in cotton wool as a few people presume the Aucks to be. That didn't faze me, those opinions. The hard work was ahead of me and they could watch it if they liked.

What really annoyed me was that Steve had appeared to take the same stand. He'd told me that it was "bad for the team" to see me always on the physio table, that it "didn't look very good". Glenn Turner, too, had felt it was an "emotional crutch". I thought it was dedication, ensuring I got the maintenance I needed; the idea is to have the fence at the top of the cliff, not the ambulance below. I was always conscious of my body and keeping it in tune like a well-oiled engine. I find it hard to accept that it was disconcerting to see me on the table all the time, thinking I was Humpty Dumpty on the verge of breaking into a thousand pieces again. And, sorry gentlemen, you just don't know what it's like to run in and bowl fast. Batsmen go out and play golf on tour, but you'll hardly ever see bowlers do that because they're so physically tired. They're the workhorses on the team, either in the nets or in the field.

I really think the demands on modern bowlers are misunderstood quite widely in the game. You see it worldwide. It was interesting to see John Hart calling for more rotational use of players in the All Black squad as their itineraries became more intense. He saw the reality of that situation as it applied to rugby. In cricket, the reality is that, this decade, the bowling brigade has needed the lion's share of physio. Not one of us in the New Zealand side this decade hasn't struggled with various niggles. The groin has publicly plagued me for the last four years of my career and the bottom line is it's harder on your body than for batters. But it was my job, I loved it and I had no qualms.

Sadly, I'm not the only player to have been criticised for getting physio regularly by batsman coaches. When Tony Blain returned to the New Zealand side in 1993 and played every game on tour, he was really crucified by Geoff Howarth for "hassling Plums so much" – but his back was shot. He needed the treatment to get up and down as a wicketkeeper all day – and then was given no rest, because he usually had to bat a long time after we'd collapsed yet again in Howarth's coaching era. We all got physio. On tour the team room sometimes had the manager in it dealing with the liaison people and in many ways Plums' room was more of a social room for us than the actual team room.

In any case, back in Devonport I locked into yet another build-up campaign for the upcoming home series against England, easing my way into club cricket and targeting Boxing Day to come back and play in the Shell Cup. I'd do my weight sessions religiously, morning and afternoon.

It was my testimonial season with Auckland Cricket and I had a celebrity day-nighter at Ericsson Stadium after the boys had got back from Pakistan. We organised a black tie dinner the evening before and it was nice to see Steve Rixon, Christopher Doig, marketing manager Neil Maxwell and a few others from New Zealand Cricket at the New Zealand table. I had a lot on my mind at the time, with these two big events on, and was chattering away in my speech at the dinner about how I was looking forward to getting fit and having part of this testimonial out of the way so I could concentrate on my cricket for New Zealand. Steve had said he'd wanted to have a word with me, to catch up, and after listening to my speech he hauled me aside and told me that he was very concerned I was an "I, I man" after the talk we'd had in Pakistan. He was very concerned I wasn't worried about the team as a unit, but about myself. I could hardly believe my ears – I knew I had always been first and foremost a team man, and was quite hurt. I really don't think he'd given himself the chance to get to know me very well by that stage. And I found it extremely strange, especially, that he'd chosen to tell me in that place, at my testimonial dinner. Something about it just wasn't right at all.

People had put together a testimonial video for me showing bits and pieces from my career and that was running at the dinner that night. Steve said, "That's how I want you to get back and bowl." Admittedly it was a few years ago, but I said I was happy to do that. I was training hard, on track and raring to go since reluctantly missing the action in Pakistan.

The more I've looked back on that testimonial night since, the more disconcerted I've felt about it. I think there was a lot more at work than I realised at the time.

Because I come from a very female-orientated background, I'd also spoken that night from the heart about my support structure – my family, wife and wife's family. People got a strong sense of that there, and of the fact that Kim had been around with me a lot on tour. In Australian cricket, the women aren't sighted much at all. Steve was from that macho Aussie school. When he'd first addressed the guys, he'd said a couple of eye-raising things that indicated he wasn't big on wives being involved in cricket at all. Maybe that counted against me, too. I came from a different culture from him, I believe that he may not have liked the fact that female influence was big for me.

One good thing about the Peter McDermott administrative era was that partners had become more involved as we set off on tour after tour, at home or overseas. The Aussie wives came over here in 1993 and said to my wife they couldn't believe how well they were treated compared to what they put up with in Australia. Some of the guys have commented to me that Steve is trying to instil some of that Aussieness, the hardness, in the New Zealand team, but while the Australians are a strong side, you can't change a culture. New Zealanders are from a different cloth and we have a totally different way of approaching our sport. And I think, looking at the All Blacks, the culture of our sport is probably OK as it is. You just have to make it work.

I think the bottom line is Steve didn't give me enough scope to get to know him, or himself to know me. I don't know what other information he was fed by whom, but I also got the impression that he had judged me on what he'd been told about our South African tour and the controversy back home.

After my testimonial match the England series started rolling. I played them in a tour match in Palmerston North to show the selectors I'd recovered. I bowled OK and, but for a couple of no-balls, would have bagged a six-for instead of a four-for. Traditionally it does take me a while to get going, but things were just about coming right. Then I played the first test at Eden Park.

Nath and I batted to save the test and it turned out to be a memorable occasion, but earlier in the match all of our bowlers had struggled, including myself. Everyone knows that we're traditionally slow starters getting into a series at home, but this time that Eden Park surface was a slow, dead wicket and it was also very hard to get in and launch from the terraces end. Darren Gough found the same problem and swapped ends, but I stuck to the terraces because it was my favourite; I got better rhythm from that end. But I was forced to jump from a sandy, shifting platform there behind the umpire so I couldn't get a decent take-off. Subsequently I was bowling along the wicket instead of getting up into my action and I didn't bowl that well. But I wasn't alone. None of us bowled well (after all, when England bowled, they couldn't even get out the world record-holder for test noughts). All of the seam bowlers went for a hundred. I talked to Steve Rixon about it, so he was aware of the problem.

Steve hadn't had a lot to say to me around that time of the test. He'd brought in Richard Hadlee to advise the bowlers and Martin Crowe for the batters before the match, so in a sense there had been limited opportunity. But I had certainly seen a bit of Ross Dykes, the convenor of selectors, and happened to be standing with our manager, John Graham, when he was speaking with Dykes. With my own ears I overheard Dykes say, "We'll probably keep the same twelve [for the next test in Wellington]. We've only bowled once in this one and we've had to save it . . ." While Nath and I were out there battling, my wife Kim had been sitting near Ross in the president's lounge in the West Stand and he'd smiled to her that he "loved it when your husband gets in this mood for the team". When the draw was official, he also went up to Kim and said her husband had made him feel "very relieved".

Having heard that the selectors didn't want to change the twelve and knowing the conditions we'd had to battle against in Auckland, it's an understatement to say I was gobsmacked when Ross Dykes rang me at the North Shore Cricket Club, where I was trying to keep ticking over while others were playing England in a tour match at Wanganui, to tell me I was dropped. I know Dyksey didn't want to ring me. His excuse was that the selectors were "trying to pick a side that could take 20 wickets".

"What?" I replied, quite astonished. "Taking wickets is my living!"

We knew the deck in Wellington was going to suit the seam bowlers. The groundsman, Warwick Sisson, had produced one that had a bit of pace all summer. As it turned out, Darren Gough, who's a similar pace and stature to me, got nine wickets there – and Cairnsie ended up bowling very little; he had ankle problems. For the balance of the side, you'd think I could have been given another crack. I was really quite angry about it, not just because of pride, but because I wanted to be there for the team and I knew I could contribute. Instead I had to watch them struggle.

Steve Rixon had publicly said upon his appointment that he didn't want a selectorial role, but all coaches have a certain amount of input. Everything went through Ross, but I'd known Ross for years – he'd been an Auckland selector when I first played for my province, had even given me my first chance back in 1984 – and you just knew when he was going lame on you. I got the strong impression that he wasn't making the decisions, that Rixon was hiding behind the selectorial screen. I just said to Dykes on the phone that you don't have to be a rocket scientist to work out who's calling the shots.

It had also been part of Steve's new, avowed protocol that guys should be given another chance to show their wares if they had a bad game. If the selectors, whoever they really were, had a problem with me, I felt they should have told me it was my last chance. Personally, I thought I could still do that job and was good enough to be in that side and take wickets at the top of the innings with the new ball. But I'd been cut off and really not given enough explanation. I really felt it was unfair, that I deserved another crack.

Shortly afterwards, on February 2, I went down to Wellington in any case for Gavin Larsen's benefit game on the Sunday. I was obviously very down. As I was leaving, Steve Rixon happened to be outside. As I made for the taxi I said, "Well, I hope to see you soon." Rixon just winked and said "So do I, mate." In that moment there was a very uncomfortable shift. You learn to trust your instinct and I felt he was being false, that he didn't want me there at all.

And then I was cut adrift. I bowled from match to match for Auckland without so much as a phone call to find out how I felt about my game. In the end, I rang Dykes myself on his mobile, while New Zealand were playing the one-day series against England and shortly before he was due to name the side to play Sri Lanka. I told him I needed to know where I stood, to at least be told what I had to do to get back in the side. I felt out of sight, out of mind – and quite dispirited. Here I was, a contracted player, but no one was even speaking to me. You felt like you had a disease.

Ross' answer was that it was "fair criticism" that I hadn't been communicated with.

Chris Drum, Justin Vaughan and myself had been sharing the wickets around for Auckland. I hadn't been taking five or six wicket bags, but I'd got a couple of three-fors and a four-for and I was bowling well with good rhythm. People around me were saying, "No, you'll be back", but I got a whole feeling that that was it for me. You just felt the door was closed.

I didn't hear from the selectors at all for the rest of the season, but in May a quick one-day tournament, the Independence Cup in India, was scheduled for the national side. During the England series most of our seam bowlers had been struck by injury. Heath Davis was struggling with his knee, Geoff Allott had broken down with stress fractures, Doully was struggling with his knee as well in Dunedin and having to carry a high workload, while Chris Cairns was able to play only as a batsman; if I stood a chance of getting back in at all, it was the classic scenario for it.

Shortly before the team was named I was working out at my mother-in-law's gym when John Reid, New Zealand's operations manager and a familiar face from Auckland cricket in earlier years, rang me. He said, "Dan, just a courtesy call from an old mate; they're going to be picking this guy Andrew Penn for India."

I said to John, "Why isn't Ross Dykes ringing to tell me this? He's the convenor of selectors, this is his job."

John just replied, "Oh, he's fairly full on at the moment."

I smiled a grim smile and said, "I can see what's happening. Steve Rixon wants to bring in a nucleus of young guys. It's the Craig McDermott scenario. I'm being phased out and unless I'm taking seven-fors I'm not going to get picked."

John started to say that he didn't think it was as black and white as all that, but I said, to be honest, I thought it was. Why else was no one else communicating with me? I was thinking, hello, Dyksey doesn't even want to speak to me now. He'd said it was fair criticism during the England series that he hadn't been in touch, then never got back in touch! I felt no one wanted to know; that they were getting rid of me sideways and no one wanted to talk to me. Rixon certainly didn't want to and now Dykes didn't, either.

I thought it was rude. You gave so much, but the loyalty wasn't returned. Instead you were suddenly cut adrift. No doubt the selectors rely on the opinions of a few people within cricket who may have watched me playing for Auckland, but what was wrong with having a talk about it with me? What was wrong with perhaps involving New Zealand Cricket's fitness panel and telling me how they saw it, where they saw me at, where they wanted me to be at? New Zealand Cricket had spent a lot of money on a medical panel of doctors and physios down in Christchurch. My surgeon had had a meeting with them in late August, after my adductor tendon release, where we'd sat down with Dayle Hadlee, the director of the academy, and discussed how I was to get back on track. It's very hard as an Aucklander to be accurately monitored by a fitness panel based in Christchurch, so where was the forum now with Steve, Dykes, me, the medical panel, Plummer, John Reid? Cricket wasn't just my sport, something I looked forward to in the summer anymore. Playing for my country was all I wanted to do. It had become my whole career, my whole living. But it all depended on the opinions of a very few people. Surely they had more responsibility than this to ensure they were right?

The next time I heard from Dykes himself was just before he was about to make a public statement about me "not being in the medium to long-term view of the selectors", as the side for the Independence Cup was announced. He said it was a shame that I'd had so many ups and downs with injuries that I hadn't consolidated my place in the side as much as I had hoped to. I felt he sounded sheepish about not having got back in touch over the previous months, but I've come to learn that whenever you put it to a selector that you're frustrated that you haven't been communicated with, the same, standard line appears; it was "fair criticism". The problem was, it had been fair criticism months, and probably years, beforehand.

It was too easy a cop-out to make a brief summary statement. I felt the reason Dykes rang me that day was because the media were about to find out I wasn't selected for the Independence Cup team and it would have looked bad if, when the reporters inevitably descended on me, I'd said to them that I hadn't heard from the selectors at all for the last few months. To be honest, I can't understand how he and the selectors – or whoever was really making the decisions – could be so confident about not needing this human resource at a time when it was clear bowlers were breaking down all over the place with little time to recover between series through the demands of both the itineraries and the job of fast bowling itself (you only had to look at the results of the inexperienced bowlers who went instead of me). It told me that it wasn't going to happen for me in Australia in 1997/98 and that even if the entire team broke down, they weren't interested. At the start of the season it had been spelt out that the selectors wanted to have a group of eight to 10 from which to pick the international bowlers, because of the demands, and as one of the few with experience I was an asset in that group. But now all that had gone out the window.

So that was it. Later that winter I was driving with Martin Snedden, as we were on our way to see Lindsay Crocker to discuss my future with Auckland Cricket. Sneds said, "You know, I can't think of anyone else in cricket's history who's been told they're not required in the long-term view of the selectors." Even in England, where there was such a revolving door policy, that didn't happen. At least I knew where I stood!

A few things continued to bother me, however. One happened when I caught up with Chris and Ruth Cairns in Auckland on the way back from their honeymoon. Chris looked at me and said, "Dan, you shouldn't have done that thing on The Footy Show".

I'd done this lighthearted skit where I asked people on the street for advice how to get back in the side. One had told me I needed some wrinkle cream for my crow's feet, I was looking too old. Another had said, "You've got an Aussie coach; you've obviously got to learn to bowl underarm." I looked at Cairnsie saying that Steve Rixon must have got quite upset – and noticed he looked scared of him, the way you're scared of the headmaster. I thought, what's going on? Cairnsie's normally a strong, determined character. I got the feeling it had been discussed, that I'd been made an example.

Another incident, involving Simon Doull, also led me to believe Steve was cultivating a fear factor in the team, and that concerns me. It's never healthy when you motivate yourself through fear instead of desire. No one feared Cuni or Wally; that didn't mean you messed them around. But I think there's a fear of Steve Rixon's power, which you can't see from the outside, but which I saw in some of the guys.

I remember standing next to Doully in the nets at the winter camp last September when he was telling Ross Dykes that, if the season went well, he'd like to be best man at his brother Lincoln's wedding. The 1997 itinerary against Sri Lanka hadn't been finalised at that point and, as he and Lincoln were very close, it obviously meant a lot to Doully to be there for him on the big day. But when that weekend rolled around, Kim happened to be running my testimonial merchandising tent at the Hamilton test match while I was away with Auckland and ran into Simon. Kim said, "I thought you were supposed to be at your brother's wedding?" It turned out the coach had said in no uncertain terms that if Simon went off to his brother's wedding he wouldn't be picked again.

I could appreciate Steve questioning where a player's loyalties lay, but it was also a blunt way of stamping authority. It was interesting to observe, more recently, Shane Warne being allowed to skip one of the Australians' Ashes tests to fly back to Australia to see his wife and new baby.

When Steve had first taken over the side, he'd said he really wanted to keep us few older, experienced guys – myself, Crowe if possible, Greatbatch – playing, but as the season progressed it seemed to me quite clear that Steve had a new regime and wanted to call the shots over young guys. I was doing my thing as a senior player and whether he felt I couldn't go down the same road as the rest of the team or not, I can't fathom. But I just felt I wasn't one of "his" players.

Unfortunately for Lee Germon, there were too many similarities between the way I was dropped after the first test against the English in 1997 and the way he was suddenly axed as a player and captain after the trials and tribulations of that series. New Zealand had ended up losing the tests 2-0, though Stephen Fleming had done well in the last test, stepping in to captain after Lee was injured. Had we played another spinner in the side, had Daniel Vettori not had to bowl a marathon spell on his own at the end, we would have won that test match, I believe, and levelled the series.

Lee came back for the one-dayers and had his best game in the last match. He was ready to carry on and even said at the press conference that he was looking forward to the challenge of Sri Lanka. But afterwards, at that game, he was abruptly told that he was out. You could tell that Lee had no idea it was coming. The whole charade came out with Ross Dykes once again; you saw how uncomfortable he looked saying it in the press conference. Then he told the media they shouldn't have given Lee such a hard time. What rubbish. Sure, the captain's in the hot seat, but that was badly handled. You really wondered what sort of communication was going on backstage, if any was going on at all. It was terribly managed – and so damaging to the game's image. Talkback went mad with criticism. But we've made so many management errors like that in recent years in New Zealand cricket. Why don't we learn?

Looking at both my and Lee's cases, the way they were handled, I don't think the people in our cricket structure are managing our resources well at all. No one enjoys being dropped. No matter what the circumstances, it's a hard time for a cricketer. At the end of the day, I don't believe I survived in the team 10 years through sheer luck. I performed well enough to earn my place in the side, clawed my way back a couple of times in the last years after injury and then had no option but to accept that it was over. But I've tried to explain the circumstances of what happened to me as best I can because my point is that as a player you're expected to maintain the highest of professional standards, but too often the standards of those in the administrative/management web let you down. I'm not the first cricketer to complain of the standard of human resources management within New Zealand cricket, and I may not be the last.

You often hear in cricket "selectors can't be accountable because they're not really getting paid for the job anyway and it's a thankless task". But they deal with people's careers and livelihoods. How can they not be professional? How could the guy hiring and firing in a company not be paid? It has to change. You end up feeling like the players are always accountable, but those on the other side of the fence aren't; it's a one-way relationship, but fully demanding of you. Then you're dumped without so much as a warning. You don't treat people who serve you like that. Even in companies where there are sudden redundancies, explanations are given. Yet New Zealand Cricket is supposed to be running "a professional sport".

After I was dropped I was suddenly in another world. On the road with Auckland, occasionally I'd see clips of the New Zealand side, bits and pieces of their one-dayers and the Sri Lankan series. It was interesting how quickly you became detached, distanced from it. There were suddenly men in New Zealand cricket uniforms that I'd never played with. I've never met Daniel Vettori, for example, though I thought it was fantastic for him to be there. Matt Horne I knew, but I'd hardly played with him in the Auckland side. It seemed a totally different environment. And it was strange seeing Cairnsie not bowling. He needed an ankle op, but Steve Rixon had told him he really wanted him to bat. It appeared to be a double standard – what had happened to the protocol? My feeling is that Cairnsie is an allrounder by nature and needs to be totally involved in the game, not half in it, to function well. Were the one-dayers in India so important that he couldn't afford to get his ankle seen to? It seemed to be a case of messing around with his career with a very demanding season, stretching from mid-September to early April this summer, ahead.

I missed playing with him, being there as the old bowling head to help guys like him along if they needed it. But also, with each passing match, I started to feel more estranged. All of us had been so intense with each other on tour, but you never lose the feeling of being workmates. I wasn't in the office anymore.

The guys feel uncomfortable talking to me now when they run into me. A couple came over to my testimonial tent at Eden Park for a rave when they were around, but the longer I was out of the side, the greater the distance became. I could see they felt uncomfortable, because I was out of that culture. Perhaps some of it was about feeling their own fears.

Late in March 1997 I happened to be driving along a road in Auckland listening to Radio Hauraki in the car when a double play came on of Pink Floyd's "Just Another Brick in the Wall" and "Comfortably Numb". I'd sensed my whole international career was coming to a close. It was the end of a 10-year adventure in my life and those two tracks summed up how I felt about the way it happened.

It was more emotional for my mother and family to see the door closing on international cricket than it was for me. Even though I'd lived and breathed the game, somehow having a testimonial season was making me feel reflective and I guess it was like when a band breaks up. To the fans, it's an awful end, but when you're inside it, it's a release.

I really did feel "comfortably numb". And "Another Brick In The Wall" reminded me of how expendable you were. Not having heard from anyone, that's how I felt.

Coach turns his back on experience

COMFORTABLY NUMB

*"The child is grown, the dream is gone
and I have become comfortably numb"*

– PINK FLOYD

Cricket's a sport that teases your emotions like no other and the most emotional moment you experience in the game is when your team clinches a test match.

The last test victory I played in seems a long time ago. It was the third test against Pakistan in 1993 at Lancaster Park. In 10 years of international cricket for New Zealand, I have, in fact, played in only five test wins. Three of them – Bombay in 1988, India at Eden Park in 1990 and Australia at the Basin Reserve in 1990 – came when Richard Hadlee was still playing. The other was against Australia at Eden Park in 1993. Since 1995 I've missed other wins over South Africa, Zimbabwe and Pakistan through injury, but I find it quite daunting to think that I've only been part of five wins from 48 test matches in my entire career. Only one every tenth test match is pretty depressing.

After the magnificent Hadlee years it all seemed to change,

usually not for the better. After Hadlee retired, there were just so many times – fourteen matches, to be precise – when I got to bowl only once in a test match, because our first innings had collapsed and we had to follow on, or had to bat out to save it. Of the 48 tests I played in total, there were an incredible 21 occasions when New Zealand bowled only once (and sometimes we batted only once, also). It just shows how inconsistent we were, trying to do the best we could with weak resources. As luck would have it, I also played in a lot of rain-affected matches, even in India. I guess when it rains, it pours.

As I've said before, batsmen and bowlers are two separate breeds. A batsman uses a completely different psyche to the fast bowler, who pounds in off 30 metres over and over again. Batters think you're a mad, thick old bear; that it's easy to run in and bowl fast, brawn over brain. It's always a batsman who tells you to step it up another gear when you've been slogging your guts out.

Dennis Lillee compared fast bowling to being an Olympic decathlete because you have to come back and perform when you're already sore from hammering your body; that's what it's like bowling for a day and a half in a test match and then coming back for the fourth or fifth day. You have to lift yourself mentally.

You see a lot of guys from the first-class level of the game try to perform in test matches without being prepared for the need to dig deep and keep going when your frame is tender. You have to be determined, to want to keep going. The greatest advantage I've had as a fast bowler is that I've had to fight to do it from the very beginning. I've always been breaking the mould, going against the dictates of my physique, so it instilled a lot of mental determination and toughness in me when I was young.

A year after my first major injury crisis Lillee said to me in Auckland in October 1985, "I don't want to see you turn into just another bowler." He was a great inspiration, not only through what he achieved, but his mana and how good he was at relating to you. But what he achieved was still important. I used to watch him playing in an Ashes series on video even when I was playing club cricket in England, studying how smooth he was as he charged in. Realising how difficult it was to keep coming back, I admired him even more.

Unless you're living and breathing it, it's hard to understand what it's about, motivating yourself to play test cricket for summers on end. It's far more a passion than about paying the bills; the money, for me, never came into it. It was more about expressing the essence of myself. And the days when you were controlled, when your rhythm was good, you were on top and everything was perfect were the days you floated on air. They really made up for all the lows that come along the way through a career.

I won't retire from the game the way Sir Richard Hadlee did, surrounded by mementos of a shining career, a roomful of great days. I'll have a few things for kids to look back on, my grandmother's scrapbooks. But mainly I'll have the knowledge that cricket taught me a lot about people and about myself, and that it brought me together with some who became friends and even family. But at some stage the door closes and a new one opens. Life goes on.

I didn't see much of a guy like Willie Watson once he finished playing, but I hope I'll be able to regenerate those relationships with people whom I played alongside now that I have more time in my life than I've had for many years. It will be nice to have a beer with Paddles.

I've been grateful for mentors, people like Martin Snedden, Murray Deaker and my family also, who have reminded me in the down times why I wanted to come back and that you must make the most of your short time in the game. Sometimes the public or media questioned your hunger, your desire to keep playing. There are times you are sluggish, and that's frustrating, but I don't think I've ever played without the intention to give it one hundred per cent. Cricket has been my total burning desire; to get back and be on that park.

There's still not a day that goes by that I don't think about the game.